Brands

Brands are everywhere: in the air, on the high street, in the kitchen, on television and, maybe, on your feet. But what kinds of things are they?

The brand, a medium of exchange between company and consumer, has become one of the key cultural forces of our time and one of the most important vehicles of globalisation. In a new approach that uses media theory to study the economy, Celia Lury offers a detailed and innovative analysis of the brand.

Illustrated with many examples, the book argues that brands:

- mediate the supply and demand of products and services in a global economy
- frame the activities of the market by functioning as an interface
- communicate interactively, selectively promoting and inhibiting communication between producers and consumers
- operate as a public currency while being legally protected as private property in law
- introduce sensation, qualities and affect into the quantitative calculations of the market
- organise the logics of global flows of products, people, images and events.

Brands: The Logos of the Global Economy will be essential reading for students of sociology, media and cultural studies, marketing and consumption.

Celia Lury is Professor of Sociology at Goldsmiths College, University of London. She has written widely on feminist theory, the culture industry, visual culture and the image.

International library of sociology

Founded by Karl Mannheim

Editor: John Urry

Lancaster University

Recent publications in this series include:

Brands

The logos of the global economy

Celia Lury

Routledge
Taylor & Francis Group

LONDON AND NEW YORK

First published 2004
by Routledge
2 Park Square, Milton Park, Abingdon, Oxon OX14 4RN

Simultaneously published in the USA and Canada
by Routledge
270 Madison Ave, New York, NY 10016

Reprinted 2005

Routledge is an imprint of the Taylor & Francis Group

Typeset in Perpetua by Wearset Ltd, Boldon, Tyne and Wear
Printed and bound in Great Britain by The Cromwell Press,
Trowbridge, Wiltshire

British Library Cataloguing in Publication Data
A catalogue record for this book is available from the British Library

Library of Congress Cataloging in Publication Data
Lury, Celia.
  Brands : the logos of the global economy / Celia Lury.
    p. cm.
  Includes bibliographical references and index.
  1. Brand name products. 2. Business names. 3. Marketing.
4. Globalization–Economic aspects. I. Title.
  HD69.B7L87 2004
  658.8'27–dc22

                                                          2004002706

ISBN 0–415–25182–6 (hbk)
ISBN 0–415–25183–4 (pbk)

Contents

Acknowledgements

I would like to thank the following for their encouragement, ideas and inspiration: Lisa Adkins, Adam Arridsson, Les Back, Anne Barron, Andrew Barry, Vikki Bell, Lauren Berlant, Kirsten Campbell, Mariam Fraser, John Frow, Monica Greco, Alexander Gutzmer, Sarah Kember, Karin Knorr Cetina, John Law, Scott Lash, Mike Michael, Liz Moor, Don Slater, Nigel Thrift, John Urry and Nicole Vitellone. I would also like to acknowledge the very many different kinds of help provided by my brothers and sister, Adam Lury, Giles Lury and Karen Lury.

Chapter 3 has been previously published as 'The interface of the brand: complex objects and partial solutions' in *Soziale Systeme 9* (2003), 2: 221–243 by Lucius & Lucius Verlag, Stuttgart, who have granted permission to reproduce the article.

Every effort has been made to contact copyright holders for their permission to reprint other material in this book. The publishers would be grateful to hear from any copyright holder who is not here acknowledged and will undertake to rectify any errors or omissions in future editions of this book.

1   Just do what?

The brand as new media object

Qu'est-ce que c'est que cette chose-là?

Ce n'est pas une chose. Ça vole.
C'est un avion. C'est mon avion.

(Antoine de Saint-Exupéry, Le Petit Prince (1946))[1]

A sociology of objects?

This book will claim that the brand is an object. What might this mean? An object, surely, is something that is external, fixed, closed; something solid that can be touched. The brand is none of these things. But the brand satisfies some other common dictionary definitions of objects. It is some-thing 'to which some feeling or action is directed'; it is an object-ive in that it is the object of 'a purpose or intention', or even a whole series of purposes; and it is also 'a noun or its equivalent acted upon by a transitive verb or by a preposition'. Put somewhat differently, the brand is the outcome of object-ives, it is produced in the tests and trials of object-ivity, and it is, sometimes, a matter of object-ion. It both is an object of information and objectifies information. But its objectivity also involves images, processes and products, and relations between products. Indeed, the preliminary definition of the brand adopted here is that it is *a set of relations between products or services*. Perhaps, then, while incorporeal or intangible (not something solid that can be touched), the brand is not immaterial. The suggestion to be developed here is that while the brand is not itself fixed in time or space in terms of presence or absence, it is a plat-form for the patterning of activity, a mode of organising activities in time and space. It is not simply either here or somewhere else, but rather is some-thing that emerges in parts. It will also be suggested that the brand is not a closed object, but is, rather, open, extending into – or better, implicating – social relations. It is some-thing that is identifiable in its doing, which is why the chapter title asks not just of Nike but of brands more generally, 'Just do *what?*'. It is implicated in everyday life, and we are – sometimes only just – implicated in it. Finally, it will be argued that the brand is not a matter of certainty, but is rather an object of possibility. These, then, are some of the things that should make the brand an object of interest to sociology.

Before developing these arguments, though, let me try to address the issue of how it is that something as abstract and intangible as a brand may be described as an object at all. To get at what might be involved in this claim, a discussion of something else whose objectivity we take for granted may be helpful: let me take the example of a car. We are easily able to accept that a car is an object, although it typically comprises many thousands of parts or components. Moreover, while each of these parts is more or less essential to the capacity of the object to move its passengers from one place to another, it is *their relation to one another* that makes the components of a car into a car. None of the individual components suffices, and the components need to be in particular relations with each other (a car is not just a heap of parts). We also tend to think of the car as a fixed or closed object, but it is a functioning car only when it is in *a controlled relation to elements of its environment*: the driver, the atmosphere and the roads. This book will suggest that both these ways of thinking about object-ivity apply to the brand. In short, the object-ivity of the brand emerges out of relations between its parts, or rather its products (or services), and in the organisation of a controlled relation to its environment – that is, to markets, competitors, the state, consumption and everyday life.

But the book will describe the brand as being more than simply a set of relations between products. It will argue that the brand is *a set of relations between products in time*. Here, the book draws implicitly on a tradition in philosophy in which time is internal to the processes by which the (physical and social) world operates (Bergson, 1991; Whitehead, 1967, 1977; Deleuze and Guattari, 1994, 1999). This is an approach in which time is dynamic, where dynamism is not an activity of fixed objects moving through static space, but a process of differentiation. In this view, any object is not fixed, but is in itself a process in time. To explore what this might mean, let me return to the example of the car. We tend to think of the components of the car as staying the same in time, or at least as all ageing at the same rate. It is only when the car breaks down that we might acknowledge – perhaps with some annoyance – that one part has aged faster than another. But some components of the car are designed to manage the temporality of the relations between themselves and other components or their relation to the environment – that is, many of the parts of the car have some kind of feedback mechanism whose effect is to manage change. In the case of the car, the hope is that the effect of this management of change is that the car will be kept stable – that is, that it will stay the same object in time (while at the same time retaining the capacity to move in space). But, so it will be argued in the case of the brand, the aim of the feedback processes in which information about competitors and the consumer is fed back into production is to make the brand itself dynamic, to put the brand into process through the management of change. The objectivity of the brand – a set of relations between products *in time* – is intended to have a dynamic unity.

To conclude this comparison of the objectivity of cars and brands, consider the case of Ford, a company that makes cars and owns a brand. In recent years, the company has come to make more money from the financial deals by which people purchase their cars than from the sale of the cars themselves (in this sense, it is a financial services provider rather than a manufacturer of cars). The majority of its profit derives not from the one-off profit it makes when a single car is sold (many times to many consumers), but from the financial arrangements in which many individuals, rather than purchase a single car, enter into an ongoing series of exchanges with the company.

> Ford would rather never sell you a car again. . . . It would rather put you in its network, so that you continually buy the experience of driving rather than buying the vehicle. And the proof is in the pudding. The renewal rate on leasing is 54%. The renewal rate in market-based transactions is 25%.
>
> (Rifkin, quoted in Borger, 2000: 4)

What is acknowledged here is that the relationship between consumer and product may be organised in a number of different ways. At the most simple, an individual acquires a car through either a one-off payment or a series of payments in time, after which that individual's relationship with the company is ended (the so-called market-based transaction mentioned by Rifkin). Increasingly, however, an individual (or indeed another company) enters into a relationship with Ford in which they may either replace the 'same' car, or acquire another car (an updated version of the previous model or a different model altogether) every three or so years. In this relationship (described by Rifkin as 'leasing'), what they are paying for is a relationship with a brand in time – that is, they are paying for the organisation of their participation in a set of relations between products (cars, financial services and perhaps other products and services) in time. In this relationship, there may be both continuity and change, sameness and difference, trust and innovation. The suggestion here is thus that the brand Ford enables the management of change in time, and in doing so it is a dynamic unity.

The brand as an object of the economy

In a series of publications (Callon, 1998a, 1999; see also Barry and Slater, 2002), Michel Callon has addressed the role of objects or technological devices in the operation of markets. It is of course economic theory that has traditionally been concerned with 'larger artificial systems: the economy and its major components, markets' (Simon, [1969] 1981: 37). But the anthropologist Callon's aim is to open up the market to multiple forms of knowledge, not simply the economic. In place of a single category, he advocates addressing the market in terms of several modalities of co-ordination or enunciation. Similarly, Benjamin Lee and Edward LiPuma draw attention to the need to address what they call 'cultures of circulation'. They suggest that one way in which the concept of culture might 'catch up' with the economic processes that go beyond it is 'through the consideration of circulation as a cultural process with its own forms of abstraction, evaluation and constraint' (2000: 192). In what follows, the brand will be understood from this perspective – that is, as an example of *a specific market modality or market cultural form*. The argument will be that *the brand mediates the supply and demand of products through the organisation, co-ordination and integration of the use of information*. The emphasis will be on the use of information to organise relations between products in time, whether those relations produce sameness or difference. It is these relations that comprise the object – or medium of translation (Latour and Woolgar, 1986) – of the brand.

In economic theory, price is seen as the mechanism that typically has the function of calibrating the market by co-ordinating supply and demand through the circulation of information. It is seen as a mechanism of dynamic, distributed knowledge. Put simply, in a market, buyers oppose sellers, and the prices that resolve this conflict are the input but also, in a sense, the output or outcome of the agents' economic calculation (adopted from Guesnerie, 1996, quoted in Callon, 1998c). Another way of saying this is that price is a mechanism by which the sameness or difference – the substitutability (or not) – of goods may be established *in quantitative terms*.

In one of the best-known sociological discussions of price – *The Philosophy of Money* ([1907] 1990) by Georg Simmel – the role of money in privileging the quantitative as a mode of abstraction, evaluation and constraint is understood in cultural terms. For Simmel, money is the representative of 'a cognitive tendency in modern science as a whole: the reduction of qualitative determinations to quantitative ones' (ibid.: 277). In short, money is responsible for the privileging of the category of quantity over that of quality. The quantitative tendency exemplified by money contributes, so Simmel argues, to the acceptance of *relativity*, in which more and more things are not simply put in

relation to one other, but are rendered equivalent in value or made uncondi-
tionally interchangeable. Money underpins

> the tendency to dissolve quality into quantity, to remove the elements
> more and more from quality, to grant them only specific forms of motion
> and interpret everything that is specifically, individually and qualitatively
> determined as the more or less, the bigger or smaller, the wider or nar-
> rower, the more or less frequent.
>
> (ibid.: 278)

This is what Simmel calls the 'merciless objectivity' (ibid.: 431) of money:
'money takes the place of the manifoldness of things and expresses all qualitative distinctions between them in the distinction of "how much"' (ibid.: 127).
It provides the conditions for the growth of calculative functions and the
emergence of a blasé attitude in people – that is, an indifference towards the
distinctions between objects (and subjects).

The brand is presented here as an alternative device for the calibration of
the market, of matching supply and demand.[2] However, the brand is not so
much a *means*, as is argued of money by Simmel in his classic study,[3] as it is a
medium. I want to draw attention to two aspects of this claim. First, the attributes of products (or production) able to function as elements of a mechanism
of exchange in the case of the brand are multiplied (that is, price is only one of
a number of product attributes able to function in this way). These attributes
typically include place, packaging, promotion and (product) qualities. Like
price, these product attributes are not fixed, but variable, and are able to act
as multiple dimensions along which the substitutability of goods may be established. The management of relations between these attributes is what produces the brand. The suggestion to be developed in this book is that this
management provides the basis for *the controlled re-introduction of quality into the
means of exchange*.[4] Second, these and other attributes are at the same time both
concrete (instantiated in specific products and services) and *part of an abstract
object*, the dynamic unity of the organisation of relations between products in
time. The brand is thus simultaneously both concrete and abstract. Another
way of putting this is to say that the contrast being drawn is that while price –
through representation – leads the economy back to the daily world, the
brand comprises (some of) the world itself (Kwinter, 2001: 44).

In the approach outlined here, the question of the *logos* of the economy
takes on a particular importance, where 'logos' is taken to mean not simply
the signs or slogans that mark brands, but the kind of thought or rationality
that organises the economy. Economists have long taken as a central concern
the organisation of a rational economic order, and some of the most dominant

economic perspectives today rely upon a notion of a calculating, self-interested individual to embody this rationality. This reliance has been criticised by sociologists and others who have sought to (re-)introduce the social – frequently understood as value, meaning or culture – into what are seen as restricted accounts of the rationality of the agents of the economy. This book suggests that the brand is an alternative or supplement to the rational order reason, or 'logos' of the economy established by price and is thus an example of an object of the economy that is already a matter of value. In particular, it is an example of an object that opens up how it is that the economy is organised, and does so in ways which introduce qualitative intensivity into the extensive but limited rationality of a conventional market economy of price.

The brand as new media object

In the approach that Callon adopts – sometimes called Actor Network Theory (or ANT) – technological devices or objects are seen as 'image instruments' or as 'media of translation' (Latour, 1987; Callon, 1986; Law, 1984). This book adopts this approach in relation to a sociological account of the economy. However, it also elaborates the notions of image, information and medium, which are sometimes left implicit in ANT. After all, the brand stands at the intersection of the diverse histories of computing, information technology and media as well as those of economics, marketing and design; as such, it is a new media object (Manovich, 2001),[5] an example of 'the "broadcast" distribution of commodities' (Rodowick, 1994).

A *first* way in which (new) media theory may contribute to an understanding of the brand is that it draws attention to *the multi-layered character of the brand's ontological existence*. Some definitions may be helpful here. For example, Fredric Jameson describes a medium as that which conjoins a specific form of aesthetic production, a technology and a social institution (1991: 67). Rosalind Krauss, in a discussion of fine art (1999), suggests that a medium comprises a relationship between a technical (or physical) support and the (recursive) conventions with which a particular genre articulates or works on that support. Put simply, the medium is a dynamic support for practice. Lev Manovich describes what he calls a new media object in terms of a physical operating system, an interface, software applications or operations, and forms or commonly used conventions for (recursively) organising the new media object as a whole (2001: 11). And the brand may similarly be seen to comprise a mode of production, a technical or physical support, and a set of conventions that articulate or work on that support. It too is a *dynamic platform or support for practice*.

Second, the notion of medium makes it possible to think of the brand in terms of *communication*. Here the book will make use of an ideal notion of communication as *the framing of exchange across disunified or disparate times and spaces* (Rodowick, 1994). This makes it possible to consider the medium of the brand in relation to the metaphors of frame, window and mirror as used in discussions of architecture, painting and cinema[6] (see Sobchack, 1992; Deleuze and Guattari, 1994: 186–199; and Manovich, 2001: 95–103 for useful discussions). The most basic definition of the frame in media theory is 'a window that opens onto a larger space that is assumed to extend beyond the frame' (Manovich, 2001: 80); alternatively, the frame may be said to separate 'two absolutely different spaces that somehow coexist' (ibid.: 95). However, the book will also draw upon the notion of the frame as it is used in analyses of the interaction order by the micro-sociologist Erving Goffman (1971), and as it has been developed in ANT by both Callon (1986, 1998a) and Bruno Latour (1996). One of the key developments in the work on cinema, however, is to consider the frame as dynamic. As Deleuze and Guattari put it, 'Frames or sections are not co-ordinates; they belong to compounds of sensations whose faces, interfaces, they constitute' (1994: 187). The suggestion here – developed in Chapter 3 – will be that the brand organises the activities of the market as if it were an interface; and in doing so, the brand presents the 'faces of a dice of sensation' (ibid.: 187).

Let me elaborate a little here. The interface – like the static frame of the window or mirror – is a surface or boundary that connects and separates two spaces: an inner and outer environment. So, as an interface, the brand is a frame that organises the two-way exchange of information between the inner and outer environments of the market in time, informing how consumers relate to producers and how producers relate to consumers. The exchange is a matter not merely of qualitative calculation, but also of affect, intensity and the re-introduction of qualities. However, although these exchanges are intensive, dynamic and two-way, they are not direct, symmetrical or reversible. The interface of the brand connects the producer and consumer *and* removes or separates them from each other; it 'is revealing of some relationships, but it keeps others very well hidden' (Pavitt, 2000b: 175). Or to put this another way, the brand as interface is a site – or diagram – of *interactivity*, not of inter-action.

From this point of view, the brand may be seen as both promoting and inhibiting 'exchange' between producers and consumers, and informs this asymmetrical exchange through a range of performances of its own. The range of performances is not entirely predetermined by the objectivity of the brand, however, but emerges in interactivity. In other words, just as the subject may be seen as an effect of performativity (Butler, 1990), so too may the ongoing object-ivity of the brand. The brand has its own (recursive) logic or performativity through which is organised a two-way, dynamic, selective and asymmetrical communication of information between producers and consumers. In Lee and LiPuma's terms, the brand is an instance of 'a self-reflexive structure of circulation built around some reciprocal social action' (2002: 193); or, alternatively, an example of a 'self-reflexive objectification' of 'temporal agency' (ibid.: 193).

The performativity of the brand

Central to the performativity of the brand as an interface are certain practices in marketing that function in an analogous way to programming techniques in both broadcasting and computing. The most significant example of these techniques is *the loop*, *a central control structure of many new media objects*. This is, then, a *third* respect in which it may be helpful to consider the brand as a new media object. As Manovich notes,

> It is relevant to recall that the loop gave birth not only to cinema but also to computer programming. Programming involves altering the flow of data through control structures, such as 'if/then' and 'repeat/while'; the loop is the most elementary of these control structures. . . . As the practice of computer programming illustrates, the loop and the sequential progression do not have to be considered mutually exclusive. A computer program progresses from start to end by executing a series of loops.
>
> (2001: xxxiii)

The marketing practices of concern here were largely developed in the second half of the twentieth century and incorporate the activities of consumers in the processes and products of production and distribution (see Chapter 2). This incorporation typically involves the marketer adopting the position of the consumer – that is, of imagining the consumer (Lury and Warde, 1996). The (historically changing) marketing knowledge or information produced in this way is used in processes of product differentiation; then, in turn, the resulting product or products themselves become marketing tools, generating further information. In other words, the brand progresses or emerges in a series of loops, an ongoing process of (product) differentiation and (brand) integration.

The book draws attention to two aspects of this looping process. The first aspect concerns the compulsory inclusiveness of subjects that the performativity of the brand involves. What is being referred to here is the ways in which the incorporation of information about the everyday activities of subjects – which may be collected with or without their knowledge or permission – is an essential part of brand-making (Barry, 2001; Poster, 2001; Lyon, 2001; and see Chapter 6). One example of this is the use of consumer profiling techniques in the collection of data (Elmer, 2000, forthcoming). Here it is important to acknowledge the roots of many developments in computing (and indirectly the brand and other informational objects) in military and state surveillance, and the development of a vision of a 'mechanized circuit of detection, decision and response' (Manovich, 2001: 101). The second aspect addressed is the way in which the looping activities make possible the introduction of qualitative possibilities into the abstract objectivity of the brand. To put this rather more concretely, information about consumers is used as a basis for multiplying the qualities or attributes of the products and managing relations between these multi-dimensional variables in time. Moreover, as Manovich points out, this looping is not necessarily a one-off (it does not, for example, necessarily have as its aim a discrete sale), but may rather be part of a sequential progression (and intended to develop a relationship). From this point of view, the brand comprises a sequence or series of loops that *entangle* the consumer (Thomas, 1991). To put this point more abstractly, the temporal reciprocity that defines the communication of the brand is defined not by instantaneity, but by managing 'the temporal delay between receiving a request and responding to it' (Rodowick, 1994; see also Butler, 1990). That is, the interface of the brand manages *the 'response time' of interactivity, the interval in time between products*.

These intervals may be organised so as to produce branded products as the same, or as different.[7] In the former case, the brand acts as a guarantor of the consistency of quality, while in the latter, the 'response time' may be organised so as to produce products as fashionable, as a part of a collection, as new or up to date, or sometimes even as an event. In short, the interface of the brand integrates, organises and co-ordinates the process of production through its qualitative possibilities – as transitions of phase or state, as the organisation of qualitative effects – not merely as price or quantity (Kwinter, 2001: 42). The emergence of the brand in this way is perhaps one of the reasons that the contemporary economy is described in terms of a *vital intensity* (Thrift, forthcoming) or as *an economy of qualities* (Callon, Meadel and Rabeharisoa, 2002).

Putting these two aspects together goes some way to identifying the specificity of the brand as a specific market modality, a particular market cultural form of 'abstraction, evaluation and constraint' (Lee and LiPuma, 2002). It is an *abstraction* that is made *concrete* in specific products and services. As a mode of evaluation, it is a mechanism both of *relativity*, as is price, and of *relationality*, as is jewellery (Simmel, [1907] 1990).[8] In other words, it is both a means of establishing the relativity or the abstract equivalence of products in space and time and it is a medium of relationality, able to support differenti-ation of both objects and subjects, products and consumers. In terms of con-straint, while the brand adds colour to the uniform colourlessness of money as described by Simmel, the potentially continuous spectrum of colour it intro-duces is reduced to a series of discontinuous terms (Coca-Cola red, Pepsi blue, BP yellow and green, Prozac green and white, and Orange orange).[9] Furthermore, as a medium of exchange it is not simply a matter of private individuals, but neither is it wholly public. It is co-ordinated by social organi-sations, principally the company or corporation[10] (although also, increasingly, voluntary organisations, charities, public bodies) and intra- and international organisations for the regulation of trade, and supra-subjective norms. Put more strongly, the rise of the brand is linked to the privatisation of the eco-nomic functions of the state (Appadurai, 2002: 24), and the growing power of multilateral agencies such as the World Bank, the International Monetary Fund (IMF)[11] and the World Intellectual Property Organization (WIPO). As such, the brand is a social currency (Zelizer, 1998), a way in which people bring meaning to various exchanges, but it is often protected in law in the form of a trade mark as private property (see Chapter 5), and is bolstered by the conventions of trade. It is thus a kind of currency by fiat.

Combining these two sets of characteristics thus reveals that the brand is an example not only of a cultural form but also of a modality of economic power. As such, it involves not simply exclusion but also inclusion, not simply the production of sameness or identity but also the production of difference, sensation and intensivity. On the one hand, then, the brand subsumes the cal-culation of symbolic (and social) capital within the calculation of economic capital (to use the terms developed by Pierre Bourdieu (1984)). On the other, the calculation of economic capital is rendered not purely quantitative – that is, it is not entirely a matter of the quantitative calculation of equivalence, but also of the qualculation (Callon and Law, 2003; Cochoy, 2002) and the pro-duction of difference and possibility. The brand is a matter not simply of *pouvoir* but also of *puissance* (Deleuze and Guattari, 1999: 174–191). It is both power as 'an instituted and reproducible relation of force' (or the actual) *and* power as 'potential, a scale of intensity or fullness of existence (that is, the virtual)' (Massumi, 1999: xvii).

Flows of disjuncture and difference

If the framing of exchange in terms of a dynamic interface is successful, the brand owner is able not simply to dominate a given market at a given moment in time, but to organise its spatial and temporal activities. In this *fourth* respect too, the notion of the medium is helpful in the attempt to describe the brand in so far as media have been widely understood *in terms of flow*, notably by Raymond Williams in his discussion of television (1974). Simmel had at the beginning of the twentieth century already described the liquidity of money. He drew attention to the importance of the rhythm of its movements – of the slow accumulation of private savings, the swings and roundabouts of corporate investment, the ups and downs of buying and selling stocks and shares, and the fluctuations of credit and debt – for the wider culture. As he puts it, 'Money is nothing but the vehicle for a movement in which everything else that is not in motion is completely extinguished' ([1907] 1990: 511). And a number of other commentators have more recently described the movements of not only money, but also people, ideas and risks in terms of flows (Appadurai, 1996; Lash and Urry, 1994; Shields, 1997). But Williams provides a precise elaboration of the logic of flow in his account of the experience of watching television (in making sense of this analogy, remember the notion of the brand as the broadcast distribution of commodities[12]).

For Williams, flow is *a sequence or serial assembly of units characterised by speed, variability and the miscellaneous*. In developing this definition, he notes the historical decline of the use of intervals between programmes in broadcasting – or rather, he draws attention to a fundamental re-evaluation of the interval. In the early days of broadcasting on radio, for example, there would be intervals of complete silence between programmes. But now, no longer dividing discrete programmes, no longer an interruption or silence, the interval plays a vital role in the management of the response gap of interactivity: it makes a sequence (or sequential progression) of programmes (or products) into a series or flow. Think here of the role of 'idents' – that is, the logos of broadcasting companies, which fill the previous gaps or silences between programmes (and sometimes now persist through programmes in the corner of the screen), making possible multiple associations within and across programmes.[13] The true sequence in broadcasting in these cases, Williams argues, is not the published sequence of programme items, but a series of differently associated units, some larger and some smaller than the individual programme. The argument proposed here is that in marketing practices, the logo is similarly able to secure the recognition of the brand *as a constantly shifting series of (variously related) products* through its positioning. It marks relations between products.

At its most basic, the repetition of a logo – which may be a name (Nike), a graphic image (the Swoosh) or a slogan ('Just do it') – means that when people are asked for examples of brands, most of them are able to give some, displaying what marketers call 'brand awareness'. But marketers argue that 'awareness' must be supported, if a brand is to be successful, by a second aspect: '*image*' (Keller, 1998). This 'image' is developed in the marketing practices of *brand positioning*, including product design, the promotion and positioning products in the media, and the management of the logo itself. The aim of such practices is to develop brand image as *the associations that a brand holds for consumers*. So, for example, as a result of the practices of brand positioning, the Nike brand image includes the associations of sports, determination and competitiveness. In so far as the practices of brand positioning are successful, the logo – or 'ident' – comes to function as a specular or speculative device for *magnifying one set of associations and then another* (Quinn, 1994; Ihde, 1995).[14] In this respect, to draw *a fifth parallel with media*, *brands may be seen as the effects of hyperlinking*, the principle that forms the basis of interactive media (Manovich, 2001: 61).

The management of brand image through the organised activity of hyperlinking – the making of one link after another, and in the process making associations – is both what makes brands not only visible and identifiable, and also gives them dynamic object-ive unity. And having a dynamic unity, the brand is able to present itself as having a *personality* or *face* (see Chapter 4), a process that has a long and complex history in the organisation of exchange. For example, Simmel explains the significance of personalisation in relation to money as capital by suggesting that the significance of a sum of money, such as 1 million marks, is more than a mere aggregate of unconnected units:

> Every sum of money has a different qualitative significance if it belongs to a number of people rather than to one person. The unit of the personality is thus the correlate or the pre-condition for all qualitative differences of possessions and their importance; here the assets of legal persons are, in terms of their function, on the same level because of the uniformity of their administration.
>
> ([1907] 1990: 271)

Simmel argues that qualitative significance arises because an aggregate sum of money forms 'a comprehensive unit in the same way as the value of a living creature, acting as a unit, [and] differs from the sum total of its individual organs' (ibid.: 272). In other words, he suggests that capital as *quantity*, as units of land, of money is capable of being realised as *quality* in certain circumstances. Similarly, the point being made here is that the *extensiveness* of capital – whether this is money or brand equity – is capable of being realised as *intensivity* when understood in terms of the singularity or dynamic unity of a person. This is of major importance in the brand's relation to consumers, since personalisation is what underpins the affective relations between brands and consumers, which typically include some degree of trust, respect and loyalty but may also include playfulness, scepticism and dislike. It is nurtured in the marketing practices that build brand relationships and brand loyalty (Chapters 2 and 6).

But 'idents' or logos are not simply the visible faces of the brand. They are also *marks of flow* or *shifters*. They are 'markers of the edge of between the aesthetic space of an image or text and the institutional space of a regime of value which frames and organizes aesthetic space' (Frow, 2002: 71). As noted on pp. 9–11, at the same time that the management of the response interval of interactivity enables a sequence of products to be made visible, these intervals are organised to produce branded products as the same (the guarantee of consistent quality), or as different, as authentic, fashionable, collectable or new. Indeed, in most cases the brand has no single temporality, but rather co-ordinates multiple temporalities. So, for example, Swatch is organised through the temporalities of both fashion and collecting, while the chocolate bar Twix has a limited edition (an orange chocolate-flavoured version that appears and then disappears) running alongside the everyday, ubiquitous temporality of its standard version. In the case of eBay, an Internet brand, a complex unity emerges from the co-ordination of the multiple temporalities of buying and selling between individuals, for whom time is a key variable. Thus, buying and selling are organised by eBay as an auction in which information not only about the product but also about the highest bid at any one time is set alongside information about how much longer the auction will be open. This may be a few months or only a few minutes. Price and time are here inter-related or mediated by the brand. The buyer is also evaluated in terms of a record of the opinions of those to whom he or she has previously sold something. This record typically includes comments not only about the accuracy of the buyer's descriptions of their goods, but also the speed with which goods were dispatched in the past. In co-ordinating the series of products that comprise the brand in these different ways, then, logos are markers of *the multiple temporalities* that contribute to the flows of disjuncture and difference that characterise the global economy (Appadurai, 1996). They are markers of the multiple logics of global flows.

The brand as an object of law

As noted on p. 10, the brand is a social currency that is neither a matter of private individuals nor entirely public. It is instead the object of private property claims in commercial and legal practices. To explore this point, it is helpful to continue the comparison between price and brand a little further. John Frow (2002) suggests that while price allows information to circulate, it requires 'a complex legal assemblage' to contain the tendency of information to proliferate freely and make possible the exaction of rent or profit. The same may be said of the brand. And it is for this reason that the book outlines some of the implications of the current legal definition in the United Kingdom of trade mark (see Chapter 5). At present, the 1994 Act defines a trade mark as 'any sign capable of being represented graphically which is capable of distinguishing the goods or services of one undertaking from those of other undertakings' (s. 1(1)). The argument put forward is that the law, like marketing, is implicated in the mediation of things – the global flows of disjuncture and difference described earlier – through the role it takes in the development of brand image. And what is important here is that the current legal definition of trade mark makes it possible that the distinctiveness of a logo is increasingly being judged in terms of linkages or associations, and not, as was the case previously, in relation to a fixed origin. To the extent that it does so, the law gives brand owners exclusive rights in the objectification of a set of associations held in the minds of consumers. In protecting the exclusive use of a sign defined in such a way, the law *not only constitutes the object the sign identifies as an object of property rights*, but also identifies it – as described on pp. 7–8 – as *a dynamic object*.

The brand is thus constituted as a mediated object, a dynamic object or artefact in legal judgments as to the distinctiveness of a trade mark. Defined in this way, the brand is not only potentially exploitable as the site of product innovation, but also legally protected as a means of corporate growth as in the practices of brand extension and brand regeneration. The law thus contributes to the emergence of an object – an image instrument – by which capital may not only extract rent from (intellectual) property (specifically through licensing or merchandising arrangements), but also build monopolies, dominate markets and secure investments in the ownership of innovation (Strathern, 1999). Alternatively put, as John Berger says of the perspectival window in painting, the market frame of the brand is 'a safe let into the wall, a safe into which the visible has been deposited' (quoted in Manovich, 2001: 105).

There is a further point to be made in relation to the role of the law, though. This is that while the associations that are protected in trade mark are held in law to be made in the minds of consumers, the consumption activities in which such associations might reasonably be assumed to be produced – at least in part – are not generally held to be objectifying. In other words, trade mark law does more than protect the mark owner from unfair forms of competition. It makes it possible for trade mark owners to establish and lay claim to property rights in new forms of object-ivity while only minimally acknowledging the implicatedness of the activities of consumers in this objectivity. The law's role in the development of the sign thus contributes not only to the asymmetrical nature of the communication that informs the objectivity of the brand, but also to its production of inequality, and to its abstraction from everyday life.

Just do *what?*

What, then, does the account of the brand outlined here raise for a soci-ological understanding of objects? The first point to have been made in this introduction is that there are multiple knowledges implicated in the brand's framing of the market – not simply the economic, but also those of marketing, design and the law. More radically, the suggestion is that the brand must also be seen in terms of the knowledge practices of images, information and the media. A second is that the objectivity of the brand is not independent of or external to these knowledge practices; they enter into the object itself. A third is that the brand is an object in movement – that is, its objectivity is not fixed, but rather is dynamic; the brand is in and of movement. A fourth point is that this dynamism can be seen as 'mixed, layered and heterogeneous images unfolding in time' (Rodowick, 1994). The fifth is that this unfolding is organ-ised in terms of an interactivity in which the recursive, looping use of informa-tion about the consumer plays a pivotal role, and sixth, contributes to the multiple logics of global flows. The seventh point is that the interactivity in which this objectivity emerges is currently organised in law so as to be not just asymmetrical but unequal.

Taken together, these points suggest that a sociology of objects should be – perhaps cannot avoid being – concerned not simply with descriptive know-ledge (with how things are), but also with the imperative (with how things should be) (Simon, [1969] 1981). In conventional sociological terms, one might say the brand's organisation of exchange is *a total and complete* social fact (Mauss, 1976), but perhaps it would be more accurate to say that it is *a totalis-ing and incomplete social fact*. The brand is simultaneously virtual and actual, abstract and concrete, a means of relativity and a medium of relationality. This is undoubtedly what makes it so effective as a mode of capital accumulation; but the incompleteness or openness of the brand also provides opportunities for consumers, sociologists and others to ask, 'Just do *what?*' (see Chapter 6). Typically, consumer organisations have made arguments for or against prod-ucts (not usually brands) in terms of price and quality, but the latter has been measured in rather limited, mechanical ways, often to do with the evaluation of a product's function, efficiency and value for money. This approach to objects seems somewhat limited; it does not acknowledge fully what it is that we do with an object when we 'just do it'. One might say of the brand, as Manovich says in relation to computer games, that they 'can pretend to be intelligent only by tricking us into using a very small part of who we are when we communicate with others' (2001: 34).[15] But the challenge for a soci-ological understanding of brands is how to contribute to the creation of inter-faces that would enable the complicity of producers and consumers (and others) in objective inequalities such as those of the brand to be challenged. The sociological imperative is to enable us to use more of ourselves in our communication with objects and introduce not only probabilities but also real possibility into the thing, the abstract object that is the brand.

Coda

In this introduction and throughout the rest of the book, I talk in terms of 'the brand' or 'branding', but I hope I will not be taken as doing so literally. There is no single thing at issue here, or even a single set of convergent processes. To understand the use of the phrase 'the brand' to imply a single, specific thing that is in all instances the same is to give what is at issue a kind of misplaced concreteness. It is to present a complex artefact as an immediate matter of fact (Haraway, 1999). To put this another way, to assume that the brand is a single thing would be to mistake the multiple and sometimes divergent layers of activity that have gone into producing the brand. Thus, the book is at some pains to outline (some of) the diverse professional activities of marketing, (graphic and product) design, accountancy, management and the law. It is not suggested that these activities are explicitly co-ordinated in the production of the brand, let alone purposefully integrated. Rather, they have multiple histories, are internally divided, in tension with each other, and may even be contradictory or opposed. It is also recognised that branding is not only a matter of relations between products and services; it also, increasingly, emerges in the management of people (David Beckham), places (Britain), charities (the Red Cross), campaigning organisations (Greenpeace), universities (Goldsmiths College) and political parties (New Labour). The method of working adopted has been working *back* from an object towards 'the system of mutual implication, the system of regularities, and the coherent network of conditions of possibilities that give the object its body and its sense' (Kwinter, 2001: 215; Haraway, 1999: 92–93, 95) and *forward* to the object as a possible set of relations and connections. The concern is to see how the 'thingyness' or 'objectivity' of the brand is something that has emerged slowly and unevenly over the past one hundred and fifty years, and then more intensively but still not always coherently (or purposively) over the past fifty or so years. The assumption is that because the brand is a happening fact (Whitehead, 1970), there is a demand – a sociological imperative – for something else to happen yet.

2 Marketing as a performative discipline and the emergence of the brand

The functioning of the economy of qualities involves the establishment of forms of organization that facilitate the intensification of collaboration between supply and demand, in a way that enables consumers to participate actively in the qualification of products. The establishment of distributed cognition devices, intended to organize real life experiments on preferences, tends to blur habitual distinctions between production, distribution and consumption. Design, as an activity that crosses through the entire organization, becomes central: the firm organizes itself to make the dynamic process of qualification and requalification of products possible and manageable.

(Callon *et al.*, 2002c: 212)

Introduction

The general argument to be developed in this chapter is that the brand is a key locus for the reconfiguring of contemporary processes of production. The focus will be on the use of information in the reflexive organisation of the market. The rise of the 'performative discipline' of marketing is central here (Callon, 1998c; Cochoy, 1998), since marketing has always concerned the definition of products both as objects within competitive market relations and as objects of consumption. In marketing, products must be defined both in terms of their similarity or difference from other objects that might occupy the same social space (in relation to competitors) and in terms of their integration in social life (in relation to consumers) (Slater, 2002a). Marketing work on product definitions thus involves destabilising and restabilising the product in terms of optimum positions within the practices of both competition and consumption (and thus also involves a de-framing and reframing of the market (Callon, 1998c)). More particularly, it is through the use of information about the market, both about competitors but also, crucially, about consumers, that the discipline of marketing has come to play an active role in the (ongoing) production of markets. Indeed, this role contributed to the growth in its pre-eminence as a management discipline in the second half of the twentieth century. The thesis of this book is that the contemporary significance of the brand as a new media object (Manovich, 2001) is in large part a consequence of this growth. However, rather than seeing the emergence of the brand[1] as the inevitable result of a single tendency ('the rise of marketing'), the more general argument will be to show the multiple processes at issue. In particular, attention will be paid to the significance of the activity of design (Chapter 3), developments in graphic and product design and media (Chapter 4) and law and accounting (Chapter 5), as well as retail management and marketing (this chapter).

The claim that information has become central to the organisation of the market is not to say that information has not always been important. In all markets, supply and demand transform each other through a sort of back-and-forth movement of information between the two, a kind of dance between the producer and the consumer (Storper, 2001). But to acknowledge this two-way relation does not presume the transparency of communication (see Chapter 7); the relationship between consumer expectations and producer performance is not now – and never has been – straightforward or direct. This and the following chapters aim to show that the involvement of many disciplines in the emergence of the brand contributes to a complex *mediation* of supply and demand, of what producers supply and what consumers demand. The argument that the brand is a medium has been made elsewhere, notably in Naomi Klein's influential book *No Logo* (2000). However, the two principal arguments to be made in this chapter elaborate this claim in particular ways. First, the contemporary brand marks a new stage in the mediated relationship between producer and consumer, and second, the understandings of information, image and media developed in the immediate post-Second World War period play a key role, fundamentally reconfiguring processes of production. The notion of the brand being developed here is thus part of a broader analysis of the implications of the use of information, image and media in the integration, co-ordination and organisation of the economy and everyday life (Baudrillard, 1997; Haraway, 1997; Manovich, 2001; Kwinter, 2001; Lash, 2002; Massumi, 2002).

Marketing as a performative discipline

The phenomena that are now described as brands are diverse, and any attempt to define the brand is caught within conflicting frameworks and is able to call upon multiple histories, each of which gives branding a different origin. But for present purposes, it will be suggested that branding becomes a visible force in the organisation of production in industrialised countries in the second half of the nineteenth century, and increases in significance – in fits and bursts – over the following one hundred and fifty years.[2] Anne McClintock (1995) shows that during this initial period, the stretching of markets over national and international space, the growth of national and international networks of circulation and distribution, together with economic rivalry between nations, created a climate within which the aggressive competition between producers became ever more intense. This competition contributed to the advertising and the first stages in the development of modern consumer culture and the early stages of the emergence of the brand as it is defined here. In England in 1884, for example, wrapped soap was sold for the first time under a brand name. McClintock argues that this event signals a major transformation in the economy: generic items formerly indistinguishable from one another – soap sold simply as soap – came to be marketed as distinctive through the use of corporate signatures or brands (such as Pears and Monkey Brand). From the 1880s onwards, corporate logos were increasingly used to promote a whole range of mass-produced products such as Rowntree's Fruit Pastilles and Fruit Gums, Bassett's Liquorice Allsorts, Campbell's soup, H. J. Heinz pickles and Quaker Oats cereal:

> Familiar personalities such as Dr Brown, Uncle Ben, Aunt Jemima, and old Grand-Dad came to replace the shopkeeper, who was traditionally measuring bulk foods for customers and acting as an advocate for products . . . a nationwide vocabulary of brand names replaced the small local shopkeeper as the interface between consumer and product.
>
> (Lupton and Abbott Miller, quoted in N. Klein, 2000: 6)

In 1886 in the United States, a medicinal product or 'nerve tonic' started being sold as Coca-Cola; as soon as the late 1890s, it was being promoted as the 'national drink'.

The early stages of the development of the brand were intended to allow the producer to speak 'directly' to the consumer through presentation, packaging and other media. In other words, the development of corporate and product personalities that characterise the early stages of the development of the modern brand was in part an attempt to circumvent or limit the role of the retailer. But it involves not simply a dis-intermediation (of the evaluative role of the retailer), but also a re-intermediation (the development of brand logos, identities or personalities to speak for the product, of which more in later chapters). Unsurprisingly, then, this period also sees the emergence of retail outlets as brands themselves: for example, large multiple stores such as Woolworths and J. C. Penney's in the United States and Thomas Lipton's stores in the United Kingdom began to standardise the quality of service in their stores. This stage in the history of brand development is thus closely linked to emerging conflicts between manufacturers and retailers, and these conflicts – and alliances – have continued to be important ever since.

It was through developments in techniques in communicating with – and acquiring knowledge about – the consumer that the discipline of marketing really begins to emerge. However, it is more appropriate to see even these early stages of the development of the brand in terms of an intervention in the system of production rather than in terms of (add-on) communication alone. While marketers were initially concerned only to describe the existing diverse ways in which products were brought to market – finding out what functions and firms were involved in making goods available to consumers – in a very short time they acquired a more active, interventionist role. In his overview of the development of marketing as a management science in the United States, Franck Cochoy identifies a series of overlapping developments:

> Firstly, marketing pioneers tried to train themselves in the empirical study of markets and to educate similar specialists. . . . Marketers reached that first objective by inventing special human and conceptual frames for market knowledge and practice. . . . From that point onward, the adepts of the discipline of marketing played the game of managers and management, of economist and the economy. . . . Eventually, they reshaped [not only] their own activity, but also the market and the economy altogether.
>
> (1998: 195)

Cochoy argues that it was not until the early twentieth century that the marketing function first began to be institutionalised alongside the emergence of a new body of industrial disciplines, regulatory bodies and management specialisms. (For example, the US Food and Drug Administration was established in 1906 to regulate corporations selling such goods.) Significantly, though, he suggests that it was the Roosevelt administration that really opened the door for marketing to participate in the increasingly technical management of market exchange in the United States. This administration co-ordinated the standardisation of market practices and organised the development of principles of industrial classification and marketing codes and conventions:

> While marketers were trying to organize themselves, by promoting the AMA [American Marketing Association] regulation over their profession, the Roosevelt administration was working to master the economy, by putting it under the State regulative action. On the one hand, the Federal

state was strongly supporting the use of industrial standardisation as a tool that could increase market visibility. The definition of industrial codes was particularly close to marketing thought: if the State aimed at the construction of conventions that could help a better identification of products . . . , marketers saw the same device as a strategic weapon for the conquest of competitive advantages: . . . the building of market conventions (at the global level) was becoming the key-tool of product differentiation and market segmentation (at the local level).

(Cochoy, 1998: 208)

This was also a period that saw a call for marketing knowledge to lead rather than to follow practice, for a shift from descriptive to prescriptive approaches, and from inductive to deductive methods of analysis (Cochoy, 1998). But this call was not taken up uniformly. There were clear differences in the development of marketing in different countries, linked to the position of this new discipline in a complex of commercial practices, including the organisation of different retail forms to capture market share (Bowlby, 1985, 1993; Nava, 1995; Winship, 2000).

In the United Kingdom in the early to mid-twentieth century, for example, the key form of retail organisation was the trade association. Such organisations were successful (from the point of view of their members) because they were able to limit forms of market competition. Thus, for example, the British trade associations persuaded manufacturers to establish resale price maintenance (RPM) in order to guarantee profits. By 1938, 27–35 per cent of all goods in the United Kingdom were sold at fixed prices. In other ways too, trade associations contributed to various forms of 'restraint on trade', with market control exercised through the placing of limits on business competition rather than through the development of either price and/or non-price forms of competition. Janice Winship writes:

Trade associations, ranking alongside 'pools, cartels, trusts, combines', found favour within British economic and political life, where ideas to moderate competition were summed up in the title of Harold Macmillan's book *The Middle Way* (1938). . . . Wiener has emphasised that by 1939 the prevalent form of organisation in the British economy was 'uncompetitive private enterprise in partnership with the British state' (1981: 109). Others have shown how the capital controlled by various public bodies or non-profit-making organisations (including the Co-op and building societies) was 'of the same order of magnitude as the aggregate capital of all joint-stock companies' (Pollard, 1983). Whether the Post Office, the BBC, the National Grid for electricity or the chain stores, these endeavours were conceived as 'public utilities' involving universal and standardised provision across the country.

(2000: 24)

In contrast, in the United States during this period, 'printed salesmanship', brand advertising and other early forms of non-price competition were more commonly adopted as the acceptable means of market control. Indeed, Winship argues that the different national histories indicated here point to an important tension between advertising-led and retail-led strategies of marketing between the United States and the United Kingdom in the first half of the twentieth century.

By the 1950s and 1960s, however, the discipline of marketing was more able to consolidate its subordination of production to a technical operationalisation of knowledge of the consumer not only in the US and the UK but more widely. Thus, 1960 saw the publication of Theodor Levitt's manifesto for a global marketing revolution. The distinction between selling and marketing was crucial to his argument. Selling, he said,

> focuses on the needs of the seller, marketing on the needs of the buyer. Selling is preoccupied with the seller's need to convert his product into cash, marketing with the idea of satisfying the needs of the customer by means of the product and the whole cluster of things associated with creating, delivering and finally consuming it.
>
> (Quoted in Mitchell, 2001: 76–77)

The consolidation of the role of marketing was linked to the changing role of retail; no longer a passive activity, driven by the manufacturer, it was increasingly becoming a complex and aggressive activity in which information about the consumer was a pivotal resource. So, for example, major retailers were able to exert greater control of the supply chain through their use of information systems technology to co-ordinate and organise store management, logistics and the distribution chain. The post-war period also sees the rise of self-service systems in retail outlets, in which the 'silent salesman' of brands, promotion and packaging was increasingly able to co-ordinate selling (Bowlby, 2000). But the increasing legitimacy of marketing was also a consequence of internal developments: the abandonment of institutional economics by marketers and the adoption of a combination of quantitative techniques and behavioural sciences (Cochoy, 1998). On the one hand, the implementation of operations research and econometrics led to the birth of marketing science, a research stream that could model and optimise market activities. On the other, the importation of statistics, psychology and behavioural analysis gave birth to what has come to be called consumer research. This involves the use of economic, social and psychographic demographics to map the target market. The combined use of these methods secured a growing authority for marketers, an authority that legitimated an increasingly important role for marketing in product development, product differentiation and product classification.

Crucially, the active role awarded to marketing involves a reorganisation of processes of what Callon calls product qualification and requalification, and puts more and more emphasis on differentiation. As Callon *et al.* say,

> The characteristics of a good are not properties which already exist and on which information simply has to be produced so that everyone can be made aware of them. Their definition or, in other words, their objectification, implies specific metrological work and heavy investment in measuring equipment. The consequence is that agreement on the characteristics is sometimes, in fact often, difficult to achieve. Not only may the list of characteristics be controversial (which characteristics ought to be taken into consideration?) but so also, above all, is the value to be given to each of them. Once agreement has been reached it will be characterized by a degree of robustness if the procedures used were objective.
>
> (2002: 198–199)

The measuring devices involved in the process of qualification-requalification (or product qualification trials) included statistical devices which increasingly showed that 'beyond prices, the result of competition depended on the management of the multi-dimensional aspects of products – above all, brands, services, packaging. It showed that one had to play on these many dimensions in order to shape the markets' (Cochoy, 1998: 213). As a consequence of the role of marketing in these qualification trials, the bundle of characteristics or attributes comprising the product was both multiplied – with attention to the so-called multi-dimensional aspects of the product – and dispersed across different stages of production and distribution. Attributes that had previously been held constant (apparently fixed properties) were now made variable. This contributed to the rise of what might be called the intensively differentiated, distributed product, in which the previously existing distinction between the processes of production (as the source of value) and those of distribution (as a means of exchange) begins to be eroded. More specifically, what emerged in this period was a widely adopted programme of marketing management. This involved the idea of the 'marketing mix', which sought to present the best marketing policy as an optimal and controlled combination of the 4 'P's – price, promotion, place and product strategies. The implementation of this programme was typically enforced through the systematic use of a Taylorian model of planning, analysis and control (Cochoy, 1998).

In the following years the commercial success of the 'marketing mix' led to further shifts in the role of marketing in the qualification and requalification of products. Marketers found ways to show that products are not adequately defined by their functional properties alone. Instead, qualification trials demonstrated that the product could not be limited to its physical characteristics – that is, they demonstrated that a product's existence extends beyond being a discrete physical good. In short, product qualification in terms of physical or functional properties was increasingly found inadequate for the disciplinary or performative purposes of marketing. Instead, the pattern of customers' needs as identified through the use of the behavioural sciences in consumer research – in particular, psychological theories of the self, such as Maslow's hierarchy of needs – were used to define a product's 'essence'. Products were classified according to the way they were perceived, used and bought by consumers, resulting in the creation of product categories such as 'convenience', 'shopping', 'speciality' and 'unsought'. The 'nature' or 'essence' of products understood in this way was thus directly linked to a framing of the market in terms of consumers' perceptions, needs and practices as construed in the knowledge practices of marketers.

Alongside the already established importance of tests of standardisation, tests of differentiation became more and more significant. By tests of standardisation is meant here the processes in which products are produced consistently in conformity to certain tests. Or to put this another way, standards are tests in which the quality of product consistency is produced. By tests of differentiation is meant the processes in which quality is subject to *experimentation*. These are process in which some of the variables (minimally including price, place, packaging and product but also design, style and service at the point of sale) of distributed production are held constant while others are intensively and systematically manipulated. In these processes of differentiation, quality (understood as the meeting of a fixed standard) is broken down and reconstituted as qualities (which may then of course be consolidated in the implementation of new, 'improved' standards). These are the processes that lead to what was described in Chapter 1 as the introduction of qualitative possibility into the brand.

This key stage in the emergence of the brand occurs in the second half of the twentieth century and is linked to a changed view of the producer–consumer relationship: no longer viewed in terms of stimulus–response, the relation was increasingly conceived of as an exchange. This changed view was advocated most explicitly by the proponents of a new organisational model for advertising agencies, one that put 'account planning' at the heart of the advertising process. This position was first developed by the London branch of J. Walter Thompson and the London agency Boase, Massimmi and Pollit in the 1960s, and was taken up more generally only slowly, first by advertising agencies in the 1980s and then by design consultancies in the 1990s (Julier, 2000). In this model, the account planner, whose role is to act as a representative of the point of view of the consumer within an agency, co-ordinates the various other aspects of the advertising process. The role was designed to offer the client an object-ive view of the consumer's experience and to ensure that the identity of the brand was maintained throughout the execution of the advertising design or creative process (ibid.: 19–20).

In the United Kingdom – and to some extent elsewhere – this attempt was associated with the rise of what was called 'creative advertising' in the 1980s and 1990s (Lash and Urry, 1994). This genre of advertising not only promoted the use of new forms of consumer research (especially lifestyle research, attitudinal and motivational research and psycho-demographics), but also aimed to construct for consumers an imaginary lifestyle within which the emotional and aesthetic values of the product were elaborated (Nixon, 1997: 195). Put in simple terms, there was an expansion of the use of qualitative methods in the market research industry; here, as in the social sciences more generally, there was an interpretative turn (Lury and Warde, 1996). There was also an increased 'reliance on sounds and shapes, which tapped into the feelings of consumers, rather than on logical propositions' (Mort, 1996: 96; Tomlinson, 1990). This in turn led to an increasing (although still marginal) acceptance of more intuitive approaches to branding:

> [Some companies] will be intuitive exponents of it, because they're learning by doing . . . I think that branding . . . is fundamentally a creative act, and therefore there are some examples of people who have done it almost accidentally . . . and those people very often aren't going to analyse it or articulate it very well because they live it and do it . . . that's because it is a making thing. It doesn't sit very well with analysis . . . it's a very difficult process for analysis to understand, if you see what I mean, in the sense that it's a bit like analysing an artist's work.
>
> (Adam Lury, quoted in Moor, 2003: 48)

From the 1970s onwards, there was also a move away from the branding of stand-alone products (that secured demand and often a price premium for the manufacturer by guaranteeing the consistency of quality) to the branding of product ranges and the branding of services. In this respect too, there is an increasing emphasis on the commercial significance of a dynamic of *product differentiation* and *brand integration*. The product mix – or brand object – that is produced in this way is sometimes said to have three dimensions: width, depth and consistency. The dimension of width refers to the number of different product lines established by a company (or brand proprietor). The depth refers to the average number of items offered by the company within each product line, while the consistency refers to how closely related the various product lines are in end use, production requirements and distribution channels. Or to put all this the other way around, the establishment and maintenance of links between a product item, a product line and a product assortment comes to be increasingly organised in relation to brands through the implementation of brand-name decisions, multi-brand decisions and brand repositioning strategies. To understand what is at issue here, think of the respective positions of the brands Wilkinson Sword and Gillette, both of which include razors in their product ranges. However, while Wilkinson Sword claims to be 'the name on the world's finest blades', Gillette says that it is 'the best a man can get' and is the brand name of a wide range of products including not only razors but also after-shaves and deodorants (G. Lury, 1998: 66). The brands respectively position themselves in the 'blades' or shaving market and the broader men's toiletries market, and have different profiles in the dimensions outlined above.

What is significant about this shift is that the brand emerges as *the organisation of a set of relations between products or services*. This is the emergence of the brand as a differential classification or system of objects (Baudrillard, 1997). A number of accounts of brands stress their role as a mark of ownership or badge intended to create trust in the consumer through the identification of an origin. And certainly there are continuing grounds to support the notion of the brand as a guarantee of a consistency of quality or sameness by reference to an origin. Thus, trade mark law is widely acknowledged to have historically been a means to secure a monopoly on the use of that mark, with the dual purpose of protecting the owner from unfair competition and the consumer from 'confusion' as to the origin of the good. Hence, trade mark is a form of intellectual property right that has historically been asserted by manufacturers of products. Importantly, though, the law has long accepted that the 'origin function' can include selection as well as manufacture. Furthermore, in many respects the notion of an origin for a product or service is increasingly difficult to sustain (see Chapter 5 for further discussion of this argument).

For example, as noted above, contemporary brands may in part be seen as a response to struggles between manufacturers and retailers. On the one hand, it is a strategy in which manufacturers may take on more and more functions of retail. These may include not only the selection and display of goods but also the planning and standardisation of methods of property acquisition and shop layout, together with control of price, stock and distribution. On the other hand, the development of retail brands gives retailers powers over manufacturers, giving them a greater role in product development, product design and pricing. The role of retailers has also been further extended through the elaboration of specific retail styles (Jackson *et al.* 2000), the profiling of customers (see Chapter 6) and the development of customer care services. In such cases, retail service (like many other services) is seen as a co-production of producer and consumer. In short, the source or origin of a product or service is increasingly unclear.

The more general point being made here is that the origin function of the trade mark does not define the brand today. Instead, the suggestion is that the brand is *the organisation of a set of multi-dimensional relations between products or services*, a set of relations that is the site of statistical testing and qualitative experimentation, subject to the rapidly changing pressures of intensive mediation, stylisation and practices of commercial calculation. The brand is thus a mechanism – or medium – for the co-construction of supply and demand (Callon *et al.*, 2002). It is not simply an add-on, a mark to identify an origin that is fixed. Instead, it is an abstract machine for the reconfiguration of production.

Once the brand is developed in this way, it is able to function as a medium for new product or new service development. For example, 'One general rule with the Levi's brand is that all innovations must be "Levi's-like". What that means is that innovations are pursued or rejected based on their compatibility with the core values and attributes of the brand' (Holloway, 1999: 71). This process of product development is sometimes described in the marketing literature as *brand extension*. Thus, for example, the Persil trademark for detergents has been extended to Persil washing-up liquid, the Mars trademark for chocolate bars has been extended to ice creams, and the Smirnoff vodka brand recently introduced a citrus-flavoured, single-serve drink, Smirnoff Ice. Similarly, starting with women's skin-care products, Nivea has been extended into men's products, including deodorants, shampoos and electric razors (that dispense moisturiser). The luxury fashion brand Versace has been extended to include a hotel and hospitality service; the product brand Lynx has established a Lynx Barbershop. In all these examples, the company makes use of the multi-dimensional objectivity of the existing brand to enter a new market more cheaply, establish the product or service more quickly and increase the overall exposure of the brand. In these and other ways, then, the brand has become a central feature of contemporary economic life.

Of course, marketers cannot be held entirely responsible for the new role (and commercial success) of brands. That the adoption of marketing was to prove so effective is in large part a consequence of its relation to other changes in the production process, notably those changes associated with the processes of flexible specialisation (Harvey, 1990; Lash and Urry, 1994; Castells, 1996). These are processes in which production is flexibly organised for specialised rather than mass production and decentralised through the use of communication media and information technologies. These changes mean that product differentiation in terms of function is less and less often able to sustain competitive advantage (because it can be imitated so quickly). At the same time, the production process is itself more flexible, more able to adapt or flexibly respond to requirements for new or differentiated products. But marketing played a key role in the *organisation of this flexibility*, especially in so far as it contributes to an active role for changing conceptions of the consumer. Marketing not only provides the rationale for increasing the rate of product differentiation (as markets are conceived to be dynamic), but also provides the framework within which product differentiation occurs (as markets are reconfigured in terms provided by marketing knowledge about the consumer). The brand must thus be seen in the context of an economy in which flexibility is a necessity, in which the dynamic differentiation of products enables the management of change.

Starbucks: 'There are no heroes. . . . What we've done is provide a safe harbor'

One example of the commercial exploitation of the multi-dimensional objectivity of the brand as it has developed in recent years is Starbucks.[3] In the post-war period, the market for coffee in the USA had been dominated by three big companies: Nestlé, General Foods, and Procter and Gamble. Together they controlled nearly 60 per cent of roasted coffee and 80 per cent of instant coffee sales. However, coffee consumption began to fall in the mid-1960s. By the late 1980s, about half the US population over the age of 10 did not consume coffee at all, and coffee consumption had fallen behind that of soft drinks. But over the same period, a speciality coffee market began to develop, although no one single company dominated the market. In this context, the aim of the soon-to-be Starbucks CEO Howard Schulz was to transform coffee from a commodity ('something to be bagged and sent home with the groceries') into a branded offering that consumers associated with (consistent) quality, service and community. In undertaking this transformation, he sought to bring about a reorganisation of the market corresponding to a shift from a commodity market to a brand market. This involved the reframing of the market in terms of consumer preferences as identified in marketing research. At this time, market research in the United States identified an increasing preference for 'natural foods' – that is, foods perceived to be less processed and more nutritious; a rise in the acceptance of 'ethnic' foods; and a greater emphasis on taste (in its full range of meanings) in consumer decision-making.

More recently, as Starbucks is expanding globally, market research in Chile suggests there is an emerging market segment of 30-something executives and media workers who eschew the traditional Chilean culture of austerity:

> 'These are the same people who now buy wine based on grape, harvest and region rather than what's on sale,' says Ricardo Grellet, a local sommelier who offers coffee-tasting classes. 'Starbucks has arrived in Chile at just the right moment.'
>
> (Mulligan and Authers, 2003: 14)

In the mid-1980s, the market research findings outlined earlier were interpreted by Schulz as requiring that special attention be paid not only to the consistency of quality of the coffee the company sold, but also to its 'authenticity'. In 1987, when Schulz – who was already running a speciality coffee retailing business – bought the company called Starbucks (which he had previously worked for), the deal bought him not only the name and six retail stores but also coffee-roasting facilities. This up-scale integration (from retail back up the supply chain to manufacturing) allowed him to control more rigorously the quality of products he sold. Slowly, quality control was further consolidated by the introduction of an organisational infrastructure that was oriented towards the production of a standardised set of products. This included a set of highly intensive quality control processes, including direct purchase of coffee from wholesalers; coffee roasting and blending by trained personnel in Starbucks facilities according to specific protocols; shipping to company stores or wholesale customers in specially designed FlavorLock Bags; and personal service by company-trained employees. For example, in the mid-1990s the employee training programme took three days, and comprised subjects including Brewing the Perfect Cup, and included the following rule: milk for cappuccinos, cafe lattes and other beverages has to be steamed to between 150° and 170°F. Each espresso shot has to be poured within 23 seconds of brewing or be thrown out. In 'Coffee Knowledge', new employees learned to distinguish between coffee made from Starbucks-sourced beans and others. In 'Retail Skills', they were taught how to clean counter equipment, weigh, measure and grind beans, fill one-pound bags, and fix the sticker with the name of the particular coffee exactly half an inch over the Starbucks logo. The quality control mechanisms also included the establishment of retail outlets in carefully selected locations. The criteria of selection included locating in places that are already 'on the way' for consumers:

> 'We want to be in highly visible locations that provide easy access for our customers. . . . You want a store located in the path of people's daily

shopping experience, their route to work, or their way home from a
movie. You want to be America's front porch, the place where people
gather to meet neighbors and friends.'

(Rubinfeld, quoted in Koehn, 2001: 244)

Other relevant factors in deciding where to locate a Starbucks store included
information about population density, residents' median age and education
level, estimated household income, information about the state of local
competition and, contentiously, the application of a principle of 'store clustering'. This is the clustering of new Starbucks stores close to each other (see
N. Klein, 2000 for a critical discussion of this practice). This apparently self-
defeating strategy is designed to attract consumer attention, lock up market
share and deter other coffee retailers, and is conducted despite the recognised
consequence of so-called cannibalisation of business in already established Starbucks stores in the locality. Once their locations are chosen, stores are also
designed by an in-house team of real-estate managers, architects, designers
and construction managers, according to fixed parameters for store design,
typically incorporating natural materials such as hardwood cabinetry and slate
flooring. The choice of both location and design of the outlet is governed by
the brand imperative for its coffee stores to become a recognised 'third place'
– a location apart from both home and work.

All these (and other) techniques, procedures and practices are what comprise the standardisation of the brand. So important is this standardisation to
the company's self-perception of the values that it promotes that Starbucks
seeks to control closely all its operations:

> Across all channels of American society and culture, there is such a frac-
> turing of values. There are no heroes. . . . There is little trust in a number
> of public institutions. . . . I am not saying Starbucks is going to save the
> world because we can't. . . . What we've done is provide a safe harbor
> for people to go. I think the brand equity of the name Starbucks has sup-
> plied a level of trust and confidence, not only in the product, the trade-
> mark, but in the experience of what Starbucks is about. At a time when
> there are very few things that people have faith in. It's a very fragile thing.
> You can't take it for granted. It's something that has to be respected and
> continually built upon.

(Schulz, quoted in Koehn, 2001: 247)

But this did not mean that there was no product differentiation within the
brand: rather, the contrary. The mid-1990s saw the development of several
new products by Starbucks, including a coffee named Blue Note Blend, a

blend that was the core of a marketing campaign that also featured jazz CDs, specially produced with Capitol Records Inc. and its Blue Note record label. What is especially interesting here is the way in which both products – coffee and music – are part of, or emerge in, processes of brand positioning.

In 1995, Frappuccino – a sweet, cold, creamy drink combining coffee, milk and ice – was sold for the first time. Two years later, Power Frappuccino®, a blended coffee drink that included protein, carbohydrates and vitamins, joined the Starbucks product mix. Through a joint venture with Pepsi-Cola, Starbucks also began selling a bottled version of Frappuccino in US supermarkets. By 1998, bottled Frappuccino was the most popular ready-to-drink coffee drink in the United States. The late 1990s saw the development of yet more products: Caramel Frappuccino, Chai Tea Latte, Caramel Apple Cider and White Chocolate Mocha, and alliances with Dreyer's Grand Ice Cream to make premium coffee-flavoured ice cream, sold in supermarkets, and alliances with Barnes and Noble and United Airlines to sell Starbucks products. These were all done with the aim of broadening Starbucks' product line, distribution channels and name recognition (that is, enhancing brand integration). In 1998, Starbucks entered a long-term licensing agreement with Kraft to accelerate the growth of Starbucks brand into the grocery channel. Under the terms of the agreement, Kraft managed all distribution, marketing and promotions for Starbucks whole-bean and ground coffee in grocery, warehouse club and mass-merchandise stores. In return, Starbucks sold Kraft the packaged products, receiving licensing fees as a percentage of sales. 'We want to expand our brand franchise to be where consumers work, travel, relax, and to help increase our customer base as the overall market develops' (Eades, quoted in Koehn, 2001: 251). So, while coffee is returned to the shelves of grocery stores, it is not as a commodity (a generic product, something to be bagged) but as a brand (a range of products with an identity, something that has been positioned in relation to consumers).

From the single store in Seattle's Pike Place Market with which it started, Starbucks today owns 3,907 stores in North America and licenses a further 1,378. It also owns 437 stores and franchises 1,180 outlets in the rest of the world. It is present in 30 countries, and was introduced to Mexico, Germany, Spain, Austria, Puerto Rico, Greece, Oman, Indonesia and southern China in 2002, while South America, including Chile, was the focus of growth in 2003. Starbuck's 'corners' or mini-outlets are found in airline offices, sports stadiums, airports, hotels and bookshops, while spin-off products include own-brand coffee beans, bottled coffee-based beverages, music recordings, ice cream and other foodstuffs. In 2002, the company reported consolidated net profits of $215 million on sales that were up 24 per cent at $3.32 billion. In the company's annual report, Schultz lays claim to 20 million customers a week (Mulligan and Authers, 2003: 14).

What distinguishes the strategy of Starbucks as a brand-led (rather than product-led) company is that the differentiation of products and services is organised in relation to the incorporation of information about consumers. This process results in the integration (or integrity) of the brand. But the use of information about consumers in brand-building is not to say that actual consumers are seen as the only, or even the best, arbiters of the qualities of products. Thus, Schulz was initially unwilling to sell coffee drinks made with skimmed milk or with added flavours – despite consumer requests – since at this stage in its development he believed this would compromise the integrity of the brand (which was, initially at least, a matter of authenticity). It was only when the brand was well established that such innovations were adopted. So, while there is a concern to identify customer response to what is offered, this response was and is intensively (and selectively) mediated. Indeed, in Chapter 3 this selectivity will be understood in terms of the performativity of the brand as an interface, a two-way, asymmetrical exchange of information. Moreover, while a particular experience is held to be at the heart of the brand, this experience is something that the company is held to have earned (see Chapter 4 for further discussion of the notion of brand relationships). The company thus can claim to have exclusive property rights in this experience or lived relation: 'We have created a set of expectations around an intimacy of experience that lies at the heart of what we are as a company and brand.' The implications for ownership and use of this identification of the lived experience of the brand as a property will be further explored in Chapter 5.

The organisation of the production process in terms of the brand

By the 1980s and 1990s, there was a rapid increase in both the branding of services and corporate branding – that is, the branding of a company rather than either particular products or services. This results in a situation in which 'the bulk of consumer spending is on corporate brands (motor cars, financial services, telecommunications and utilities) rather than on product brands' (Mottram, 1998: 63). For example, Mitsubishi is the brand of a company that manufactures cars, stereos, medical equipment and textiles, as well as being in the shipbuilding and banking industries. The Virgin brand includes air and rail travel services, a music company, financial services, mobile telephones, fashion, cosmetics and drinks. As a consequence of such developments, it became possible for marketers to claim that 'Many of the brands that are emerging today are succeeding because they do not focus on a specific product, but instead communicate clear values which can extend across a plethora of different products and services' (Hart, 1998: 208). At the same time, marketing becomes increasingly central to the internal organisation of firms, and brands come to have a dual role: in organising the exchange between producers and consumers, and in organising relations within the company itself, between employers and employees. This latter role is sometimes described as 'internal marketing'. As the brand management company Interbrand puts it:

> A corporate brand stands for the relationship that an organization has with its employees, as much as it represents the relationship that it has with its customers through its product and service offerings. For a brand to come to life with customers, the organization must be internally aligned to deliver the brand promise through the organization's culture, reward systems, key success activities and structure. In other words, employees must 'live' the brand values in their day-to-day interactions.
>
> (Interbrand Insights, 2001, www.Interbrand.co.uk)

In the 1980s, a famous slogan for what was then called British Rail – 'We're Getting There' – was widely known to be as much a message to those who worked for this much-maligned service as to its passengers (or customers, as they have since come to be known). Elements of the visual identity of the brand British Rail were also part of an organisational strategy to change working practices. The brand may thus be seen as one of a growing number of devices to monitor and control the performance of the employee, including productivity monitoring, video surveillance and so-called active-badge systems. So, for example, a 'silver swallow' was part of the visual design identity produced for Inter-City by the company Newell and Sorell in 1986, and was an element of the visual design identity that was applied to the trains as well as to literature and publicity. Employees were encouraged to 'earn' a 'silver swallow' badge as part of a drive to raise standards (Mollerup, 1997: 46–47).

By the last decade of the twentieth century, brand management was no longer the responsibility of the marketing department alone, but permeated the organisation of companies more widely. In 2000, a survey of 200 senior UK managers revealed that 73 per cent anticipated restructuring their companies, building the working structure of the firm around the brand (Manuelli, 2000, quoted in Julier, 2000: 193). Indeed, the role for the brand within a company has become increasingly widespread, such that it is now claimed that 'The 4 "P"s (product, price, promotion and placement) are all replicable by competitors; the only thing not replicable is the fifth P, the personality of the organization, or its people' (Kevin Thomas, President of MCA Communicates, quoted in Webster, 2003). This of course makes brand management a problem of management in general:

> How does the company make sure that there is a perfect match between values and behaviour? Products, buildings and machines – even ideas – can be copied, but the only unique elements in a company are its people. They constitute the soul of the brand. The first step to creating brand authenticity is therefore to ensure that its core values are clear and have been fully internalised by those who work within the company. That is not to say everyone has to be identical – that would be impossible and undesirable. But there should be certain values that they share *as part of their own core values*.
>
> (Marzano, 2000: 58; emphasis added)

In this regard, consider the ways in which the management of the brand informs the organisation of the work process through the mobilisation of constructions of the market in terms of information about the consumer (as Bourdieu (1984) remarks, the act of classifying acts back on those who classify). The point being made here is that the creation of market hierarchies in terms of classifications of the consumer provides resources for techniques of control in the management of the work process, and the incorporation, marginalisation and exclusion of particular social groups *as producers or workers*. This occurs as a consequence of the ways in which organisations of the market in terms of consumer characteristics, behaviours and tastes provide the resources for the definition of jobs, the organisation of the work process, and competition between groups of workers as well as that between individual workers.

Most importantly, markets are increasingly seen as dynamic. The imagining, mapping and anticipation of this dynamism provide the basis for new forms of competition and control in the workplace. So, for example, the creation of the taste pyramid (Mort, 1996), market niches, and taste groups by marketers provided a constantly shifting set of new resources not only for product innovation but also for the management of employees. In recounting the history of Philips, a designer suggests that the company has moved from meeting the needs of people relating to the lower rungs of Maslow's scale – food, shelter, work – to those concerning the higher levels, such as self-actualisation and cultural well-being (Marzano, 2000: 59). The skills required to meet these needs may include not only those acquired through specialist training, but also the employee's knowledge of themselves, their interests and even their fan orientations, as skill recognition is conducted in relation to the aim of satisfying certain target markets (groups of consumers). To put this another way, conceiving the market as dynamic, as constantly shifting, provides grounds – or organisational resources – not only for constant innovation, but also for an insecure, high-pressure working environment.

The mobilisation of constructions of the market in the organisation of the work process may involve addressing (potential) employees as if they were brand ambassadors, partners (as do Starbucks) or even consumers. Typically, it requires employees to consider their work as a means of adding value to themselves (du Gay, 1996; Pettinger, forthcoming). The McDonald's slogan – 'I work for McDonald's. McDonald's works for me' (www.mcdonalds.com) – is symptomatic here. The employee is required to interpret and constitute themselves and their interests in relation to the goals of the company, and this may involve participating in a company philosophy or brand mission statement (a more recent slogan that adorns McDonald's uniforms is 'I'm lovin' it'). Sometimes the identification of employees as consumers is achieved straight-forwardly, as when a company employs members of the social group to whom it wishes to sell, as is supposedly the case with the Italian fashion company Diesel, or sports retailers such as Athlete's Foot or Shoe Science. The recruit-ment process at Pret A Manger requires prospective employees not only to complete an interview process successfully, but also to undergo peer review by working for one day at a Pret store. The employees of that store then con-tribute to the final decision as to whether the prospective employee is hired or not. The company believes that this is a way of ensuring that employees have the appropriate Pret attitude. And while the alignment of employees with a brand usually happens more indirectly than in the case of Pret A Manger, the management of brands increasingly has implications for who gets hired or not, who gets promoted or not, and thus who prospers or not.

However, while the dynamism of the market may provide a basis for product or service innovation, what is acknowledged to be innovative or cre-ative in any particular company is not necessarily immediately apparent as such. Not all difference or change will be perceived as innovative. Whether and how change is recognised, named, owned and exploited is typically a matter of contestation. It both reflects and reinforces divisions within and between occupations. In very general terms, Castells (2000) argues that there is a division of labour into two categories within the global economy. The first category includes what he calls *self-programmable labour* – that is, labour which is equipped with the ability to retrain itself, and adapt to new tasks, new processes and new sources of information, as technology, demand and man-agement speed up their rate of exchange. Similarly, in relation more specifi-cally to the culture industry, a number of writers (du Gay, 1996; Lash and Urry, 1994; McRobbie, 1998, 1999; Nixon, 2003) have argued that one of the key workplace assets in the so-called talent- or design-intensive economy is the ability to claim that a job is creative or innovative.[4]

A striking example of this is to be found in the management literature that explicitly advises white-collar employees to present themselves as brands (so-called personal branding). Consider how Tom Peters describes the project of becoming 'brand you' in *The Brand You 50: Fifty Ways to Transform Yourself from an 'Employee' into a Brand That Shouts Distinction, Commitment, and Passion!* (1999). He outlines a number of exercises for those wishing to turn themselves into brands: make a personal brand equity evaluation; develop a one-eighth (or one-quarter) page Yellow Pages ad for brand you/me and co.; create an eight-word personal positioning statement; and devise a bumper sticker that describes your essence. As the back cover makes clear, Peters believes the choice to take up this opportunity is driven by the need for survival in a changing labour market.

> In today's wired world, you're distinct . . . or extinct. Survive, thrive, triumph by becoming **Brand You!**
>
> The fundamental unit in today's economy is the individual, a.k.a. YOU! Jobs are performed by temporary networks that disband when the project is done. So to succeed you have to think of yourself as a freelance contractor – **Brand You!** Someone who is savvy, informed, always learning and growing, who knows how to sell herself, and – most important – **does work that matters**.

The fate facing those who fail in (or can never aspire to) such an enterprise is to fall into Castells's second category, so-called *generic* (or *commodity*) *labour*. This labour is easily substitutable and disposable, is institutionalised in organisationally sanctioned scripts, and co-exists in circuits with machines and unskilled labour from around the world (Hochschild, 1983; Gabriel, 1995; Ritzer, 1993). It is also often subject to intensive surveillance and particularly invasive forms of workplace control. Such employees' personal characteristics are frequently linked to their 'suitability' evaluated in relation to quality service imperatives (Adkins, 1995, 2002; Adkins and Lury, 1999; Pettinger, forthcoming). Indeed, their labour is increasingly drawn into and considered integral to the 'hardware' of the company:

> In this way, for some companies in the 'style' labour market, such as design-led hotels, style bars and cafés and designer fashion retailers, staff are intended to be the embodiment of the company, at which point the human software is transformed into the corporate hardware and becomes in this process an important part of what the customer consumes.
>
> (Nickson *et al.*, 2001: 176)

The rise of the brand has heightened this hierarchical division of labour (although to see it as a binary divide undoubtedly overstates the simplicity of the hierarchy), with design-intensive producers located at the top of the hierarchy and many of those actually involved in manufacturing the products or delivering the service at the bottom. For example, only a few pennies of the price of a Starbucks cappuccino goes to pay for the labour of those who harvest and roast coffee beans, and not many more are paid to those who serve the drinks. The remainder accrues to those able to assert the value of their contribution to the brand in terms of creativity, product innovation or design activity (see Chapter 3).

Brands as events and activities

The commercial success of the marketing management model outlined in this chapter has been such that the brand has been extended *in and beyond business* through the invention of '*social marketing*'. In relation to business, this is an approach which proposes that companies should acknowledge their 'strong social influence on a society's sense of purpose, direction and economic growth' (Hart, 1998: 213).

> Since brands play such a fundamental role in society, we believe it is the responsibility of brand owners to begin to ask themselves more wide-ranging and searching questions: rather than ask a straightforward question such as 'Will it sell?' they must ask a series of more complex questions: 'Will it make a contribution to our customer's success?' 'Will it improve the customer's and society's well-being?' 'Does it add to our country's cultural stock or bring pride to our nation?'
>
> (ibid.: 213–214)

Outside business, it has involved a tendency for 'non-business' organisations such as universities, political parties, charities, football clubs, voluntary and campaigning groups (see Szersynski, 1997) places, and individual people to be presented as brands. As Cochoy (1998) notes, social marketing is oriented towards fundamental research, towards the study of the consumer for his or her own sake as it were, rather than towards the study of the consumer for the optimisation of markets. And certainly the figure of the customer, the consumer or the user is central to many recent attempts to reconstruct institutions and practices in both the public and the private sectors (Keat *et al.*, 1994; du Gay, 1996).

In this pursuit of the consumer, contemporary marketing makes use of an ever-increasing set of approaches, including those developed in anthropology, sociology, cultural studies and semiotics. Marketing and advertising executives – with job titles such as 'Experience Officer' – are themselves increasingly drawn from those with educational qualifications in these fields. The openness of the marketing discipline to such approaches has been linked by Adam

Arvidsson (forthcoming) to an analysis of the changing environment of the brand, notably the intensification of processes of mediation and re-mediation.[5] This includes, most importantly, the continuing expansion and differentiation of television culture, and the growing use of home computers, video, computer games, the Internet and personal stereos. In an article written just as television had taken over radio's position as the main marketing channel, Gardner and Levy (1955, cited in Arvidsson) argued that marketers needed to invest more in positioning brands within media culture and less in attempting directly to persuade consumers to buy products. But it is only now, Arvidsson argues that it is now widely accepted in marketing thought that sales are most effectively made as a consequence of *the positioning of the brand* (see Chapter 4). This is what has become an increasingly media-intensive culture, in which the distinction between advertising and media message is increasingly blurred. And as a former director of HHCL advertising agency says, 'everything is unpaid media if you want to use it in that kind of way' (A. Lury, quoted in Moor, 2003: 45).

Arvidsson argues that this shift in perspective happens in part because advertising is assumed to have lost most of its (or never had much) capacity to persuade consumers. The industry's own research had undermined faith in the established linear sequential models of the communication process.[6] These rested on the presupposition that consumers are more or less passive subjects to be moved by advertising through various behavioural stages from product awareness to buying decision. In contrast, marketers have increasingly become advocates of the view that consumers are active and reflexive. In relation to this active, or reflexive, consumer, Arvidsson notes that so-called post-modern marketing posits a different logic of value from that of the classic marketing approach: the 'semiotic logic of value' (Firat and Venkatesh, 1993, cited in Arvidsson). In this approach, consumers value products according to the position they occupy in the flow of media culture. Value is principally derived from brand image; and the relation between product, image and value is reversed (Firat and Schultz, 1997, cited in Arvidsson; Franklin *et al.*, 2000). Moreover, so Arvidsson argues, this view of the consumer has also undermined – to some extent at least – the utility of traditional tools of market segmentation. Instead of a desire to keep up with the Joneses, consumers are believed to be more concerned with finding meaning in their lives. For example, British marketing expert John Grant suggests that the aim of 'the new marketing' is to seek to fill the 'great gaps of meaning that exist in people's lives' and to propose brands as 'ideas that people can live by' (1999: 15).

The use of 'cultural' approaches by not only brand management and design agencies but also the marketing personnel in large corporate firms contributes to a more situated model of the consumer, supplementing and deepening previous constructions of the individuated, rational consumer. A well-known example of the commercial benefits of this approach is Sony's development of portable televisions:

> The American company General Electric had conducted a survey by judging people's responses to mock-up televisions to estimate demand for a small portable TV, the conclusion of which was that the 'people do not place a high value on portability of the television set' (General Electric, quoted in Lorenz 1986: 34). By contrast, Sony looked at people's behavioural patterns at home and the number and type of TV channels available. Using this data they anticipated that a portable TV would actually suit changes in these patterns. Following the success of their portable TV, they then went on to do precisely the same with the video cassette recorder, the Walkman personal stereo and the Watchman flat-tube TV.
>
> (Julier, 2000: 100)

Sometimes, consumers' conscious knowledge of their own needs, desires and wants is explicitly described as inadequate for the purposes of marketing. The rise of social marketing also contributes to a devaluing of what has come pejoratively to be called rear-view marketing and the rise of the aspiration among marketers to be able to provide future knowledge of consumer behaviour. A designer at Philips, the electronic goods company, notes:

> Technologies are increasingly shared among companies, so that the real differentiating factor is the way technology is shaped. This is more than a question of styling. To design is to shape the future. The Italian for design is *progetto*, or *architetturra* – project, or architecture. These expressions clearly convey how design gives physical shape to ideas that will affect people's lives. Viewed in this way, design is a continuous attempt to create future civilisation – no small undertaking.
>
> (Marzano, 2000: 59)

In seeking to develop this 'Vision of the future' (a 1996 slogan), Philips makes use of practices of modelling or simulating everyday life. Multi-disciplinary teams are brought together to develop 'scenarios' – that is, 'short stories describing a product concept and its use'. Such scenarios are then evaluated in relation to four 'domains' that 'represent all aspects of everyday life': 'personal', 'domestic', 'public' and 'mobile'. New products are then proposed for production in the form of 'tangible models, simulations of interfaces and short films'. Companies such as The Future Laboratory seek to present information about the future to clients such as the BBC, Procter and Gamble and Marks and Spencer. This company provides information about key changes in consumer and lifestyle trends, edits a magazine called *Viewpoint*, and uses video-makers, photographers and 'guerrilla researchers' to produce custom-made reports for clients.

The development of a more situated model of the consumer has also been fed by the development of retail management and retail design, 'theming', event-based and ambient-marketing sub-disciplines, in all of which the brand is staged as a performance or an event of some kind. For example, the aim of contemporary 'brandscaping', according to architect Johannes Ringer, is to 'provide a space where consumers and retailers can interact' (Riewoldt, 2002: 104, quoted in Arvidsson, forthcoming). Niketowns are designed to encourage consumer activity in the space of the store: visitors are invited to try on shoes and clothing, test athletic equipment, watch videos, listen to music and, in some stores, use an indoor basketball space. In discussing the use of the Niketown in Chicago, Arvidsson notes:

> [I]nteraction frequently takes place across generations, as the store is full of parents who bring their children. Consumers are thus not just awed by the Michael Jordan statue, but that awe is communicated from parents to children. Together they perform an event where the truth of Nike values – that you can 'Just do it' – acquires a significance that goes far beyond the accomplishments of a particular athlete.
>
> (forthcoming)

Other examples of dedicated retail stores that function as marketing devices include Original Levi's Stores, which are said to provide 'an invaluable test-bed for new ideas, such as powerful point-of-sale strategies related to our advertising campaigns' (Holloway, 1999: 76). Sony showrooms located in global cities such as Tokyo, New York and Paris are furnished with 'lifestyle settings' such as bedrooms, offices and lounges, and consumers are encouraged to play with Sony products.

> Their behaviour and preferences are closely monitored by Sony staff. The showroom thus becomes a laboratory for analysing consumer reactions to different products. This information is passed on to Sony headquarters which then feeds into subsequent product research and development.
>
> (Julier, 2000: 106)

Event-based marketing is now common and includes sponsoring existing music, sporting or arts events, as well as specially arranging events (Moor, 2003). Sometimes the specially organised event may be a sporting occasion

(Nike fun-runs), a leisure activity (Playstation club nights), art events (joint exhibitions between the Victoria and Albert Museum in London and the department store Selfridges), or even the opening of a new shop:

> In its ambitious plan to cover the globe with spectacular architecture, Prada is nothing if not methodical. The SoHo store was designed by Rem Koolhaas, the prince of daringly prosaic design; ever since it opened in late 2001, tourists have come along just to check out the dressing rooms outfitted with the latest interactive technologies. Now a new store in Tokyo is advancing the Prada cause. Designed by Jacques Herzog and Pierre de Meuron of Switzerland, the store, which opened on June 6, is a six-storey, freestanding mirror of the Prada gestalt.
>
> (Vlovine, 2003: 12)

Sometimes the event may just be the launch of an (expensive) advertisement, such as the annual launch of Levi's new advertising campaign: for example, the 60-second advertisement, entitled 'Swap', and costing just under $1 million to make, was launched across 13 European countries on 13 February in 2003:

> The story of Swap is bizarre, but put simply, runs something like this. The new jean, Type 1, is a bold jean, and is represented and worn by a group of very bold characters: mutant 'mice-men'. These are part-human, part-mouse to varying degrees, and barge their way around Los Angeles, before kidnapping an old lady's cat and holding it to ransom.
>
> (O'Connell, 2003: 8)

In the case documented by Liz Moor (2003), a whole new music-based 'sister' brand, Witnness, was created by the marketing department of Guinness Ireland for the drink-based brand Guinness in collaboration with the music department of a London-based international marketing agency, KLP Euro RSCG. The campaign involved hosting a summer music festival and a series of music events over three years. Moor writes:

> These events, it was argued, should not be presented under the Guinness name (even though they were being used to promote Guinness), but should have a separate brand identity, which could metonymically represent the Guinness brand, whilst simultaneously losing – so it was hoped – its (negative) product-specific connotations. Moreover, as a brand rather than specific product or event, Witnness would retain the option of developing its activities in new directions at a later stage.
>
> (2003: 41–42)

In such practices, the brand seeks to incorporate not only (aspects of) the consumer but also (aspects of) the context of use or wider environment, inserting itself into activities and entities that exceed the individual consumer and are understood in terms of collectives such as fans, lifestyles or communities. Or to reverse this point of view, points of access to the brand have now come to include not simply the point of purchase and associated advertising and promotion, but also 'special' events.

Such events – openings, launches, visits, specially arranged performances and happenings – extend the openness of product–product and product–consumer interaction. In these and other ways, the brand is explicitly presented as open-ended, as question-generating, in process and requiring completion (Knorr Cetina, 2000). Thus, for example, Phil Knight, the Nike CEO, describes the consequences of the self-recognition of the company as a marketing company in terms of a re-evaluation of the product – as a marketing tool. This view of the product was also implicit in the actions of Microsoft when it sent out 350,000 beta-tests of Windows 98 to computer users. At an estimated labour cost of around $3,000 per test, the net customer contribution to the development of Windows 98 has been calculated to be in the region of £1 billion, probably more than Microsoft itself invested in the development of this new product (Mitchell, 2001: 230). Similarly, in March 1999, personal computer manufacturer Compaq, under its 'FreePC' scheme, began to give consumers 'free' computers in exchange for information on consumption habits (Mackenzie, 2002: 151). In Britain, the energy drink Red Bull was given away 'free' at clubs and dance music festivals before it was marketed or sold anywhere else. It appeared in the Playstation game Wipeout, and was available in chill-out rooms at these venues with a soundtrack by the Chemical Brothers. Only when the brand had become part of dance music culture, was it marketed – as a 'cool' drink – to the general public (Grant, 1999 in Arvidsson, forthcoming).

A similar shift in perspective was also made by Levi's, as illustrated by the Levi's 'Personal Pair'™ programme. This is a mass customisation programme, introduced in 1995, in which a consumer's measurements are taken and entered into a computer. This information is sent directly to a factory and personally fitted jeans are produced and delivered on a pair-by-pair basis within two weeks, resulting in what Levi's describes as 'a genuine one-on-one relationship with our target consumers'. However:

> The programme is also important for another reason: size, style and colour preference details of each consumer can be stored and accessed, giving the company a wealth of valuable information about each Personal Pair consumer. Since these individuals tend to be some of the most

motivated and loyal Levi's brand consumers, our ability to know who they are and what they want most provides us with a powerful way to ensure their continued engagement with the Levi's brand today and in the future.

(Holloway, 1999: 71)

Consumers are here explicitly adopted as salespeople and as marketing tools. Another much discussed example of this is the practice of cool-hunting and 'bro-ing' as developed by consultancies such as Sputnik, The L. Report and Bureau de Style. 'Bro-ing' is the name given to the practice of 'giving' prototype shoes and clothing to selected individuals in black inner-city neighbourhoods in New York, Philadelphia and Chicago by Nike marketers in order to evaluate their likely success (N. Klein, 2000: 72–75). In another example of the same strategy, in 1998, the Korean car manufacturer Daewoo hired 2,000 college students on 200 US campuses 'to talk up the cars to their friends' (Klein, 1999: 80). In another, some market researchers working for Nike asked schoolchildren to undertake research, by, for example, collecting and presenting evidence of 'their favorite place to hang out' (N. Klein, 2000: 94). More generally, as Michael Dell (of Dell computers) puts it, 'Our best customers aren't necessarily the ones that are the largest, the ones that buy the most from us, or the ones that require little help or service. . . . Our best customers are those we learn the most from' (quoted in Mitchell, 2001: 230).

At the same time, with the intensification of consumerism and the development of hybrid forums (including consumer advice organisations), consumers are themselves acquiring greater knowledge of marketing and can increasingly position their own consumption choices in terms of marketing practices. As Callon *et al.* says:

The forum . . . the great divide between specialists and laypersons is redistributed. It creates material conditions for co-operation between laboratory research performed by experts and specialists, on the one hand, and research 'in the wild' that makes it possible for laypersons to be vigilant and sometimes prompts them to propose guidelines for new research.

(2002: 196)

Alternatively, as a partner in one British advertising agency puts it,

Forty years of commercial television means that [consumers] are smarter; not only are they media literate but they are 'market literate'. They watch and learn. They know about product life-cycles, product similarity, pricing strategies – 'You're buying a lot of off-peak air-time' a 24-year-old observes in a focus group discussion.

(HHCL, 1995: 13)

This consumer reflexivity is sometimes described as what is called 'co-training', as, for example, when Amazon.com recommends books to a customer on the basis of previous purchases. As Mitchell puts it, 'The customer realizes he is training Amazon.com as to his tastes and preferences, while Amazon.com trains the customer to get most value from its services and infrastructure' (2001: 230). More generally, consumer market reflexivity has contributed to the proposal by marketers for the practices of marketing to be deployed to develop 'deep' relationships with consumers, so-called relationship marketing. This is said to involve moving beyond a one-way model of exchange or communication and a single-stage transaction model of consumption to the advocacy of an ongoing 'dialogue' between producers and consumers. Following the use of the neologism 'distributed production', this might be described as consuming production. In this and other ways, brands are now developed as a response to – and as a means of managing – a relation that is constituted by marketing practices as not merely two-way, but also long-term, inherently dynamic, and *interactive* (see Chapter 6).

In the past, the moment of purchase was the end of the sale. Suppose, however, that buying something is only the first step. Think of the initial purchase as an application for brand membership. . . .

Constructed with care a community is a creation that customers will want to belong to, not something that happens by definition or default. It can, and should, encourage spontaneous participation often outside the formal network established by the brand. . . .

If the [branding] agency is to enrich the experience that customers have of its clients' brands, it will need to find new ways of including them, enfranchising them and empowering them.

It will need to learn ways of increasing customer interaction and of working outside the broadcast media.

This entails looking at disciplines that have responsiveness 'built in' – disciplines such as sales promotion and direct marketing. . . .

It's going to need a highly demanding set of principles. The company will need a competitive approach on all fronts. In particular it will need innovative strategic and creative skills. It will require a radically new approach to problem solving, one based on a collaborative working methodology that encourages and facilitates cross-discipline working, and one that incorporates the customer into the process.

(HHCL, 1994: 21, 25, 29, 31)

The point here is to make consumers think of the brand as something that inspires loyalty, as 'the centre of social organization' (Schmitt, 1999: 188, quoted in Arvidsson, forthcoming). Arvidsson (forthcoming) gives many examples:

> Tesco's and Sainsbury's both create ties to their customers through membership cards, special discounts, direct mailing and company publications. They make ties between customers possible through social events like cooking courses, gourmet dinners and wine tasting. . . . Some brands like Jeep and Harley Davidson routinely organize 'brandfests' where users can come together, improve their skills at using the product and, most importantly, socialize and create community ties. Harley Davidson has been particularly successful in creating a feeling of community around the brand, defined by a particular 'biker ethos' contingent on participation in a branded Harley gathering. . . . Amazon.com encourages users to review and discuss books: MTV's site has chat and dating services.

As he concludes, 'For a company no longer clearly located in one physical space or even one legal entity, a brand can provide different sorts of boundaries for the (imaginary) organization' (forthcoming).

Coda

In mapping out this schematic history of the contribution of marketing to the organisation of the brand, what has been emphasised is that as marketing has increased its influence as a management discipline, the brand has become increasingly important to the economy. Marketing has become the principal means by which information about the consumer can be identified, owned and exploited in the co-ordination of the qualification–requalification of products (Callon *et al.*, 2002). As Cochoy puts it, 'Half-way between producers and consumers, half-way between economics and managerial practices, marketing specialists have gradually re-invented the fundamental actors and processes; they have succeeded in disciplining (mastering/codifying) the market economy' (1998: 195).

And the brand has been a key locus for marketing strategies. As a consequence, the past thirty years or so has seen the emergence of the brand as a medium for the organisation of products and production activities over time and space. In this regard, consider not only the well-known consumer product brands Microsoft and Ford, McDonald's and Nokia, Monsanto and MTV, Prozac and Coca-Cola, but also OOCL – Orient Overseas Container Line. On the one hand, the brand OOCL may be described in terms of a set of quality assurance processes. So, the company brand managers claim that 'the five petals of our plum blossom logo represent the five components of our quality assurance process: customer satisfaction, management commitment, employee participation, quality partnership and continuous improvement'. But they also argue that they seek to make the processes of quality assurance more than simply a guarantee of certain kinds of service; instead, they 'want our slogan, "We take it personally", eventually to become the norm in everything OOCL does world-wide'.

Five main points have emerged here. First, brands enable their owners to reach 'over the shoulder of the retailer straight to the consumer' (H. G. Wells, quoted in Murphy, 1998: 4). This prevents the product simply becoming a commodity that is bought (and sold on) by an intermediary, such as retailing or distribution chains, and thus, through its management of the distributed product, the brand has become a key asset to manufacturers in their transactions with retailers. Conversely, of course, some retailers have developed their own brands to strengthen their own position *vis-à-vis* manufacturers. In relation to both developments, then, *production is distributed, product attributes are multiplied, and more and more attributes are made variable.* To put this another way, product (and service) attributes are no longer necessarily fixed in relation to an origin, but rather are produced dynamically, in the course of being brought to market.

Second, *the brand is a mechanism for the co-ordination, organisation and integration of the processes of standardisation and differentiation of products and services.* These processes are trials or experiments that introduce qualitative differentiation into the abstract, integrated object that is the brand. To put this another way, *the objectivity of the brand emerges in the organisation, co-ordination and integration of dynamic, multi-dimensional relations between products.*

Third, *the brand is associated with an increasing emphasis on – and valuation of – innovation and creativity in the workplace.* This is associated with transformations in the organisation of the work process deriving from changes in the ways in which intra- and inter-firm competitiveness is organised. It is not only that competition is framed in terms of product innovation and creativity, but that *innovation itself is understood in terms of constructions of – and interventions in – a market organised in terms of information about the consumer.*

Fourth, *the brand is a mechanism by which products and services may be presented as more or less open-ended, as in a process of completion.* It is a means by which products enter into a processual relationship both with individuals and with entities, activities or fields that exceed the individual, providing the basis for a sustained, ongoing relationship between 'production' and 'consumption'. In this process, it is not only the distinction between producers and consumers that is blurred, but also that between objects and subjects. The economy brought into being by the brand is thus not a two-step process with a production phase followed by a distribution or exchange phase (Lee and LiPuma, 2002). While it sometimes seems that the functions of marketing are simply added on to production, or that production is a series of transactions or exchanges happening in sequence along a time-line, one after the other, culminating in consumption, this model is not adequate to describe the organisation of the brand as it has been outlined here. To jump ahead, one of the principal claims to be advanced in this book is that the rise of the brand has contributed to a fundamental reconfiguring of the temporality of production. To put this the other way round, the brand is the object of a process of production that is non-linear, a dynamic set of relations of power or force, with each moment or stage of production occurring in relation to every other.

Putting all these points together, what emerges is that brands are a name for cutting into and making manageable an increasingly dynamic production process. Significant stages or moments in this process identified here are: relations between producers and retailers; the management of processes of product standardisation and differentiation; the use of information about the consumer; and the emergence of the branded product as open-ended, generative of questions and in a dynamic relation with its environment. But none of these moments is primary, and none can be completed or fixed independently of the others. The variety and varying character of the inter-relationships between different moments in production helps explain the myriad forms of brand that currently exist (for example, single-product brands, multi-product brands and company brands). And the myriad forms of brands help make the space and time(s) of particular brands according to the disjunctures and differences of the flows of the global economy (Appadurai, 1996).

As Manovich says of the new media object, the brand 'is not something fixed once and for all, but something that can exist in different, potentially infinite versions' (2001: 36). The indeterminacy, openness or potential of the brand is visible in the ways that it incorporates the heterogeneity of labour, co-ordinates product qualification and re-qualification trials, valorises creativity and innovation, reconstitutes the product as a marketing tool, and subsumes consumer activities into itself. As something that can exist in different versions, the brand is thus one example of the introduction of possibility into the thing that is the object of contemporary capitalism (Massumi, 2002). It is a part of the rise of a virtual economy, an economy in which feedback systems of information, communication and control fundamentally reconfigure the temporality of production and processes of object-ification.

3 The interface of the brand

Complex objects, interactivity and partial solutions

The mass production of standardized commodities in the Fordist era could count on an adequate demand and thus had little need to 'listen' to the market. A feedback circuit from consumption to production did allow changes in the market to spur changes in productive engineering, but this communication circuit was restricted (owing to the fixed and compartmentalized channels of planning and design structures) and slow (owing to the rigidity of the technologies and procedures of mass production).

Toyotism is based on an inversion of the Fordist structure of communication between production and consumption. Ideally, according to this model, production planning will communicate with markets constantly and immediately. Factories will maintain zero stock, and commodities will be produced just in time according to the present demand of the existing markets. This model thus involves not simply a more rapid feedback but an inversion of the relationship because, at least in theory, the production decision actually comes after and in reaction to the market decision. . . . In general, however, it would be more accurate to conceive the model as striving toward a continual interactivity or rapid communication between production and consumption.

(Hardt and Negri, 2000: 290)

Introduction

This chapter will outline and develop the claim that the brand is a complex object. This will be done by focusing on the argument that what has come to define the brand in the contemporary era is the organisation and functioning of *a dynamic set of relations between products*. These relations will be understood as complex – that is, as *probabilistic*, *global* and *transductive* (these terms will be explained in what follows). It will be suggested that the complexity of these relations is a consequence of the functioning of the brand as an *interface* of communication between producers and consumer. In general terms, an interface is the organisation of data by one system for communication with another (Manovich, 2001). It is the activity or functioning of this interface which introduces qualitative possibility into the abstract thing that is the brand (Massumi, 2002). And it is the introduction of qualitative possibility that makes the emergence of the brand – a complex object – a significant development in the contemporary economy.

The interface of the brand

So far, it has been suggested that the brand is an image instrument, a medium of translation or a new media object. In this chapter, it will be suggested that the brand is an object of the artificial sciences, an artefact. This is a term taken from the economist Herbert Simon ([1969] 1981), who developed an approach to the study of economics that drew on information theory and non-linear concepts in order to address issues of power in the economy (see Hayles, 1999 for an illuminating account of information theory).[1] In his influential discussion of the economy as an artificial system,[2] Simon provides the following fourfold definition of artefacts:

> Artificial things are synthesized (though not always or usually with full forethought) by man [sic].
>   Artificial things may imitate appearances in natural things while lacking, in one or many respects, the reality of the latter.
>   Artificial things can be characterised in terms of functions, goals, adaptation.
>   Artificial things are often discussed, particularly when they are being designed, in terms of imperatives as well as descriptives.
>
> ([1969] 1981: 8)

He argues that an artefact can be thought of as a meeting point – *an interface* – 'between an "inner" environment, the substance and organisation of the artefact itself, and an "outer" environment, the surroundings in which it operates.' (To continue with the example of the car introduced in Chapter 1, think of its interface in terms of, minimally, the windows, the steering wheel and the pedals.) 'If the inner environment is appropriate to the outer environment, or vice versa, the artifact will serve its intended purpose' ([1969] 1981: 9) (that is, the car will transport its driver safely from A to B). For Simon, design is understood as the organisation of an (artificial) entity in terms of an intended purpose – that is, it is the organisation of an interface or surface of communication between inner and outer environments. As he says, the 'description of an artifice in terms of its organisation and functioning – its interface between inner and outer environments – is a major objective of invention and design activity' (ibid.: 13).

The main claim to be advanced in this chapter is that the management of the brand may be understood in terms of such an object-ive.[3] In this way, the brand is located as an artefact, or an interior milieu, in an artificial system: the economy. The aim of designers, marketers and brand managers to describe the brand (an object of the artificial system of the economy) organises what Simon calls the inner environment of production, while consumption or everyday life is constituted in this process as the outer environment. The object-ive is the organisation of an artefact that functions as a medium of exchange between inner and outer environments, 'producers' and 'consumers'. In other words, Simon's notion of design activity (and the pursuit of this object-ive) is used here to describe not simply the organisation of the functioning of specific products (such as a car), but the organisation of the brand. The surface of the brand is described as a meeting point or interface for the communication of information between 'producers' and 'consumers'.

The chapter will focus on the particular properties of the brand as they are produced by the communication of the interface, but before moving on to this let me make a number of preliminary points about the notions of the interface and design activity used here. First, the interface is an example of a frame, a term given by Erving Goffman (1971) to a boundary within which interaction takes place more or less independently of its surrounding context. The frame is a communicative surface or boundary that both connects and separates disunified or disparate spaces (Rodowick, 1994). The interface of the brand is not, however, to be located in a single place, at a single time. Rather, like the interface of the Internet, it is distributed across a number of surfaces (of, for example, products and packaging), screens (television, computers, cinemas) or sites (retail outlets, advertising hoardings, and so on).

Second, the interface is a particular kind of frame. It connects the producer and consumer and removes or separates them from each other in particular ways. Thus, on the one hand, brands have been widely argued to contribute to processes of identity formation by consumers; on the other hand, 'The tendency to emphasise the relationship between identity and consumer behaviour eclipses another crucial relationship – with those employed to produce the goods we consume.' In short, the interface of the brand 'is revealing of some relationships, but it keeps others very well hidden' (Pavitt, 2000b: 175). The interface is the basis of two-way exchanges between producers and consumers, informing how consumers relate to producers and how producers relate to consumers, but these exchanges, though they are two-way and dynamic, are not direct, symmetrical or reversible. Rather, the interface is a site – or diagram – of intense mediation or, more accurately, interactivity (a term to be discussed in more detail in Chapter 6).

Third, the interface has its own (recursive) logic or 'artificial depth', through which is organised a two-way, dynamic and selective communication of information. As Ezio Manzini puts it,

> The idea of a mute and static border is . . . replaced by an idea of the surface as an interface between two ambients, with a role involving an exchange of energy and information between the substances put into contact. The surface as semiotic membrane capable of promoting or inhibiting such an exchange thus becomes a component of the object . . . capable of standing between the inside and outside of the object itself, or to provide a range of performances of its own.
>
> (1989: 183)

From this point of view, then, the interface of the brand may be seen as both promoting and inhibiting 'exchange' between producers and consumers, and informing this asymmetrical exchange through 'a range of performances of its own'. The focus in this chapter is on the performativity of the interface of the brand.

Fourth, while the claim that the brand is the outcome of design activity provides a way of acknowledging the purposive strategies of those involved in brand management, it relates that activity to the performativity of the brand. The argument here is that as the brand emerges as a set of relations between products, it begins to acquire a self-organising, recursive logic that cannot be reduced to the strategies of social actors. Or to put this another way, while there may be a struggle between social actors to impose specific goals, the functioning of an interface means that the properties of the brand cannot be reduced to the strategies of individual actors. In other words, the account of the activities of the marketers presented in Chapter 2 does not adequately describe the brand. Nor indeed would an account of the practices of designers (although it is undoubtedly relevant – see Julier, 2000), or a description of the activities of consumers. While all these accounts are a necessary part of describing the brand, they are not sufficient even when added together. They privilege purposive actions, and do not acknowledge the significance of the self-organising elements of the brand as a complex, indeterminate or open object.

A fifth point is that since design activity understood in this way is not defined in relation to a final goal, it inevitably leads to a continual reformulation of goals. This definition of design activity thus enables the emergence of the brand to be seen in relation to a production process that has no final goals, no natural target or final user, but rather continuously feeds on itself (Krippendorff, 1994). Another way of putting this is that through the activity of design the process of production provides information for itself about itself.[4] Simon writes:

> [O]ne goal of planning may be the design activity itself. The act of envisioning possibilities and elaborating them is itself a pleasurable and valuable experience. Just as realised plans may be a source of new experiences, so new prospects are opened up at each step in the process of design. Designing is a kind of mental window shopping. Purchases do not have to be made to get pleasure from it.
>
> ([1969] 1981: 188)

The significance of this point is that while brands may be set up in terms of some initial conditions, rules or procedures, the functioning of these procedures leads to the generation of new information, and this in turn contributes to the emergence of further behaviours. The correlate of this is that the organising logic described here may be understood in terms of a patterning of space and time, a logic of flows, and products and services themselves may be seen as (more or less frozen or fixed) manifestations of emergent patterns. The book seeks to explore the emergence and significance of some of these patterns in space and time – *the logic of flows* – that follows from describing brands as not simply objects but artefacts.

To some extent, a recognition of the importance of design activity as outlined here underpins a number of recent accounts of the contemporary economy in terms of flows (Lash and Urry, 1994; Castells, 1996; Appadurai, 1996; Lash, 2002; Callon *et al.*, 2002; Urry, 2003). As Callon *et al.*, put it, 'Design, as an activity that crosses through the entire organization [of production], is central' (2002: 212). What will be stressed here, though, is that it is helpful to see the brand as an increasingly powerful object-ive organisation of the logics of flow. This is largely because of the ways in which the organisation of the functioning of the set of relations that comprise the brand do not simply *mark*, but rather *make* time and space (Miller, 1987; Appadurai, 1996; Lury, 1999). Another way of putting this is to say that the brand has been a successful commercial strategy because it is produced interactively, because it is an artefact in which the dynamic qualities of relationality are managed in a process of design intensivity.

The interface as the organisation of asymmetrical communication

In what follows, the performativity of the brand will be described by focusing on the distinguishing characteristics or 'advantages' that Simon identifies in the organisation of all artificial systems. In the terms of the argument being developed here, these characteristics derive from the particular ways in which the brand divides and connects the inner environment of the process of production from the outer environment of consumption and everyday life. While Simon describes these characteristics as 'advantages', they are not necessarily advantageous (in the sense of beneficial) for everyone or indeed anyone involved. The paradoxical nature of the exchanges between producers and consumers that characterise the interface of the brand – of asymmetry, of partial separation and connection, of dynamism – is what makes it distinctive and commercially successful. But it does not mean that such exchanges are beneficial for those participating (actively or passively) in the economy or for society as a whole. Nevertheless, these characteristics usefully identify some of the distinctive properties or capacities of the performativity of the brand; they identify the key dynamics of its organisation of communication.

They are identified most clearly if they are explored first from the perspective of *outside in* (see the first of the following subsections), and then, second, from the perspective of *inside out* (see the second subsection). Both these views – from *outside in* and *inside out* – are analytical perspectives of 'the sciences of the artificial' (Simon, [1969] 1981); they are not to be equated with those of real consumers and real producers. Rather, they have as their concern the description of the interface of the brand as artefact. They have analytical purchase precisely because they recognise the significance of the asymmetrical communication of information that an interface affords an artificial system such as the economy, and provide a way of understanding the principles of this asymmetry.

Outside in

One consequence of dividing outer from inner environment in an artificial system is that behaviour can be predicted from knowledge of the system's goals and its outer environment, *with only minimal assumptions about the inner environment*. Two advantages follow from this for Simon. The first of these is that it is possible for those involved in design activity to identify and exploit quite different inner environments accomplishing identical or similar goals in relation to identical or similar outer environments. But in what sense can brands be understood in terms of this advantage or characteristic, and what is its commercial value? Consider the interfaces of the brands Swatch and Nike in this regard.

First, Swatch. A key component of the logo of the brand Swatch from 'outside in' is a consistent self-identification in relation to Switzerland. Swatch watches display not only the name Swatch (itself a contraction of 'Swiss' and 'watch') and the Swiss flag, but also the description 'Swiss' on their faces. In addition, much of the promotional literature accompanying products makes reference to the Swissness of the Swatch ethos. Such references are widely held to have the effect of strengthening consumer perceptions of trust in the quality of Swatch products in what is perceived to be a risky global commercial environment. Thus, Nicolas Hayek, one-time Swatch CEO, has gone so far as to claim that the buyers of Swatch are 'sympathetic' to the Swiss: 'We're nice people from a small country. We have nice mountains and clear water.' Indeed, he attributes the company's success to the fact that

> We are not just offering people a style. We are offering them a message. . . . Emotional products are about message – a strong, exciting, distinct, authentic message that tells people who you are and why you do what you do. There are many elements that make up the Swatch message. High quality. Low cost. Provocative. Joy of life. But the most important element of the Swatch message is the hardest for others to copy. Ultimately, we are not just offering watches. We are offering our personal culture.
>
> (Quoted in Taylor, 1993)

Here Hayek describes the way in which a place of origin may be deliberately designed into the interface of a brand. This design activity enables Swatch products to sell by securing the trust of (certain) consumers, providing a guarantee of quality, by tying the brand to an origin (a 'personal culture'). This guarantee requires – or at least implies – the use of Swiss labour in the manufacture of Swatch products. It thus limits the extent to which the Swatch company is able to move production of Swatch-branded products to take advantage of lower labour costs outside Swiss national territory. What is at issue is a limit (both enabling and restrictive) to do with the internal environment of the interface.[5] The location of the majority of the required labour force in a single country, Switzerland, is thus one aspect of the inner environment that functions 'as a necessity' (in Simon's phrase) in relation to the Swatch interface. It suggests that Swatch is best seen as a national, territorial brand.

In contrast, the origin-ality of the Nike interface is less clearly tied to a single national place of origin, or indeed to an origin at all. To some extent, the physical location of the company itself, dedicated retail outlets such as Niketowns and sports events sponsored by the company may serve as such an origin. Certainly this perception of the flagship retail outlets, Niketowns, as origins is encouraged not only by the highly charged design of the stores, but also by the greater range of stock available, typically including all the most recent models of shoes, clothes and accessories. Alongside such intense and exclusive sites, however, Nike presents itself as original in relation to the almost endless multiplicity of the sites of its products' uses through the brand's elevation (and ownership) of an ethos of competition, determination and individuality. 'Just do it' is the brand injunction, and in this 'doing', multiple origins for the brand are brought into being. Of course, it is possible to argue that a culture of competition, determination and individuality is the national culture of the United States, and in this sense there is a parallel between the interfaces of the Nike and Swatch brands. But what makes the interface of the Nike brand so distinctive is that it appears as if there is no need to locate this ethos within territorial boundaries in order to secure its owner-ship or claim its effects. The interface is not tied to any specific inner environ-ment in this regard; it is deterritorialising.

Another way of putting this is to say that the relations between different stages of the processes of distributed production as presented at the Nike inter-face are *global*. That is, *the relations between stages of production are not presented at the interface as occurring in a discrete, sequential or step-by-step fashion* (resulting in a finished product with a fixed origin in a specific territory), but are intended to have their effect all at once, *in each and every presentation or use of the brand*. The commercial advantage to be derived from this is that since the brand's origins are not visibly tied to specific places of production, the Nike company is able to exercise enormous spatial flexibility in relation to the place of manufacturing of its products. This in turn is linked to the use of information and communication technologies, without which the precise control required to co-ordinate very complicated processes of production and distribution could not be exercised at a distance. Famously, or rather infamously, the Nike company has in fact continually shifted the sites of production from country to country within East Asia in such a way as to be able to take advantage of the low-cost and poorly protected workforces in these countries. However, while this account may support the view that Nike is a global rather than a national, territorial brand, it is not meant to suggest that the consequences of this spatial flexibility have been entirely beneficial for the company. The point of this comparison is not that the Nike brand functions without limits (see Chapter 7 for further discussion of the notion of limits). Rather, the aim has been to show that the performativity of the interface is such that the relation of a brand to an origin may be organised in many different ways.

A second advantage of the organisation of the surface of communication of the brand as an interface is that the face of an artefact may connote 'perceptual similarity but essential difference, resemblances from without rather than within' (Simon, [1969] 1981: 17). This, like the first advantage described above, follows from the fact that it is possible for those involved in design activity to identify different inner environments accomplishing similar goals in relation to similar outer environments. This second advantage enables the brand to function as *a mechanism of modelling, imitation or simulation*. Thus, Simon argues that

> the artificial object imitates the real by turning *the same face* to the outer system, by adapting, relative to the same goals, to comparable ranges of external tasks. Imitation is possible because distinct physical systems can be organized to exhibit nearly identical behaviour.
>
> (ibid.: 17; emphasis added)

Simon recognises that the artificial characteristic of simulation is viewed ambivalently in many quarters (see Baudrillard, 1994). He notes that the synonyms of artificial in the dictionary – affected, factitious, manufactured, pretended, sham, simulated, spurious, trumped up, unnatural – reflect 'man's [sic] deep distrust of his own products' (Simon, [1969] 1981: 6). But he is determined to use artificial in 'as neutral a sense as possible, as meaning man-made [sic] as opposed to natural' (ibid.: 6). He further notes that because of its abstract character and its 'symbol manipulating generality', the computer has greatly extended the range of systems whose behaviour can be simulated. And rather than seeing simulation in terms of representational models alone, he argues that phenomena such as the computer (and by implication the brand) are no less real for being abstract symbol-manipulating machines for generating simulations. As he says, 'Computers have transported symbol systems from the platonic heaven of ideas to the empirical world of actual processes carried out by machine or brains, or by the two of them working together' (ibid.: 28).

In the case of the brand, the face (see Chapter 4) presented to the outer environment is typically a logo or logos – the Swatch name, the Nike Swoosh. And in many cases the abstraction and generality of this face means that the brand is able to function as a machine for the simulation of product innovation. In other words, brand innovation need not derive or emerge from innovation in the organisation of the production process. Instead, it may be produced in the practices of simulation or behaviour modelling – that is, through qualification trials in which products are experimentally tested in relation to the goal or aim of reaching a target market.[6] (These processes will be described in more detail in Chapter 4 in terms of brand positioning.) What is being suggested here is that innovation is no longer as tied to the production process, or indeed to the making better of specific products, but rather is understood in relation to meeting the needs of the market, understood in terms of information about the consumer.

A number of developments in the processes of production have made this mode of innovating more possible, including transformations in 'the material of invention'. In a book of this title, Manzini (1989) examines the changing way in which matter becomes material — that is, he looks at how matter becomes capable of being integrated into design activity, and in the end becomes products. He describes a move from a period in which technological knowledge was such that there was an 'enforced' complexity (in which the heterogeneity of materials such as wood and stone limited the possibilities of craft skills, enforcing certain kinds of uses of materials) to one in which complexity is first 'controlled' and now is 'managed'. Manzini describes this shift in modes of complexity as an historical increase in 'the depth of the artificial'. Formal properties such as flexibility, heaviness and heat- and stress resistance are, he says, no longer determining. Instead, materials are available that can relatively easily be adapted to the problems of design activity as described by Simon. In this process, the identity of products becomes a matter of (surface) communication. This is as a consequence of 'the increase in intensity of the information contained in matter' (Manzini, 1989: 45):

> Matter is no longer a system of classification of given and well-defined materials, but a continuum of possibilities — based upon which it is possible to design new materials as they are needed, with desired properties.
>
> This structure gives rise to materials 'made to order', with properties that are determined by altering their microstructures . . . the material does not exist prior to the object in which it is to be integrated. The material exists only after the manufacturing process, as a component of the finished product.
>
> (ibid.: 38)

Manzini points out that some materials — such as many composites — do not exist independently of either the object or the manufacturing process for which they were developed, and for this reason he suggests that design should be considered as a 'material–process system' (ibid.: 41). An exemplary case here is engineering plastics and super polymers, terms referring to a wide range of materials that have not only 'plastic' but also mechanical, thermal and even electrical properties. Discussing such examples, he concludes, 'In this context, a characteristic of invention and innovation is the profound integration between materials and processes' (ibid.: 70). In summarising the implications of these developments, Manzini, like Simon, argues for the centrality of the artificial to design:

> A new form of knowledge of the real is developing, whose code of reference is no longer that of the classification of materials according to their properties and intrinsic cultural meanings. Instead, the reference has become a recognition of the level of performances and of the evocative images generated as integrating parts of a manufactured product.
>
> (ibid.: 31)

Let me illustrate the possibilities of the simulation or modelling of innovation with the example of Nike. The origins of Nike are in a company called Blue Ribbon Sports, which Phil Knight, a former runner at the University of Oregon and now Nike CEO, and Bill Bowerman, Knight's former track coach, created in 1962. The company initially did no more than distribute running shoes in the United States for a Japanese company (Onitsuka Tiger track shoes[7]). However, it soon shifted to designing its own shoes and outsourcing their production to East Asia (although the company did have factories in Exeter, New Hampshire, and Saco, Maine, until the early 1980s). At this stage in its history, the company's market competitiveness was characterised by a series of functional product innovations linked to developments in the production process – most famously the 'waffle' method of aerating the rubber sole of shoes – and an early mastery of the spatial dynamics of out-sourcing.[8] But in the mid-1980s, there was a turning point in the company's fortunes. Nike's growth during this period was fuelled by the expansion of its market brought about by the rise of jogging as a national pastime in the United States, but in the mid-1980s the company suddenly lost its footing. It was overtaken in market share by Reebok, which had tapped into the growing (female) aerobics market, deploying a new understanding of the trainer as accessory or fashion good. As Knight comments,

> We made an aerobics shoe that was functionally superior to Reebok's, but we missed the styling. Reebok's shoe was sleek and attractive, while ours was sturdy and chunky. We also decided against using garment leather, as Reebok had done, because it wasn't durable. By the time we developed a leather that was both strong and soft, Reebok had established a brand, won a huge chunk of sales, and gained the momentum to go right by us.
>
> (Quoted in Willigan, 1992: 92)

Nike was forced to accept a reframing of the market, in which the organising principles of product qualification were to do not with function, but with identity and communication with specific target groups of consumers. The setback was a defining moment in company history, as Knight outlines in his description of the ensuing transformation in the company's understanding of itself:

> For years, we thought of ourselves as a production-oriented company, meaning we put all our emphasis on designing and manufacturing the product. But now we understand that the most important thing we do is market the product. We've come around to saying that Nike is a marketing company, and the product is our most important marketing tool. What I mean is that marketing knits the whole organization together. The design elements and functional characteristics of the product itself are just part of the overall marketing process.
>
> We used to think that everything started in the lab. Now we realize that everything spins off the consumer. And while technology is still important, the consumer has to lead innovation. We have to innovate for a specific reason, and that reason comes from the market. Otherwise we'll end up making museum pieces.
>
> (Quoted in Willigan, 1992: 92)

However, the consumer may be represented in more than one way. Rather than accept the organisation of the market in terms of the dynamic but arbitrary system of fashion, Nike adopted a strategy in which it sought to frame the market in terms of a little-developed (at the time) consumer category, the (sports) fan or enthusiast. This category was itself a largely media-based understanding of the consumer (see Chapter 2), and was linked to the growing importance of sport in television and other media schedules.

At one level, the self-transformation of Nike simply involved more promotion and more advertising (already in 1980, Nike had started what was to be a long-standing – and unusually close – relationship with advertising agency Wieden and Kennedy, also based in Portland, Oregon). Nike spent $5 million between 1984 and 1986 advertising a coloured leather shoe, the Air Jordan. In 1987, it launched a 10-model 'Air' line. The overarching aim of this advertising was to build an 'emotional tie' with the fan that would provide the basis for repeated purchase. But the increase in advertising was tied to a number of other transformations in the processes of product differentiation, led by innovations in design linked to a growing role for marketers within the company structure. In the years 1985–1988, Nike doubled its design staff and tripled its research and development budget, and its three hundred designers sustained a relentless flow of new product technologies and designs. As Knight puts it,

> Even though 60% of our product is bought by people who don't use it for the actual sport, everything we did was aimed at the top. We said, if we

get the people at the top, we'll get the others because they'll know the shoe can perform.

But that was an oversimplification.

. . . we do a lot of work at grass-roots level. We go to amateur sports events and spend time at gyms and tennis courts talking to people.

Beyond that, we do some fairly typical kinds of market research, but lots of it – spending time in stores and watching what happens across the counter, getting reports from dealers, doing focus groups, tracking responses to our ads. We just sort of factor all that information into the computer between the ears and come up with conclusions.

(Quoted in Willigan, 1992: 94)

The redefinition of the company as a marketing company was successful: in 1991, Nike – a real, abstract, symbol-manipulating machine for generating simulations – held 29 per cent of the global market for trainers, and sales topped $3 billion.

The commercial value of innovation by simulation more generally is that it provides a focus for the organisation of production for 'increasing returns' (Waldrop, 1994; Urry, 2003). At the most basic level, relatively small differences in brand preference – if shared widely among a significant group of consumers – can lead to large differences in product choice and therefore in the value of a brand to a firm. In other words, 'a brand need not be "powerful" (in the sense that consumers believe it dramatically superior and refuse all substitutes) to be extremely valuable to the business' (Barwise *et al.*, 2000: 89). There is no necessary proportionality between causes and effects here; instead, an economic calculus (or rationality) of statistical *probability* is at work. The potential for (disproportionately) capitalising on differences in preference is multiplied in the case of the brand in so far as it provides a mechanism for the exploitation of differentiation across product lines. This is one characteristic of the complexity of the brand noted above: the *probabilistic* effects of innovation as it is amplified in the relations between products (where probabilistic refers to statistical correlations between elements of a population). The amplification of slight transformations in the design, styling, promotion and delivery of a particular product (or service) has the potential consequence of non-linear increases in returns as it is exploited in the multiple relations between products that comprise the brand. 'The key here is that wealth comes not from scarcity, as in conventional economics, but from abundance' (Urry, 2003: 53).

The probabilities of benefiting from increasing returns are further increased by the exploitation of a number of linked brands by a firm, although such exploitation is typically organised in different ways in different industries.

Many industries (industrial products, industrial services, consumer services, frequently bought consumer products) market largely under a single corporate or umbrella brand, often with sub-brands or other detailed product descriptions. But more expensive, infrequently bought consumer goods are more often marketed by a company as two or more product lines at very different price ranges. These are often separately branded. Examples here include the car companies Toyota, Nissan and Honda, which have all launched luxury car ranges under separate brand names to their volume car ranges. Another current example of this kind of car-brand portfolio is VW's four-brand strategy (Audi, VW, Seat, Skoda) using a limited number of manufacturing platforms shared across the brands (Barwise *et al.*, 2000: 91–92). So-called diffusion fashion brands provide another example. As described by Smith (1997) and Moore (2000), successful American designers such as Ralph Lauren and Calvin Klein have been adept in the development of a portfolio of brands, each of which is promoted using a distinct brand name, while still retaining some connection with the designer's name.[9] Each of the brands has a distinct visual identity and is manufactured, managed and distributed using quite separate channels to distinct customer groups. Moore emphasises the exploitation of a set of related distribution techniques to reach the middle retail market:

> Where previously a fashion designer's store typically offered between two and three hundred product lines a season, the introduction of a diffusion brand at Ralph Lauren has swelled that company's product range to more than 6,000 lines per season. And where previously the fashion designer's ranges were distributed through a small number of company-owned stores in the fashion capitals of Paris, London, Milan and New York, as well as select department stores world-wide, the desire to attract the middle retail market has required that they adopt less narrow distribution methods. A more extensive market coverage has been achieved largely through the development of wholesale distribution to third party stockists. Through the extensive use of wholesaling, the Polo Ralph Lauren brand is now sold in over 1,600 department and speciality stores, as well as through 200 Polo Ralph Lauren shops and outlet stores world-wide, the majority of which are operated under franchise arrangements with local partners in over twenty countries.
>
> (2000: 267)

He further notes that many diffusion brands have become lifestyle brands, and some diffusion stores carry ranges that extend beyond clothing and include jewellery, perfume, eyewear (spectacles), luggage, furniture, paint, fabrics, sheets, towels and bedding. He writes, 'The primary aim of this product line extension is to allow a greater number of customers access to the brand, be it through a $5 candle, a $3 bottle of (branded) mineral water, or a $500 suit' (ibid.: 269). Similarly, the analysis presented here would suggest that what is important in a production process such as this is the management of relations between products rather than the products themselves. What emerges from the exploitation of such relations in the case of diffusion or lifestyle brands cannot simply be equated with the sum of the exchange of individual products, but is a consequence of specific system effects when one or more of the products becomes successful. Such effects do not stand in direct or proportional relation to specific causes. Thus, while diffusion ranges account for between 50 per cent and 60 per cent of companies' sales turnover, their contribution to gross profit may be as high as 90 per cent (ibid.: 267).

In all these cases, what is at issue is a particular mode of innovating (the simulation of innovation), linked to constructions of the market framed by information about the consumer. As was noted in Chapter 2, the effects of the brand are commonly attributed in the business community to creativity. Or rather, designers, producers and marketers claim that their contribution to the management of the brand or their design activity is the source of innovation (Nixon, 2003). But it may be helpful here to distinguish, as Andrew Barry (2001) does, between *innovation* and *invention*. He argues (following the social theory of Gabriel Tarde) that invention may be defined not as technical change but as a particular form of change that opens up new possibilities for action. It is possible to argue that the simulation of innovation, seen in these terms, *may have anti-inventive as well as inventive implications.* In any case, this mode of innovating cannot be exclusively linked to the purposive action of any particular individual or individuals at any particular moment or particular site, such as new product development or the marketing department. Rather, it is a consequence both of the organisation of the brand as an interface and of contestation within the production process. For example, the framing of the market as fast-moving is both an innovation itself and the basis of further innovation. As was described in Chapter 2, it was at the heart of many of the strategies during the 1980s and 1990s in which marketing experts systematically and repeatedly recategorised and fragmented target markets, combining, cross-tabulating and elaborating previously standard demographic variables to create multiple new permutations, market niches or lifestyles. In the terms adopted here, the activities of targeting provided a constantly changing set of goals or tasks, intensifying the pace of design activity and multiplying the possibilities for innovation. But the privileging of the simulation of innovation is a specific consequence of the performativity of the interface and the opportunities (or lack of them) this affords.

Inside out

Simon goes on to identify a further characteristic of the division of a system into goals, inner environment and outer environment, this time from the standpoint of the inner environment. He points out that in very many cases, whether a particular system will achieve a particular goal or adaptation *depends on only a few characteristics of the outer environment and not at all on the detail of that environment.* As a consequence, it is possible that the inner system – the production process in this case – may be insulated from the environment, so that an invariant relation may be maintained between inner system and goal, independent of a wide range of parameters that characterise the outer environment. Various forms of passive insulation maintain such quasi-independence from the outer environment, including reactive negative feedback, predictive adaptation (or feed-forward), or various combinations of these. As Simon points out, biologists are familiar with this property of adaptive systems under the label of homeostasis, but economists also recognise the price mechanism as another instance of an adaptive artifice. The suggestion here is that the brand is another.

Let me try to elaborate this claim by developing the comparison with price. In discussing the importance of the limits to market processes posed by the human capacity for information processing, Simon quotes from the Austrian neo-classical economist Friedrich von Hayek:[10]

> We must look at the price system as such a mechanism for communicating information if we want to understand its real function. . . . The most significant fact about this system is the economy of knowledge with which it operates, or how little the individual participants need to know in order to be able to take the right action. In abbreviated form, by a kind of symbol, only the most essential information is passed on, and passed on only to those concerned. It is more than a metaphor to describe the price system as a kind of machinery for registering change.
>
> (1945, quoted in Simon, [1969] 1981: 42)

From Simon's point of view, what is most striking about Hayek's formulation is that the price system is presented as a distributed cognitive device; it reduces and localises informational and computational requirements. Within this model, 'markets may be seen as rich information networks – even as a kind of "conversation" between buyers and sellers' (Slater and Tonkiss, 2001: 53). The brand, it is suggested here, is also a framing of this conversation, but in a number of very particular ways. It provides 'a communicative middle term – a meta-stability – affording exchanges and transmitting tension across many and varied systems of influence' (Kwinter, 2001: 47). As a consequence, the conversation between buyers and sellers may be seen as *interactive*, as noisy rather than mute.[11]

As is well known, Hayek was an exponent of the view that economics should concern itself not with stationary models, but with '"an explanation of the economic process as it proceeds through time"' (quoted in Slater and Tonkiss, 2001: 52). And what might also be noted is Hayek's formulation of price as not simply a mechanism for communicating information, but also 'a kind of machinery for registering change'. If we adapt these terms, the interface of the brand may be seen as a mechanism for communicating information in a market that is (performed or brought into being as) *dynamic and noisy*. What is fundamental here, as Manovich (2001) notes in his discussion of the new media object, is the use of looping techniques. The developments in the brand described in earlier chapters in relation to marketing – the application of the marketing mix, the use of information about the consumer in the qualitative differentiation of products, and the use of the product as a marketing tool – are absolutely fundamental in this regard. In these developments, the brand emerges from attempts to address and manage precisely those aspects of relations between buyers and sellers that are not governed by price through the use of information about the consumer in product qualification trials. It is in this sense that the brand may be understood in terms of *transductive* relations, where transduction is 'a process whereby a disparity or difference is topologically and temporally restructured across some interface' (Simondon, quoted in Mackenzie, 2002: 25).

Let me elaborate what is involved here in more detail, once more by way of comparison of Swatch and Nike. In an early formulation underpinning its development, what was to become the brand Swatch was described as an '"economical" watch that was also desirable': a cheap watch that everyone would want to own. The production of such a watch was not itself antithetical to the Swiss watch-making industry, as the historical example of the 'Proletariat' suggests. This was a watch designed by a famous Swiss watchmaker, Abraham Louis Breuget, in the late nineteenth century, manufactured to give the working class an individual means of access to clock time.[12] Crucially, however, the economical watch of the end of the twentieth century was intended not so much as an affordable time-telling device for the thrifty worker as an expendable accessory for the fashion-conscious consumer. Indeed, it is this temporal framing of the market that defines the many characteristics of the interface of Swatch:

> It was a decision from the start to promote the Swatch as an accessory, following a study made in 1980 by one of the big marketing consultants which had confirmed the up-and-coming popularity of the fashion acces-

sory. To make the product so that it would fulfil this requirement was an important point; it was something to be worn, to match clothing, mood, occupation, and easily changeable, like a scarf or a tie. Needless to say all of these ideas had been discussed, written down and drummed into everyone working on the 'non-watch' project, long before they had started to design anything concrete.

(Carrera, 1991: 55)

What was innovative about Swatch then was that its reframing of the market for the Swiss watch-making industry concerned its temporal (and spatial) ordering.

The desire for production of a variety of models was integral to the design of Swatch from the very beginning. Franz Sprecher, a marketing expert brought in from outside the watch-making industry, prescribed a principle of unity-in-variation for the organisation of the qualification trials of Swatch products: 'they should be restrained but at the same time have an attractive appearance, with sufficient variety to please all tastes. Transforming the "crazy" idea into a mass-produced item' (quoted in Carrera, 1991). But while the introduction of the principle of fashion was systematic right from the start – the selection of colours adopted for the first range of Swatch was made after visiting the Paris ready-to-wear clothing fair – it has been hugely intensified over the course of the past twenty or so years. So, for example, Swatch, like the fashion industry, now typically organises the introduction of new models via 'seasons'. Each season's offerings are illustrated in brochures which are then differentiated by theme (for example, 'Irony') and then distinguished still further by type ('Big', 'Medium', 'Scuba', 'Chrono' and 'Ladylady'). Additionally, some new models are launched independently of these long-standing types; for example, some ranges are differentiated by the attribution of their design to named artists; others still are made available in special packaging. The annually renewable membership of the Swatch Club includes ownership of a limited-edition Swatch, a newsletter and opportunities to participate in 'a world of Swatch collecting'. In short, a distinctive feature of the Swatch is its reconstruction of the temporality of the market; indeed, it provided Swatch with not only the basis for a distinctive ongoing relationship with consumers, but also a distinct competitive advantage *vis-à-vis* competitors. This reconstruction is made visible in the attempt by Swatch to introduce its own time – the Swatch Beat – fixed in relation to its place of origin.

Swatch has invented a new universal concept of time that eliminates time zones and geographical differences: the Swatch Internet Time. Swatch divides the 24 hours of the day into 1,000 units. A unit is called a Beat.

Each day has 000 to 999 Beats. Each Beat lasts 1 minute 26.4 seconds. Internet time is displayed by @ and three digits and starts at midnight (wintertime) in Biel, the home of Swatch, with @000.

Everybody all over the world then talks about time in Beats, no matter what actual time it may be in their time zone.

(Publicity leaflet)

As an accessory – and not a time-telling mechanism – the brand Swatch has a very different biography or life cycle from that of the watch as it had been traditionally understood, and consequently it tells a different time. It is a contraction of tradition and innovation, an intervention in the (spatio-) temporality of the production of making, buying and owning watches. Swatch does not simply mark the stages of life – coming of age, birthdays, marriage, retirement; it is not only an index of such rituals. Instead, the Swatch name is also the mark – or symbol – of the ways in which the brand's organisation of relations between products *makes* time, notably the temporalities of fashion, collection and the ordered regimentation of the Beat.

In contrast to the relatively ordered world produced by Swatch in this way, the temporal restructuring of the market that characterises Nike as a brand has emerged in stages, many of which overlap, but others of which diverge, producing multiple markets or syncopated external environments, presenting both problems and opportunities. Fashion is one of the ways in which the dynamism of the market is imagined for Nike as well as for Swatch. So, Knight (the CEO) notes, 'We have people who tell us what colors are going to be in for 1993, for instance, and we incorporate them'. But what really distinguishes Nike as a brand is that it has simultaneously sought to escape the remorseless competitiveness of the fashion market. It does not simply attempt to anticipate the future through the realisation of the possible; instead, it seeks to approach the virtual, the limit of objectivity, the staging of time as event. In this regard, the decision to rename the company as Nike, the Greek goddess of victory,[13] was especially apposite. As described by Marina Warner,

The figure of Nike, flying in to land on the victor's ship or hovering overhead with the garland of victory, cancels time's inauspicious vigil on her subjects' lives; she materializes as form in art at the point at which the destiny of a single person converges auspiciously with time. Like time she is travelling at speed, but unlike time, she is not moving regardless of us. She has become conscious of our passage into the future. The arrest of Nike in mid-flight, her halt over the head of the victor folds together the moment of unutterable good fortune when we come to the attention of destiny instead of hurtling on willy-nilly while undifferentiated time streams by. When she comes to a standstill in mid-flight over us she tells us that time now augurs well. And for a moment time's dread fades.

(1987: 134–135)

Let me give two examples of how Nike does not attempt to come first in a race of product fashions but, rather, is organised so as to displace the temporality of fashion altogether: the artificial limitation of the availability of Nike products and the use of event marketing.[14]

First, consider the unpredictable and discontinuous availability of Nike products and those of some other brands. Alongside the compulsive innovation of a yearly cycle in which there may be as many as four seasons, Adidas recently reissued a 1984 shoe in very limited numbers (600 pairs in the United Kingdom). In 1996, Reebok trickled out 5,000 pairs of 'The Question', a hundred-dollar name shoe, before releasing an initial shipment of 250,000. Later that year, Converse distributed limited numbers of a shoe: 'The brand needs life injected into it. . . . We want edge and image. Market share will come with that' (Solomon, quoted in Vanderbilt, 1998: 73). For a long time, the company Nike routinely allocated limited numbers of Air Jordans to keep customers wanting. Additionally, Nike is said (but refuses to acknowledge the fact officially) to 'probe' the market, by letting it be known, by word of mouth, that a very small number of a certain kind of shoe (perhaps no more than three or four pairs) will be available at a certain retail outlet. In early 2001, Nike sought to tantalise its most avid consumers: it was promising, but not yet delivering, a shoe designed in collaboration with Junya Watanbe of Comme des Garçons. It had only been sighted 'in Japan and on the web' (Hill, 2000: 9). Putting all this together it becomes clear that as a brand Nike is available as both a matter of course and a matter of chance.

Production has always involved a temporal framing of the market, but what is involved here is not the artificial limitation of the products in relation to artistic notions of uniqueness, authenticity or specialness, as in the case of Swatch. Rather, it is the multiplication of points of access to a complex object organised as a set of relations structured in terms of pattern and randomness, rather than presence and absence (Hayles, 1999). While the occurrence of randomness might be thought to undermine object-ivity, it is clear that brands such as Nike rely – to some extent at least – upon unpredictability as they monitor, respond to and sometimes appropriate the unintended effects of their products in use.

Second, consider the case of the use of event marketing by Nike (see Moor, 2003 for an interesting discussion of event marketing by Guinness). This includes both the sponsoring of already existing events, and the organisation of events by Nike itself. In both practices, Nike frames the market through the co-ordination of a series of occasions in which it seeks to ensure that time is on its side. In describing the Goddess Nike, Warner writes:

> Nike belongs to the salubrious, sunlit, upper air, and her wings mark her out as otherworldly, at one with the sky above and a spirit of concord and harmony. . . . But, most importantly, she represents a power for whom speed is of the essence, yet who hallows and glorifies the spot of her temporary halt. This makes Nike resemble an aspect of time itself, or more precisely a way we see her relation to time. She represents the propitious event that interrupts the ordinary flow and singles out the lucky winner.
>
> (1987: 133)

The attempt by Nike to resemble an aspect of time itself – to interrupt the ordinary flow – involves what might be called (un)control (Massumi, 2002). The 1998 World Cup saw ten national squads bearing the Nike insignia: the Netherlands, Italy, South Korea, the Czech Republic, Poland, Russia, the United States, Portugal, Nigeria and Brazil. The last of these were the championship favourites. However, when the Brazilian national team returned home, after losing the final (to France), they were met at the airport by disappointed fans holding the national flag modified so that in place of the slogan 'Order and Progress' was the word 'Nike'. In January 2001, the Brazilian footballer Ronaldo was questioned by parliamentary investigators on the role that Nike had played in the performance of the national team. He was asked by congressmen why Brazil lost the 1998 World Cup final 3-0 to France. 'We lost,' he said, 'because we didn't win.' Questions focused on whether Ronaldo (who had a personal sponsorship deal with Nike), who had a convulsion (and had taken a tranquilliser) before the final, had been forced to play by Nike against medical advice. It was also suggested that without pressure from Nike, the player would not have had a convulsion at all. The commission called 125 witnesses, including other players, the team doctors and former FIFA president João Havelange. But the testimonies did not incriminate Nike; as Ronaldo put it,

> 'There is no clause [in the contract with Nike] saying what I had to do during the World Cup. My relationship with Nike is very good. They never demanded me to do anything. The only thing they wanted was for me to score some goals wearing their boots.'
>
> (Quoted in Bellos, 2001b)

Instead, criticism was ultimately directed towards the Confederação Brasileira de Futebol (CBF). The final report presented evidence to prosecute 33 people for corruption including CBF president Ricardo Teixeira (the former son-in-law of João Havelange) on 13 counts of fraud. The communist congressman Aldo Rebelo, who had called for the commission, commented, 'Disney didn't sell Mickey Mouse, but the CBF sold the national team to Nike. It should have sold the spectacle, not the product' (quoted in Bellos, 2001c). But the organisation of the Nike brand as an event is such that the spectacle is not of a different order to, or detachable from the product.

What is suggested by way of this last comparison of Nike and Swatch is that marketing is neither an image stuck on top of a product or something added on to production, in a linear fashion; rather, it may lead to a reconfiguring of its temporality. In comparison with price, the brand is a mechanism not simply for registering change and thus enabling reactive feedback, but also for anticipating, indeed producing, change and thus enabling predictive adaptation or feed-forward. In other words, the interface of the brand integrates, organises and co-ordinates the phenomenon of production through its qualitative possibilities – as transitions of phase or state, as the organisation of effects, not as price or quantities (Kwinter, 2001: 42). From this point of view – the inside out – the brand is thus a means of performing production not as a homogenising but as a (more or less) heterogenising process; not as a linear, but as a (more or less) non-linear process.

Complex objects and partial solutions

As a consequence of its ability to function as an interface in the market, the brand is both dynamic and indeterminate. It emerges as a real, abstract symbol-manipulating machine for the simulation of product innovation; it is an artefact that adapts through continuous feedback and feed-forward. As such, it is a complex object – or, more precisely, an artefact of managed complexity (Manzini, 1989). Simon suggests that in 'the best of all possible worlds', it might be possible to combine the two sets of advantages described above – that is, those deriving from the viewpoint of the outer environment, and that deriving from the viewpoint of the inner environment. He says:

> We might hope to be able to characterise the main properties of the system and its behaviour without elaborating the detail of either the outer or inner environments. We might look toward a science of the artificial that would depend on the relative simplicity of the interface as its primary source of abstraction and generality.
>
> ([1969] 1981: 12)

This is one way of describing the aims of the artificial science(s) of brand management. It holds up the possibility that the brand might enable the communication of information relating to a continuously evolving multi-dimensional system, including its ability to mutate in time (Kwinter, 2001: 47). That this aspiration is even conceivable is a consequence of the increasing role of information in the co-ordination and conduct of the processes of production (Castells, 1996, 2000; Hardt and Negri, 2000; Lash, 2002; Mackenzie, 2002).[15]

However, while the informational economy is sometimes described in terms of real-time instantaneity, this temporality is typically restricted to certain highly invested spheres of activity (such as foreign exchange markets). Elsewhere, there remains a speed differential. Indeed, Adrian Mackenzie argues that time differentials are essential to the contemporary economy:

> Insisting on value, the very principle (and principal) of capital resides in different delays. Although the value of information rests in its speed, this speed only makes sense as a differential. There must be differences in speed for information to have any value.
>
> (2002: 160)

Drawing on Guy Debord's analysis in *The Society of the Spectacle* ([1967] 2002), Mackenzie argues that there must be different speeds of access to information or different rates of movement of information if capital is to market spectacle to consumers as a form of merchandise. The brand provides one mechanism by which such differences in speed may be staged as a modulation of production: the stylisation of power (Massumi, 2002: 88), not only as 'again and again', or as 'faster', 'sooner', but also as anticipation and nostalgia, fashion and collection, and, at its limit, as event.[16]

To talk in these terms is not to celebrate brands; nor is to suggest that the development of brands is the best response to the question of how to organise the economy in a rational way (the question that economics sets itself as a discipline). Simon is at pains to stress that while the conception of design he outlines is about the generation of solutions to problems, the solutions so produced will not necessarily be optimal (for any or all of the parties involved). Thus in relation to the operations of the price mechanism, he writes:

> One can marvel that the productive efforts and consumption activities of a great population can be brought into patterned order simply by allowing people to exchange goods at prices mutually agreed upon, without agreeing that the pattern will have optimal properties.
>
> ([1969] 1981: 40)

In a similar way, to describe the interface of the brand as a machine for generating solutions does not imply that the solutions it provides to the problems posed by the management of the economy are optimal. It is in any case a characteristic of complex artificial systems that there is no fixed criterion of optimality, but the performance of contemporary brands suggests that the (multiple) solutions they provide are not simply not optimal, but less than satisfactory for many. Put baldly, brands do not produce more 'perfect' information than price.

This less than optimal performance is clear when considering the brand both as an object within competitive market relations and as an object of consumption (Slater, 2002a). On the one hand, brands do not necessarily enhance competition between firms. Rather more often than not, the reverse is true – that is, brands allow markets to be controlled more effectively. For example, successful brands (for example, Microsoft, Coca-Cola, Heinz) provide the basis for long-standing monopolies or dominance of certain markets and afford protection of long-term investment against risk. At the same time, the rise of brands has contributed to the emergence of a market environment in which the costs of new product development have developed so that they are more or less prohibitive in many cases. Thus, while around sixteen thousand new products are launched in the United States every year, 95 per cent of them are launched as extensions of existing brands (Murphy, 1998: 5).

There are many examples of the use of the dominant position of one brand in a market to enter (and dominate) others. Perhaps one of the clearest examples of this is that of Microsoft, whose operating-system software is used to run between 80 per cent and 90 per cent of the world's computers.[17] Microsoft also controls nearly the same market share for applications such as word processors, spreadsheets, presentation graphic programmes and relational databases – the components of the suite of office applications that the company 'bundles' together to consumers. The company's practices have been the subject of a long and bitterly fought anti-trust case in both the United States and Europe (type in 'Microsoft' and 'anti-trust' to your preferred search engine and read!). In an attempt to gain control of linked markets, Microsoft is said by its critics to have used its strong brand identity and control over the PC operating system to eliminate or dominate a number of rivals in markets for desktop applications. Alleged tactics include selectively disseminating information about the operating systems's current and future functionality, thus requiring companies to enter into unequal relations with the company if they are to be able to design functional products; giving away copies of its proprietary browser, Microsoft Internet Explorer (MSIE), to undermine its main rival, Netscape (MSIE is now included in the Microsoft basic operating system); pre-announcement of non-existent products sometimes described as 'vaporware') to discourage consumer purchase of rival products; and predatory pricing of products to deprive rivals of revenue. The effect of such strategies, it is argued, is to drive rivals out of the market; to deter future entrants; to control a wide range of operating standards; and to play too large a part in the regulation of the Internet in relation to issues such as surveillance, copyright, personal privacy and the ability of Internet users to avoid commercial content. Supporters of Microsoft argue that the effect of its strategies is to reduce prices and reduce consumer uncertainty, while its critics believe it has stifled invention and reduced choice. While the case of Microsoft is unusual, it does seem that the brand organises 'a certain structuration of competition, which acts both as a constraint and a resource for the collective qualification–requalification of products' (Callon *et al.*, 2002: 201) – and that it does so in such a way as to extend the forms of market control exercised by large corporations.

On the other hand, while brands are sometimes represented as being more in the interest of consumers than commodities, this is also not necessarily so. For example, Stephen King of J. Walter Thompson claims, 'The difference between products and brands is fundamental. A product is something that is made in a factory; a brand is something that is bought by a consumer' (quoted in Pavitt, 2000b: 73–75). And it is the performative discipline of marketing that is commonly held to have a pivotal role in the communication of what it is the consumer wants. But it is commonly argued – even by some within marketing – that the actual role of marketers has remained that of an adjunct to sellers, that marketing continues to be seller-centric (Mitchell, 2001; see also Chapter 5).

> Marketing teaches that organized efforts are needed to bring an understanding of the outside, of society, economy and customer, to the inside of the organization and to make it the foundation for strategy and policy. Yet marketing has rarely performed that grand task. Instead it has become a tool to support selling. It does not start out with 'who is the customer?' but 'what do we want to sell?' It is aimed at getting people to buy the things you want to make.
>
> (Drucker, 1998, quoted in Mitchell, 2001: 78)

So, for example, while the setting up and development of Swatch was dependent on market research, its 'non-watch' product is not used to mark the stages in the life cycle of the consumer. Instead, the time of the consumer is created in the relations between the products that comprise the brand: fashion, collection and the Beat. Similarly, while Nike may be described as a brand characterised by uncontrol, the managers of the brand do not respond to all the uses to which consumers wish to put its products. Indeed, the company clearly wishes to disassociate itself from some of its uses. At the same time, brand owners are able to lay claim to the exclusive ownership of brands – including the multiplicity of their possible uses – through the legal protection afforded by trade mark (see Chapter 5). In short, while the account presented so far has suggested that information about the consumer is vital to the emergence of the brand, it has not implied that the exchange between producers and consumers is direct, impartial or symmetrical in its effects; rather the reverse.

Coda

Rather than seeing the activities of producers and consumers as the sole focus of analysis, this account has sought to show the importance of *the systemic properties of the relations between products* for an understanding of the brand's economic, political and cultural implications. The aim is to describe a dynamic, multi-dimensional model of the economy in which the brand functions as a complex object. It is thus a contribution to the discussion of the economy in terms of a circuit of production and consumption, or 'circuit of culture' (Johnson, 1986; du Gay *et al.*, 1997; Julier, 2000). Rather than seeing relations in terms of either determination or articulation, however, the suggestion is that the brand has the potential to function probabilistically, globally and transductively. As a consequence, it is able to work within certain *margins of indeterminacy* afforded by its abstraction and generality. This is what enables it to organise design intensity, to manage the system of relations between products in such a way as to produce non-linear effects, and to co-ordinate the flows of disjuncture and difference of contemporary capital (Appadurai, 1996; Lee and LiPuma, 2002; Knorr Cetina, 2003). The argument being developed here is thus that the brand is an artefact of an economy in which the relations between the products or stages of production are not linear, but complex – that is, probabilistic, global and transductive. But this chapter has also suggested that the functioning of the brand as a complex object or artefact does not necessarily lead to more competitive relations between firms, or to greater equality in the relations between producers and consumers. For this reason, it is important to identify the social mechanisms for expanding the margins of indeterminacy (see Chapters 5 and 6). Intervening in such margins provides the possibility of effective social and political intervention in the objectivity of the brand.

4 Logos

From relations to relationships, or, the face of the interface

A horror story, the face is a horror story. It is certain that the signifier does not construct the wall that it needs all by itself; it is certain that subjectivity does not dig its hole all alone. Concrete faces cannot be assumed to come ready-made. They are engendered by an abstract machine of faciality (visagéité), which produces them at the same time as it gives the signifier its white wall and subjectivity its black hole. Thus the black hole/white wall system is, to begin with, not a face but the abstract machine that produces faces according to the changeable combinations of its cogwheels. Do not expect the abstract machine to resemble what it produces, or will produce.

(Deleuze and Guattari, 1999: 168)

Introduction

So far, this book has developed the argument that the brand is an object or medium for the exchange of information between 'producers' and 'consumers'. The interface of the brand organises the exchange of information or communication so as to produce relations between products as constancy, fashion, collection, novelty or even as event. The brand emerges as a complex object or artefact in this reconfiguring of the temporality of production. But this complex object is intangible or incorporeal; as such it is not immediately identifiable in everyday encounters. Instead, a face – that is, the logo or logos – makes the brand visible.

Well-known examples of logos in use today include names of products – Surf, Fairy Liquid, Snickers, Intel, Kleenex; names and monograms of companies – Nike, Microsoft, IBM, Nokia, Disney, Virgin, Shell and BP; graphic images – the representation of a white propellor blade against a blue sky in the BMW logo, the tyres of the Michelin man, the Lloyds black horse, the Nike Swoosh, the Orange orange square; and tag-lines – 'the real thing', 'Just do it', 'Where do you want to go today?', 'United Colors of Benetton' and

'Think different'. But the use of marks to identify, describe and create value has a long history. Some commentators suggest that the use of brands to mark livestock has been going on for at least five thousand years, and that over two thousand years ago the Romans used marks to distinguish pottery made or owned by different individuals (Mollerup, 1997). Early modern examples of the use of marks in Europe are to be found in *ars heraldica*, the art of the herald – that is, the official at medieval tournaments of arms who was responsible for the identification of fighting knights.[1] Marks were also used in a number of occupations and trades, including farming (branding and earmarks), ceramics (*dipiti* – pen- or brush-made marks; and *graffiti* – incised marks), stone-masonry, printing, papermaking (watermarks), silver- and gold-smithing (the term 'hallmark' refers to Goldsmiths Hall in London, where articles of gold, silver and platinum were traditionally assayed and stamped) and furniture-making, among others. These marks were primarily used to distinguish the products and property of an organisation or individual, but were also designed to produce attention value, to exert a kind of holding power, as well as, some-times, to describe or present information about the organisation or individual (ibid.). In these uses them, marks or logos organise a process of identification, presenting a mark as social identity, as ownership and as origin (ibid.).

While having their modern roots in this artisanal or craft practice, marks or logos became more and more widespread in Europe and the United States in the second half of the nineteenth century as they were increasingly used to dis-tinguish industrial, manufactured, packaged products from one another. As part of a growing set of industrial conventions for the regulation of liability, they came to function as marks of quality assurance. By the second half of the twentieth century, however, there is a shift from the use of logos as guaran-tors of quality to a role in which the logo contributes more actively to the value of the brand. This is the period in which the use of logos as marks of social identities is extended through their iconic presentation as personalities, persona or *faces*. This use of logos is now pervasive, and it will be the focus of discussion in this chapter.

Before embarking on this analysis, though, the chapter will outline the account of the sign developed in the approach to the study of signs known as semiotics. This is a study of signs that aims to restore the immanence of move-ment to the logic of the image, sign and narration; it is not a linguistics, but a logic.[2] Crucially, although Peirce maintains that the world can be known only through its signs,[3] he also maintains that signs qua images are real. Here Peirce (and then Deleuze) draws on a notion of the image in general – the Image as a mobile material, as universal variation, the identity of matter with movement and light (Bergson, 1991; Rochberg-Halton, 1986; Rodowick, 1997[4]). *The relation of signs to the real here is not one of representation, but one of implication.* In what follows, this approach to the study of the sign will be applied to the development of the logo by marketers in terms of two aspects: 'awareness' and 'image'. 'Awareness' will be considered as a strategy of self-referencing, while 'image' will be addressed in conjunction with developments in the media, and here the notion of the logo as persona or face will be elaborated. The aim is not to present the logo as the culmination of developments in the media, or as some kind of avant-garde form of the image, but rather to point out how logos may be understood in relation to changes in other forms of communication. In conclusion, the chapter will consider the logo as an image of the organisation of the logics of flow – the movements of people, products and ideas – that are characteristic of a global (media) economy.

The logo as sign: a semiotic approach

The brand has been described so far as a set of relations between products in time. On the one hand, branded products are themselves discrete; on the other, in so far as they are branded, they have a kind of unity in their relation to one another. The brand is thus a unity that is more than the sum of its parts (or products). It is this indivisible thing that is signified by the logo. As a sign, the logo may be understood in terms of the semiotics proposed by Peirce (1978) and adapted in the writings of Deleuze (1986, 1989). From this perspective, the logo is not exceptional in its dynamism; rather, all signs may be said to be in and of movement. For Peirce, the image is not a unified or closed whole (it is not a fixed relationship between signifier and signified), but rather an ensemble or set of logical relations that are in a state of continual transformation. That these logical relations are what constitute signs is made clear in his famous definition of a sign as:

> something which stands to somebody for something in some respect or capacity. It addresses somebody, that is, creates in the mind of that person an equivalent sign, or perhaps a more developed sign. That sign which it creates I call the interpretant of the first sign. The sign stands for something, its object. It stands for that object, not in all respects, but in reference to a sort of idea, which I have sometimes called the ground of the representamen.

> (1978: 99)

Because all signs occur in time and are framed within a normative community of interpretation, a sign is by definition a sign-process, a communicative act. Because the interpretant is also another sign, it in turn 'addresses' another interpretant, in a continuing process of interpretative communication

(Rochberg-Halton, 1986). This continuous framing is what, for Peirce, makes the sign inherently and necessarily dynamic.

As noted earlier, the sign never represents the real for Peirce, in the sense of fixing the meaning of something that exists elsewhere; rather, it enfolds or implies it. He identifies three principal modes in which the real appears or is implicated in signification: Firstness, Secondness and Thirdness. Peirce says:

> Signs are divisible by three trichotomies; first, according as the sign itself is a mere quality, is an actual existent, or is a general law; secondly, according as the relation of the sign to its object consists in the sign's having some character in itself, or in some existential relation to that object, or in its relation to an interpretant; thirdly, according as its interpretant represents it as a sign of possibility or as a sign of fact or a sign of reason.
>
> (1978: 101)

Each of these three modes may in turn be distinguished in three ways: as a sign in itself, in the relation of the sign to its object, and in how the interpretant represents the sign. While Peirce distinguishes the three modes in which the real appears or is implicated in signification analytically, they do not appear in isolation from one another in practice.

Firstness is 'a mere quality', a quali-sign, such as 'red, bitter, tedious, hard, noble' (Peirce, quoted in Marks, 2000: 196). It is something so emergent that it is not yet quite a sign, for it is perceptible only as it appears in other signs. So, for example, we do not ever perceive only the quality of red, or only the quality of bitterness; rather, we perceive these as a complex with other signs. As Peirce puts it, '[Firstness] cannot actually act as a sign until it is embodied; but the embodiment has nothing to do with its character as a sign' (1978: 101). The relation of the quali-sign to its object is *iconic* – that is, the sign denotes the object by being like it; and the interpretant represents the sign as a rheme (or Deleuze's reume) – that is, a sign of qualitative possibility. Peirce writes, 'An Icon is a sign which refers to the Object that it denotes merely by virtue of characters of its own, and which it possesses, just the same, whether any such Object actually exists or not' (ibid.: 102). The interpretant represents the sign as a sign of *qualitative possibility*, the icon is 'a mere may-be' (ibid.: 81).

In relation to Secondness, Peirce speaks of an actual thing or event as a sin-sign ('where the syllable "sin" is taken as meaning "being only once", as in single, simple, Latin, semel, etc.' (1978: 101)). It can be so through its qualities, so that it involves several quali-signs. Or to put this the other way round, it is in the realm of Secondness, of 'brute facts', that qualities become attributes of objects and events, which are perceived in their individuality and in opposition (or 'struggle') to everything else. The relation of this sign to its object is *indexical* – that is, the sign denotes the object *through an existential connection to it*. As Peirce puts it, 'An Index is a sign which refers to the Object that it denotes by virtue of being really affected by that Object' (ibid.: 102). The Interpretant represents the sign as a sign of *actual existence*.

Thirdness is the realm of interpretation and symbolisation, of general statements about qualities and events. Rather than being indicative, it is declarative. The legi-sign is a law that is a sign. It is not a single thing, but a general type which, it is agreed through convention, shall be significant. Every legi-sign signifies through an instance of its application, which Pierce calls a replica of it. The relation of sign to its object is *symbolic* – that is, the sign denotes the object through its relation to an interpretant. Peirce writes, 'A Symbol is a sign which refers to the Object that it denotes by virtue of a law, usually an association of general ideas, which operates to cause the Symbol to be interpreted as referring to that Object' (1978: 102). The interpretant represents the *sign as an argument*.

Brand image: the logo as symbol

Logos are examples of legi-signs or symbols. They are agreed, general typifications; the relation of the logo to its object, the brand, is established in relation to an interpretant; and the interpretant represents the logo as an argument. But, so it will be argued here, as a symbol or mode of Thirdness, the logo as legi-sign mediates both Secondness and Firstness. On the one hand, the agreement that secures the logo as a symbol is typically little more than a recognition (a mark of 'brand awareness') that is achieved through the repetitive placing of a logo on products, promotion and packaging. On the other hand, much of brand management involves the management of the ability of such signs to mediate aspects of Secondness and Firstness (in the creation of 'brand image'). This mediation provides the basis for the 'argument' of the logo, such as it is. It is what enables the logo to act as 'the border and limit of a rationalist discourse' (Quinn, 1994: 8).

As an application of marketing practice, logos are ubiquitous, constantly presented to us on products, on packaging and promotion, on hoardings, on the sides of buses, taxis and buildings, on bags and people's clothing, on screens in the cinema, television and computers, and as signage and orientation devices. The presentation of a particular logo may be varied in size, colour and in other aspects over time. So, for example, the words 'Coca-Cola' have been written in a number of different scripts throughout the brand's history, while the Penguin 'penguin' has metamorphosed in shape, as has the Shell 'shell', the double 'RR' mark that signifies Rolls-Royce, and almost any logo that has a long history. The logo or corporate personality Betty Crocker, whose handwritten 'signature' marks a number of products (currently over 130), has had a portrait painted on at least seven occasions during the eighty or so years of her (imaginary) existence. In 1921, she was just a signature; in 1924, she acquired a voice and appeared on radio for the first time; in 1936, her portrait was painted for the first time. In 1941, she became a brand name on product packaging, and was known to nine out of ten American housewives. By 1945, she was the best-known woman in the United States next to Eleanor Roosevelt. In her latest portrait, 75 photographs of Betty Crocker product-users were superimposed to create a new, modern image (G. Lury, 1998: 40–41). Nevertheless, while her dress, hairstyle and make-up change with the period, Betty herself does not grow older. The repetition of a recognisable logo (a mark recognisable as itself) remains constant.

Rather than referring to a (pre-existing) set of meanings or practices, repetition is a *strategy of self-reference*. In repetition, a descriptor or nonsense word (such as Kleenex or Kodak) 'acquires a semantic autonomy and a force of memory which transform it into a self-signifying proper name' (Frow, 2002: 64; Quinn, 1994). This is perhaps most evident in those promotions in which a logo is initially presented without reference to the products or services that it will later be found to mark. This was the case with the promotion of Orange, a telecommunications service that was launched in the United Kingdom with a series of posters featuring only a small square of orange on which was written the word 'orange' in lowercase white lettering, and the words 'Laugh', 'Cry', 'Listen' and 'Talk'. As a marketing strategy, repetition produces the certainty of a reference in a process in which each instance is encountered as a more or less effective representation of itself. To put this another way, repetition secures the familiarity of a brand, that which is constant despite changes. It is what makes possible the *'awareness'* of a brand, one of the two key aspects of brand equity identified by brand consultant Kevin Keller (1998, quoted in Barwise *et al.*, 2000: 75–82). Brand awareness means that when most people are asked for examples of brands they are able to give a list of examples. In Europe and United States, these typically include Coca-Cola ('Coca-Cola' is said to be the second-best-known word in the world, 'OK' being the first), McDonald's, Levi's, Ford, Heinz, Nike, Disney, the BBC, Nokia, Microsoft and perhaps now Orange. However, Keller argues that 'awareness' must, if the brand is to be successful, be supported by a second aspect, *'image'*. And it is in building brand image, this chapter will suggest, that aspects of Secondness and Firstness are introduced into the logo.

Brand image: the logo as index and icon

Brand image, Keller argues, includes *the associations that a brand holds for a consumer*. For Coca-Cola these associations are likely to be America, 'the real thing' and the colours red and white. For Microsoft they would include Windows, Bill Gates and the slogan, 'Where do you want to go today?' Orange might make us think of the colour orange and, perhaps, communication or interaction. The expanded set of marketing activities described in Chapter 2 is heavily implicated in the management of these associations, but perhaps most important in the development of brand image are the practices of *brand positioning*. This is the activities (to be described further in what follows) that a company adopts to give its brand a distinctive position and ensure that consumers in the target market can tell that brand apart from others. In so far as these activities are successful, the logo comes to function as a specular or speculative device for magnifying one set of associations and then another (Quinn, 1994), creating a set of associations in the mind of the consumer. The effect of marketing activities, then, is that at the same time that it is recognisable as itself only, the logo is able to focus and channel sense and meaning.

Historically, aspects of what Peirce calls Secondness were introduced into the logo through the ways in which some marks denote their relation to the brand *through an existential connection to the processes of production*. In these cases, the logo is typically used to function *as an index*, a (more or less genuine or degenerate, in Peirce's terminology) trace of the producer, and in this way is able to act as a guarantee of a certain consistency of standards or quality. As an index of the person, corporation or process of production, the logo as index is able to act as a guarantee of authenticity and serves to repudiate forgery. The logo as index is sometimes (a reproduction of) the actual signature of the individual who makes the product; more usually it is the mark of the organisation that is responsible for the process of production. In these cases, the marks sometimes implicate the organisation as if it were itself an individual,[5] as in the case of Paul Smith (whose name logo is presented as his own signature but was handwritten by a friend) and the Betty Crocker logo described in the previous section. In the latter case, not only does the name Betty Crocker mark a range of products, but it also authorises recipes, and, as noted above, someone performing this personality has appeared on radio programmes as if the logo were indeed the trace of a real individual.

Certainly, the knowledge that there is a real, live individual standing behind the brand gives it vitality, but such an individual may behave in ways that will undermine the reputation of the brand. In any case, a real-life individual will, in the short or long run, die. Sometimes then the company that bears the founder's name is still (partly) owned and run by members of the family; sometimes there is no longer any family connection at all. In all cases, the question of continuity is important for the ability of a logo to act as an index; as Giorgio Armani says,

> Obviously, the company is very tied to my name and it would be very selfish of me to think, 'OK, tomorrow I'm not going to be here, so, that's it. That's the end of everything.' So I do have to think about it. There are different solutions and one could be to associate myself with a [luxury goods] group – in some way which could guarantee a certain continuance to the brand.
>
> (Quoted in Rushton, 2003: 10)

Alternatively, the organisation of some brands – such as that of Martha Stewart – seems to presume that the individual person who initially gave life to the brand may come to live through it (as if the brand were some kind of life-support machine):

KELLY: Management guru Tom Peters preaches the 'brand of you' – if there is anyone this applies to, it's you. What happens if you get hit by a bus? Does the brand of you continue?

STEWART: I'm trying to make sure that my brand extension is broad enough that if anything happens, or I decide to check out, it can continue. We have taken the next five years of photographs of me already, so if anything happened to me we have those closets full of photos.

KELLY: You could have yourself scanned to create a virtual character.

STEWART: Cloning hasn't worked yet, but I'll be the first. The first human Dolly [the name of the first cloned sheep] will be me.

> (Kelly, 1998: 114)

As this last example indicates, there is more to logos than indexicality alone. Indeed, the focus of many recent attempts of brand management to control and channel the brand image may be understood in terms of the creations of *icons*, or the implication of Firstness in the logo. In some accounts of the icon, its distinctiveness as a sign resides in its resemblance to that which it represents. But as outlined above, for Peirce the icon is understood not so much in terms of visual similitude but in terms of the quality, suchness or Firstness of the object that is conveyed by the sign.

As Sanford Kwinter (1998) points out, historically, some qualities – such as colour – once so overwhelmed perception that they were removed from the remit of scientific inquiry as effects of the subjective. This is evident in the long-standing distinction in the philosophy of science (from John Locke onwards) between so-called primary and secondary qualities. Secondary qualities (such as colour, sound, scent and others) were deemed by the philosophy of science not to be properties of objects as such, but were rather held to be a function of subjective sense perception alone. This view sets up two opposed sites of investigation, the object-ive and the subject-ive, or 'a field of perception devoid of any data for its own interpretation' on the one hand, and 'a system of interpretation devoid of any reason for the concurrence of its factors' on the other (Whitehead, 1978: 9). This object–subject opposition was nonetheless also the prompt for a steady stream of studies seeking to bridge the gap between the two sites. Thus, this distinction fuelled the 'age-old search for material equivalences to match the qualitative feel of elusive inner states', which has included 'the pursuit of color correspondences . . . and [research] into how people are affected by distinctive odors' (Stafford, 2001: 156).

For much of the nineteenth and twentieth centuries, such endeavours were deemed to be marginal, unscientific, impractical, but the situation is changing as part of a wider cultural shift across science, philosophy and the arts as well as business. Across all these domains, the dynamism of relations or situations between object and subject are being re-addressed, and made the site of explicit intervention. Kwinter writes:

> The modern, rationalizing mind . . . set out to organize the world so that it could become apprehensible to, and manipulable by, rational operations. Today these operations have begun to approach the point of radically diminishing returns. . . . the mysteries of the qualitative world are necessarily beginning to recapture attention. The difference is that today we have a scaffold of mental technologies with which to investigate the qualitative world in a relatively systematic manner.
>
> (1998: 42)

From this perspective, brand positioning is one such mental technology, an organisation of the capacity for conjecturing, for making abductive inferences about the possibilities of objects and then submitting them to deductive and inductive tests in an ongoing process of practical experimentation with subjects. 'The world is turning orange', as the tag-line for the Orange mobile telephone company informs us.[6] Or to put this another way, the brand is a series of qualification trials in which the active possibilities – or 'mere may-bes' of products – are investigated (Callon *et al.*, 2002), *differentiated* in particular products and then *integrated* in product ranges, series or lines and, ultimately, the abstract object–subject, the brand.

Brian Massumi (2002) provides an example of an early precursor of such trials in his description of a psychological experiment (conducted a hundred or so years ago now) to study the effect of memory on colour constancy. In this study, subjects were required to match colours, including, for example, the black of a subject's hat, the red of his own lips, the brown of the bricks of the house he lived in, and the blue of a certain friend's eyes. Massumi notes that the subjects almost always selected a colour that was '"too bright to match a bright object", "too dark to match a dark object", and "too saturated to match an object which is known to have a distinct hue"' (ibid.: 210). Massumi goes on to point out that this excess was understood by the experimenter to be subjective (the effect of the subject), while colour was retained as a constant quality of the objective circumstances of the experiment. However, Massumi himself suggests that 'The remembering of a colour is not effectively a reproduction of a perception, but a transformation or a becoming of it. The memory of the friend's eyes is in some way "too blue": excess' (ibid.: 210). From this more recent perspective, colours such as blue (or orange or red) may be seen to attest to 'a self-activity of experience' (ibid.: 211), and belong to the joint situation of the experimenter, the experiment and the subject.[7] Marketing may be seen in this context as a similar kind of experiment, albeit one conducted outside the laboratory and on a mass scale. The production of the effect of 'too-blueness', self-activity or 'excess' is precisely what is desired in such experiments. In other words, the brand is the staging of an experiment in which qualities are no longer pre-emptorily divided into primary and secondary groups but rather are deliberately provoked into existence in trails of product qualification. The object, the subject and the pervasive quality of their relation become a site of systematic manipulation and intervention. There is a recognition in such investigations that the logo as icon is a qualitative mode of communication not reducible to convention, and that 'participation precedes recognition' (ibid.: 231);[8] in other words, that 'image' precedes 'awareness'.

The case of the development of a logo for the Orange telecommunications brand (www.orange.com) is outlined here to illustrate what is involved in the development of iconicity in rather more detail. Before this telecommunications service was launched in 1994, the company's trading name was Microtel (the company was itself owned by HWL Telecommunications). A team including Microtel, corporate identity specialists Wolff Olins and advertising agency WCRS was commissioned to create 'a clear strong voice for the brand'. The team encapsulated the core brand proposition in three ideas: 'my world', 'my manager' and 'my friend'. The composite idea was 'It's my life'. A short list of names that were held to suit this proposition were identified, including Pecan, Gemini, Egg, Miro and Orange. The last of these was chosen because it was held to have connotations of hope, fun and freedom. Following the decision of the name, the orange square logo was designed. Michael Wolff, co-founder of the agency Wolff Olins, describes his understanding of the use of the colour orange (which he first used in 1965 for Camden Council) in the following terms:

> Orange is a way of using red without its stridency, urgency and alarm – it keeps the vibrancy but is warm and cheery.
>
> Tesco's red means cheap but Sainsbury's orange is red, but not quite.

Other marketers say, 'Orange is attention-grabbing without being aggressive. . . . It can be calm, warm and rich as well as fresh and healthy' (Marksteen Adamson, international creative director of Interbrand), and 'Orange is warm and friendly as opposed to the cold, blue tones used by telecoms companies and banks' (Robbie Lawson, Wolff Olins's creative director) (all quoted in Day, 2001). The strap-line for the launch advertising campaign was, 'The future's bright. The future's Orange.' Market research found that people believed the name Orange to be distinctive, friendly, extrovert, modern and powerful, and attempts were made to incorporate these values in the Orange promotional ethos.

> **Refreshing**. We constantly look to do things differently and in a better way. We give colour to all that we do. We are ready to push the boundaries and take risks.
>
> **Honest**. We are always open and honest. We say what we do and we do what we say. We have nothing to hide and we behave responsibly.
>
> **Straightforward**. For us, clarity comes through simplicity. We recognise that we are people communicating with other people. We are always direct and easy to understand.
>
> **Dynamic**. We want to make a difference to people's lives. Our optimism is contagious. We are passionate about what we do and we have confidence in ourselves.
>
> **Friendly**. We enjoy working and succeeding together by building close relationships. While we have a sense of purpose, we also have a sense of humour. We consider the needs both of our customers and of each other.

The brand values were said to be represented in the service's billing policy to its customers: while a rival service, Mercury One-2-One, offered 'free time' to its consumers, Orange provided bundled tariff packages and per-second billing (this policy was described as 'honest' and 'straightforward'). The Orange campaign won a Gold award from the Institute of Practitioners in Advertising Effectiveness Awards. This was for 'its success in creating a brand identity that captured consumers' imaginations, allowing the company to take on its competitors in a short space of time even though it was a late entrant in the mobile market'. Since then, the name 'Orange', the specific shade of orange used (in a specific shape, a square) and the word 'wirefree' have been trademarked. The Orange brand was floated successfully on the stock market in 1996 and has been successful in Switzerland, Israel, Australia, Belgium and Hong Kong; in 2002, Mobilix became the first company in the Orange group to be rebranded Orange.

Inevitably, the real-life 'experiments' of marketing are not always success-ful. For example, in 1996 Pepsi spent approximately $500 million on a cam-paign to change the colour with which its products were associated: from red (the colour also associated with its main rival, Coca-Cola) to electric blue. This campaign ('Project Blue') included the most expensive commercial ever made, the most expensive press conference ever held (400 journalists were flown to Gatwick, London, from around the world), the painting blue of Concorde for a year, and a plan to change every single can of Pepsi around the world on the same day. Yet according to a recent survey (conducted by Marks and Clerk, a firm of trade mark and patent attorneys), while 48 per cent of businesspeople think that Coca-Cola's red is a highly valuable and recognisable colour, only 2 per cent think this of Pepsi's blue (www.wnim.com/issue14). Despite the apparent failure of this particular example, the point being made here is that the logo is a device (an image-instrument) for experimentation in the sciences of the artificial (Simon, [1969] 1981), the arts of the possible (Massumi, 2002) *and* the markets of the mere may-be (Peirce, 1978).

Brand positioning: differentiation and integration

The logo is also the mark of the marketing practices of brand positioning, which may themselves be understood in terms of the two axes of signification identified by Deleuze (1986, 1989; Rodowick, 1997).[9] The first is a vertical axis of *differentiation and integration*, and the second a horizontal axis of *association*, in which images are linked through principles of contiguity, contrast and opposi-tion. The organisation of these two axes underpins the emergence of a qualitat-ive ratio(nality) between time and space, and in relation to the brand provide a basis for the re-introduction of qualities into the (logos of the) economy.

Let me address the vertical axis first. Central to the performativity of the brand described in these chapters are those marketing techniques that function in an analogous way to programming in both broadcasting and computing. As Manovich describes it, for example (2001: xxxiii), computer programming involves altering the flow of data through the organisation of a series of control loops such as 'if/then' and 'repeat/while'. The suggestion put forward here is that marketing practices are in some respects analogous to the control loops of new media objects. That is, these practices enable the activities of consumers to be internalised in the processes and products of production and distribution. This internalisation typically involves the marketer adopting the position of the consumer – that is, of imagining the consumer (Lury and Warde, 1996). The marketing knowledge or information produced in this way is used in processes of product differentiation, then, in turn, the resulting product or products themselves become marketing tools for a brand which thus progresses or emerges in a series of loops. In relation to a vertical axis of signification, then, this looping may be seen in terms of *a process of (product) differentiation and (brand) integration*. This is a process in which 'related images are internalized into a conceptual whole whose movement expresses a qualitative change: the whole is different from the sum of the parts' (Rodowick, 1997: 10).

Here it is interesting to note that the development of brand image through the looping incorporation of information about the consumer is not confined to the management of the logo alone. As was noted in Chapter 3, there have been changes in the ways in which matter becomes capable of being integrated in design activity such that this is now described as a matter–process system and the relations between products may be described as a flow (Manzini, 1989). Such changes have made it increasingly possible for the practices of brand positioning to involve product design as well as promotion and product positioning in (or as) the media. One example of a development in design activity that is relevant here is the approach called 'product semantics'. This term, first used by Krippendorf and Butter in 1984, has been described as 'designing by association'. As Julier (2000) notes, its emergence in this period coincided with developments in manufacturing – notably the increase in the use of microchip technology for products – that enabled the miniaturisation of the internal workings of many electronic goods. Julier gives a number of examples of the design thinking (and practice) that lie behind such developments, including the Cranbrook Academy of Art in Illinois and the Memphis projects of Milanese designers in the 1980s. He also describes the more recent approach of Hsiao and Chen in South Korea, who have developed a semantic and shape grammar-based approach to individual features of office chair design:

> They explored the semantic values of various forms abstracted from the basic typology of the office chair by marrying particular shapes with their associated emotional effects. From this they then produced a computer program which pieced together separate formal components according to the emotional characteristics they wished to imbue in the object.
>
> (Julier, 2000: 94–95)

In other words, while the changes described here may mean that designers have greater freedom in relation to the use of materials, this freedom is simultaneously curtailed by another set of requirements. Designers are increasingly obliged to 'ascertain what emotional values they [or their employers] want the consumer to attach to the product. They then develop forms which instigate the associations to, hopefully, inculcate those feelings' (ibid.: 94).

This shift in design practice is, however, merely one aspect of what is in marketing discourse described as brand positioning: the intensification of the values with which the brand is associated through practices of targeting and positioning. The aim of brand positioning is to 'monitor the current brand images that exist in the different types or "segments" of the consumer market and try to highlight some and sideline others, while continuously introducing new, positive associations' (Barwise *et al.*, 2000: 75–78). It typically includes the intensive use of more traditional media to stage the logo, including the computer screen, television, film and print, as well as packaging, signage, sponsored events and the built environment. And it is often in these practices that the very distinction between object-ive properties and subject-ive values is blurred: 'For consumers, brands and brand values are a way to "feel" the product as part of their own personalities' (Renzo Russo, President and Founder of Diesel, quoted in Pavitt, 2000b: 64). This approach to positioning attempts to brand manage the role of emotion in forging enduring brand relations (or joint situations):

> Emotion is an unlimited resource with unlimited power. Neurologist Donald Calne put it brilliantly, 'The essential difference between emotion and reason is that emotion leads to action while reason leads to conclusions.'. . . In the crucible of emotion, Saatchi & Saatchi developed Lovemarks – powerful emotional connections between a company, its people, its brand and its customers. . . . The outcome is the ultimate premium profit generator – a brand that earns loyalty beyond reason. . . . What started as a transaction and deepened into a relationship has moved on. In the new reality, successful business will be a conversation of the spirit. The paradox of less is more. Less logic. Less research. Less analysis. More mystery. More sensuality. More intimacy. Less head. More heart.
>
> (www.lovemarks.com)

In this way of thinking, the logo is produced in the movements of 'face, rhythm and line' (Klein, 1993: 5); or, as Kevin Roberts, the chief advocate of Lovemarks, puts it, 'Sensuality is not about cool functionality, it's about curves and swings, push and pull' (www.lovemarks.com).

Brand positioning: association

The horizontal axis of signification is concerned with the principles of association involved in the creation of the logo as icon, and here the notion of *the interval* is absolutely fundamental to the (media) economy in which the brand operates. Let me try to elaborate what is at issue here by returning to some of the points made just now. As described then, the looping activities of brand positioning make possible the introduction of qualitative possibilities into the abstract objectivity of the brand. To put this rather more concretely, information about consumers is used as a basis for multiplying the qualities or attributes of the products (including design, style and image) and managing relations between these multi-dimensional variables. This was described just now in terms of the vertical processes of (product) differentiation and (brand) integration, but may also be understood in terms of horizontal linkage or association, since the logo acquires a meaning in relation to *a sequence or series* of products, images and events. What is important here is that the temporal reciprocity that defines the communication of the brand is defined not by instantaneity, but by managing 'the temporal delay between receiving a request and responding to it' (Rodowick, 1994). That is, the performativity of the brand organises the 'response time' of interactivity, the interval in time between products. This is important to an understanding of the iconicity of the logo since 'What is specific to the image . . . is to make perceptible, to make visible, relationships of time which cannot be seen in the represented object and do not allow themselves to be reduced to the present' (Deleuze, 1989: xii).

How, then, is the productivity of the interval to be understood? In his influential account of the experience of watching television (1974), Raymond Williams notes the historical decline of the use of intervals between programmes in broadcasting. Or rather, he draws attention to the changing role of the interval between programmes. In the early days of broadcasting on radio, for example, there would be intervals of total silence between programmes. But now, no longer dividing discrete programmes, the interval plays a different role: it no longer divides but relates what it also separates, and in doing so it makes a sequence or sequential progression of programmes or products into a flow. This changed use means that the true sequence or flow is not the published sequence of discrete programme items, but a series of differently related units, some larger and some smaller than the programme, a shifting series of products, images or events. In short, Williams argues that a transformed notion of the interval produces an organisation of time as a sequence or serial assembly of units characterised by speed, variability and the miscellaneous – that is, as flow. And the argument being proposed here is that the logo is a mark of this new operationality of the interval[10] in relation to the broadcast distribution of the commodity (Rodowick, 1994), the organisation of space and time as a flow of disjuncture and difference.

To explore this idea further, let me consider the corporate 'idents' of television companies, since they quite obviously fill the space or interval between programmes, organising the perception of movement or series (Morse, 1998; Meech, 1996; K. Lury, 2002). One of the most famous cases here is the CBS pictographic eye designed by William Golden, which first appeared as an on-air logo on 16 November 1951:

> According to Phillip Meggs, a historian of graphic design, the eye 'was superimposed over a cloud-filled sky and projected an almost surreal sense of an eye in the sky . . . Translucent and hovering . . . it symbolizes the awesome power of images projected through air into every home.' I myself have heard several people tell stories about their uncanny feeling in childhood that the CBS logo was looking back.
>
> (Morse, 1996: 73)

Peter Meech describes the effects of 'idents' in a similar way in his discussion of Scottish television logos:

> From their introduction they have performed cognitive and affective functions. They have informed or reminded viewers of the channel they have selected, a straightforward enough function in the days of one, two, three or even four terrestrial channels. But even then, whether in still or animated form, they have also sought to express – visually and audibly – aspects of the broadcasting company's self-perception as an organization in the hope of creating a favourable image and attitude among its audience.
>
> (1996: 69)

Another example is the 'ident' for the children's television channel, Nick Junior. This is a representation of a face, given a voice (who says 'I'm face') and features (eyes and mouth, sometimes with tongue), and (varied) colour, but whose outline is always that of the television screen itself. The very title of the style magazine *The Face* is another example. The changing faces of particular individuals on the front cover of many women's magazines similarly present a constant identity to the magazine, marking not simply the beginning of a new edition of the magazine, but associations between and within editions.

Examples that involve the use of a face to represent the management of movement is not accidental here. Flow is never itself visible or legible: the flows of the brand can only be 'seen' – made identifiable – through the inter-mediaries of space and movement. What marketers call personalisation, the production of a personality, is once again involved here.[11] This is because a personality, figure or a face is the most easily identifiable, intelligible and perhaps also the most powerfully persuasive configuration of space and move-ment.[12] But this use of personalisation is not the signification of the individual as the origin of the product which the logo marks (as in the description of the logo as index above), but rather an iconic signification of the brand. This means that the personality that sustains the iconic logo need not necessarily be embodied in an individual, fictional or real, alive or dead, but is instead an abstract amalgam of qualities. It is a signification of the indeterminate compos-ite of values that are commonly associated with individuals in the abstract.[13]

Nike may be used as an example in order to illustrate this process in rela-tion to the brand as an abstract economic entity or legal 'person' (see Chapter 5). Dan Wieden (of Wieden and Kennedy, an advertising agency that has worked very closely with Nike, Coca-Cola and Microsoft), says, 'In the busi-ness world, brand-building creates the personality that allows people to bond. The Nike brand, for instance, is very complex . . . but it's always as it were coming from the same person.' Nike marketing and advertising is explicitly intended 'to create a lasting emotional tie with consumers', and to this end Nike 'uses athletes repeatedly throughout their careers and present[s] them as whole people. So consumers feel that they know them' (Knight, quoted in Willigan, 1992). In short, Nike makes extensive use of the marketing tech-nique of personification, in which the properties of a product (or series of products) are associated with the characteristics of a person. This technique operates at many levels, including the sponsorship of individual sports figures and teams, the use of individuals in advertising campaigns ('Bo knows', 'I am Tiger Woods'), as well as in the naming and design of products linked to particular individuals. Consider, for example, this account of the design of a shoe:

> When I was designing the first cross-training shoe for Bo [Jackson], I watched him play sports, I read about him, I absorbed everything I could about him. Bo reminded me of a cartoon character. Not a goofy one, but a powerful one. His muscles are big, his face is big – he's larger than life. To me, he was like Mighty Mouse. So we designed a shoe called the Air Trainer that embodied characteristics of Bo Jackson and Mighty Mouse. Whenever you see Mighty Mouse, he's moving forward. He's got a slant to him. So the shoe needed to look like it was in motion, it had to be kind of inflated looking and brightly colored, and its features had to be exag-gerated. That's how we came up with the larger-than-life, brightly

colored Stability Outrigger and the similarly colored, inflated-looking rubber tongue top.

(Hatfield, 2003)

But the personality implicated in the Nike logo is not always that of a real individual. Think here of the Swoosh, the tick that supposedly represents the wings of the goddess Nike.[14] This graphic sign has no (or very little) individuality and is not an index, but is rather an abstract personification – in this case, first of desire, the desire for success, and then of its realisation, success itself (Warner, 1987: 129).

In this and the other cases, what is at issue is what Deleuze and Guattari describe as *facialisation* – that is, 'a very special mechanism' most emerges *at the intersection of the two axes of signification* outlined here.

> Even a use-object may come to be facialized: you might say that a house, utensil or object, an article of clothing, etc., is *watching me*, not because it resembles a face, but because it is taken up in the white wall/black hole process, because it connects to the abstract machine of facialization.
>
> (1999: 175)

Margaret Morse describes something similar when she suggests that the 'ident' or logo is a clock-like mechanism (1998: 72), organising, co-ordinating and integrating activities over time and space (see also Poster, 2001).[15] Certainly the persuasive force of the face is widely recognised in marketing, even in this abstract sense:[16] as Stephen King, Director of Planning at J. Walter Thompson, argued in an influential speech to the Advertising Association in 1970:

> People choose their brands as they choose their friends. You choose your friends not usually because of specific skills or physical attributes (though of course these come into it) but simply because you like them as people. It is the total person you choose, not a compendium of virtues or vices.
>
> (Quoted in G. Lury, 1998: 3)

Or as another marketing consultant puts it,

> People have names; so do brands. People belong to families; so do brands. People project a certain style and image; have unique personalities; have physical characteristics that distinguish them; so do brands. You can tell a person by their friends and associates; so too with brands. People experience a life cycle; so do brands. Our perception of a person is determined by our interaction with them. Their attitude and behaviour

towards us often determines ours to them. So it is with brands. Our relationships with people are built on honesty, trustworthiness, reliability and
predictability. So it is with brands. The essence of a person's character is
displayed by the values they chose to cherish or ignore. These values
guide and determine their behaviour. So it is with a brand.

. . . So what can we apply from the 'brand as person' metaphor? Essentially that relationships are everything!

(Bibby, 2003)

As this last sentence indicates, the presentation of the logo as an iconic personality or face is designed to transform a one-off exchange relation between producer and consumer into an ongoing relationship. It enables the brand to
appear 'to address, to recognize and thereby "to love" the consumer' (Berlant,
1993: 186; see also Haug, 1986). Indeed, there is now a set of well-
established techniques in brand management that seek to sustain the brand-as-
relationship (see, for example, Aacker, 1996: 153–170), to build brand
authenticity and consumer trust and loyalty (Lury, 2003).

The face, the frame and the flow

In what has been said so far, it has been suggested that the effectiveness of the
logo as symbol is supplemented by the use of metonyms of the person that
may be both indexical and/or iconic. On the one hand, as an index such
metonyms denote their object through an existential connection to the process
of production; on the other hand, as icons they are signs of qualitative possibility, 'expressions' of affect. An example of a logo that combines these two
aspects of signification is Virgin, a brand that is signified by the figure of the
company's CEO, Richard Branson:

The chief mechanism for the diversification of the Virgin brand is the
personality of Richard Branson himself. He is presented as a kind of
'Everyman', with the best interest of us, his consumers, at heart. He per-
sonalises what could otherwise be a faceless corporation, gaining our trust
along with our custom. Branson keeps the Virgin brand constantly in the
public eye with his personal pursuits, such as ballooning, that reinforce
the non-conformist values of the brand itself.

(Williams, 2000a: 61)

It was further suggested that the iconic aspects of logos may be understood in
terms of the physiognomics proposed by Deleuze, in which qualitative possibility is 'expressed' in a face. However, it has also been suggested that icons

are *marks of flow*. For example, the 'living brand' Martha Stewart is described in the following terms:

> [W]ith a 2.3 million-circulation magazine and syndicated column bearing her name, *a river of books, and a stream of television shows*, Martha Stewart is a force of nature, the most influential person alive giving shape to our living spaces.

> (Kelly, 1998: 114; emphasis added)

In the final section of this chapter, this aspect of logos is further explored. This involves considering the operation of logos as shifters, 'markers of the edge between the aesthetic space of an image or text and the institutional space of a regime of value which frames and organizes aesthetic space' (Frow, 2002: 71).

Shifters or *indicateurs* are indicators of positionality in space (here/there) and time (now/then). From some points of view, such as that of the linguist Emile Benveniste, they are tokens, empty placeholders of subjectivity and position. But for Deleuze and Lyotard, they indicate a correlative function between the body of a subject and space, a function that is incommensurable with the experience of language.[17] For Lyotard, 'language is pierced with holes where the gaze insinuates itself, the gaze sees outside and anchors itself there, but this "outside" is itself returned to the primary intimacy of the body, its space (and time)' (quoted in Rodowick, 2001: 7). For Deleuze and Guattari, the abstract machine of faciality (*visagéitié*) 'constructs the wall that the signifier needs in order to bounce off of; it constitutes the wall of the signifier, the frame or screen' (1999: 168). But at the same time, faces are not basically individual; instead, they 'define zones of frequency or probability, delimit a field that neutralizes in advance any expressions or connections un-amenable to the appropriate significations' (ibid.: 168). What has been suggested here is that it is the management of the interval – understood as the production of association through linkage, the management of the response gap of inter-activity – that enables the series of programmes or items to be personified in the face of the brand. But at the same time, these intervals are organised to produce the relations between branded products as constancy (the guarantee of sameness), authenticity, fashion, novelty or event (the guarantee of difference). These are the ways in which looping and sequential progression are combined in the logo. It is this combination that underpins the multiple logics of the global flows of branded products, what Kwinter describes as the 'irreducible actualizing duration that inflects, combines and separates' (1998: 39).

In the case of logos, the management of the interval or the response time of interactivity produces linkages not only within specific media (such as a film or television series), but also across and between media. As film historians have argued, from very early on in the twentieth century, the shop window and the frame of the movie screen borrowed one another's functions in the distributed production or broadcast mediation of commodities (Eckert, 1978; Allen, 1980; Ewen, 1980; Doane, 1989). This movement or relay between frames across media is further extended in the dynamic framing activity of the logo. Think here of the relation between figure and ground, with the logo as the figure and the (dynamic) frames or screens being sites in media as diverse as a poster, a window display, a television advertisement, a film, a sponsored event, as well, of course, as products. In these cases, the logo may acquire a face, but it is also a sign of a liquidity that flows through old and new media, across windows, products, signs, screens and (computer) interfaces (Simmel, [1907] 1990; Morse, 1990; Manovich, 2001). It marks the edge between a specific frame and the distributed system or flow of production of which it is a part (Frow, 2002). In the co-ordination of these movements, the brand contributes to a condition of transitivity, what Massumi (2002) describes as the dominant mode of power in the contemporary economy.

Let me return to the example of Nike. One of the things that makes it possible for the Swoosh logo to personify success, as described earlier, is its ability to make us see (and do) movement in particular ways. This in turn is a consequence of the activity of the interval – the division between frames, shots, sequences that are part of the editing of seeing – and how the organisation of these intervals informs the spatial representation of time (Rodowick, 1997: 8; Massumi, 2002). This is managed in marketing by the organisation of spaces of display, the ways in which the logo is able to frame the activity it marks, and extend this framing beyond conventional media.[18] In this and other cases, the logo not only integrates its surroundings the way a lens focuses and intensifies light, but also integrates the differential events in the ambient environment that function as a kind of motor for it, a potential to be tapped (Kwinter, 1998). In the management of the intervals that create brand image, logos may be not only active and flexible, but also in ongoing communication with their environment. In other words, logos may constitute within themselves such a dense system of self-referencing, co-relations and exchanges that they can throw up a boundary of order, a frame or a discontinuity between themselves and the world that surrounds them. At the same time, the discontinuity introduced by the framing effect of the logo enables it to open on to a series of non-present spaces, a sequence of linked products, placements, promotions and events also marked by the logo.

Such exchanges are not restricted to the frames of display and promotion co-ordinated in the purposive practices of brand positioning. Consider in this regard some observations of Nike logos in everyday situations (Lury, 1999), in which the Nike logo is the sign of a mobile frame that is not simply visually delimited, but in whose dynamism there is a recalibration of the relations between the senses. Consider a scene at the beach in Los Angeles. It is late afternoon: the shadows are lengthening. Two boys are playing in the waves. Both are wearing Nike shorts, the letters NI and KE on each leg of their matching shorts. One is bigger, one is smaller: the shorts are what unite them; the boys are larger and smaller versions of each other. The shorts give a flickering message as the boys run in and out of the water. This is a visual message, but it also has a rhythmic accompaniment: a bit like a football chant, a crowd chant. NI-KE, NI-KE. The eye focuses, pinpoints, abstracts, locating the object and viewer in physical space, organising depth through the lens of perspective, but the ear is attuned to sound from any direction. In the wearing of Nike shorts, the brothers are lifted out of their background, the pictorial space of beach, and relocated in a dynamic, acoustic space, 'always in flux, creating its own dimensions moment by moment' (McLuhan, 1997: 41). To put this another way, the ubiquity of Nike is such that it is able to insert its logos transparently into everyday scenes, transforming the field into what might be described as a *mise en ordre sensible* (Hosokawa, 1984: 178) in which the logo both informs and is informed by what is going on, what surrounds it. In both its promotional and everyday uses, then, the Nike logos present observers with manifold ensembles of signs in movement; and in the organisation of this movement, the personality of the logo acquires a face.

Consider another scene. As you sit by the boulevard, as you fail to notice the sun going down until you suddenly feel the chill, you can watch people going by. Some are cycling, some roller-skating, some roller-blading; the insignia on their clothes are usually too small to see until they have passed. You too would have to be on the move to see whether it was Adidas or Nike. If you were on blades, you could move up behind people, overtake, hang back, or turn around to get a second look. Then you would be able to see that insignia are communication in movement, moving communication; not turn-taking, but turn and turn about, as fronts and backs of people move past and around each other. In this movement, the placing of insignia on the back of clothing makes sense: you still have a face, even when your back is turned. Look also at how, as you leave the beach, in shopping malls, in movements up and down escalators, in hesitations outside windows, the careful positioning of Nike logos situates the wearer's body in space. The marks or logos are often at right angles to each other, as is clear observing a woman sitting down, with one leg at a right angle to the other, the ankle of one leg resting on the top of the knee of the other. There is a Swoosh in a contrasting colour on the sole of the shoe, looking out, as it were, watching you. This proper, perpendicular space is also apparent when watching people walking by, wearing shorts and socks, the Swoosh riding high on the outside of their ankles. Yet although their legs move in sequential time, while the roller-bladers are clearly in three-dimensional space, they are simultaneously repositioned by the logos or marks. The mark of the brand collapses the foreground into the background, and slides now into then, brings the future into the present. It offers an opening into the flow, a multiple mediated field in which subject and object may take up shifting positions. The window-shoppers and roller-bladers are moving into and out of multiple planes in space and multiple frames of time. The logo – as a conceptual outline – is seemingly pressed against an enveloping surround of space and time that can simultaneously seem far away *and* near, right here *and* already gone, over there. It operates in such a way that the environment is not only a space in which foreground and background can be brought into and out of focus, but a space in which we are in and at a distance from. It is a mark of an object – and a subject – that is not simply either present or absent, but a mark of a logic of flow, of pattern and randomness (Hayles, 1999), of disjuncture and difference (Appadurai, 1996).

Coda

It has been argued here that the power of the logo as symbol is supplemented by both indexical and iconic elements, but that the latter have become increasingly important. In this staging of the logo as icon, the qualities of the object of the brand are intensified, developed experimentally in the joint situation of object and subject. On the one hand, qualitative possibility is introduced into the brand, while on the other, the activities of the consumer are linked – or looped – into the process of building the brand ever more intensively in the activities of brand positioning. Importantly, however, in the insistent monitoring, measuring, interpretation and evaluation of the uses of (branded) products and the presentation of such uses as the possible effects of brands, marketing professionals are able to ascribe the logo a causality of its own (Franklin *et al.*, 2000). As a consequence, in the development of brand image, 'the mark or emblem is not just the designation of a valuable product, but [becomes] a valuable product in its own right' (Frow, 2002: 66).

To describe the building of brand image in this way is not, however, to suggest that it is entirely within the control of a brand manager, a company or indeed any single entity. As the accounts above suggest, processes of mediation and re-mediation (Bolter and Grusin, 1999) are such that the flow of images is characterised by speed, variability and the miscellaneous. These characteristics have intensified since the time Williams wrote, with the proliferation, globalisation and deregulation of media in the United Kingdom and elsewhere. Moreover, there are plenty of critical commentaries – from both within and outside the marketing industry – which argue that the management of brand image is little more than an *ad hoc*, inferential or intuitive process. Certainly the history of most brands indicates that their image is not coherent over time, that many campaigns are unsuccessful, and/or that there is little agreement as to what counts as success. Nevertheless, one of the things that distinguishes particular brands is how – or under what circumstances – this movement is acknowledged, regulated and incorporated. The next two chapters will explore further what it means for the logo of a brand to be represented as a face, and suggest that the brand is best understood not in terms of face-to-face communication or interaction, but rather in terms of *face-to-profile communication or interactivity*.

5 The brand as a property form of relationality

Or, trade mark as a way of fixing things

A new notion of 'commons' will have to emerge on this terrain. Deleuze and Guattari claim . . . that in the contemporary era, and in the context of communicative and interactive production, the construction of concepts is not only an epistemological[1] operation but equally an ontological project. Constructing concepts and what they call 'common names' is really an activity that combines the intelligence and the action of the multitude, making them work together. Constructing concepts means making exist in reality a project that is a community. There is no other way to construct concepts but to work in a common way. This commonality is, from the standpoint of the phenomenology of production, from the standpoint of the epistemology of the concept, and from the standpoint of practice, a project in which the multitude is completely invested.

(Hardt and Negri, 2000: 302–303)

Introduction

So far, the notion of the brand that has been developed is that it is the dynamic organisation of a system of relations between products. It has been further suggested that the framing of the market by the interface of the brand contributes to the emergence of a non-linear process of production. In Chapter 4, I argued that the performativity of the brand is signified in a logo or logos. Attention was drawn there to the processes of personalisation and the ways in which logos may be seen as the face of the brand. In this chapter, the discussion will focus on how the logo as a sign of the brand is legally constituted as a kind of intellectual property[1] and how this legal constitution as property has supported the valuation and exploitation of the brand as a commercial asset. In this respect, the law makes a specific contribution to the objectivity of the brand – that is, to the operation of the brand as a new market modality or cultural form. It will be suggested that the law is one of the most significant actors in the organisation of the asymmetry of the relations between producers and consumers, operating so as to consolidate and legitimate the use of the brand as an object or mode of capital accumulation.

Trade mark: its definition and purpose

As is widely known, the signs that comprise logos may be legally recognised as trade marks, a type of intellectual property, the law relating to which is currently governed in the United Kingdom by the Trade Marks Act 1994 (TMA 1994). The earliest trade marks recognized by statute law in England were the hallmarks used by the cutlers of Hallamshire, Sheffield. Regulations regarding the use of such hallmarks were first drawn up during the reign of Elizabeth I and codified by the Cutler's Company Act of 1623. It was not until 1875, however, that the first British Trade Marks Act was passed. The first mark registered under the Act was the red triangle for Bass pale ale, and since then over 2 million marks have been registered (with 400,000 still in force). The 1875 Act has been amended several times, notably in 1938 and again in 1986, when the provision of statutory protection was extended to owners of service marks. The 1994 Act defines a trade mark as 'any sign capable of being represented graphically which is capable of distinguishing the goods or services of one undertaking from those of other undertakings' (s. 1(1)).

This legal statement can be broken down into three components. First, the legal object of a registered trade mark *is a sign*. As such, it may include logos such as the word 'Nike' or the 'swoosh' with which the Nike corporation marks its goods. Many brands make use of a number of trade marks. In the case of Coca-Cola, these include the word 'Coca-Cola', its distinctive font style, the 'Dynamic Ribbon device', the contour bottle, a number of slogans including 'It's the real thing', and also its distinctive colour combination (red and white). Similarly, the Lego brand makes use of a combination of trade marks, including the word 'Lego', a chunky logotype and the 'retaining' rectangle. As these examples indicate, any sign – not just words – may legally serve as a trade mark provided it can be represented graphically and does not breach any of the specified legal grounds for refusal of registration. The TMA 1994 states, 'A trade mark may, in particular, consist of words (including personal names), designs, letters, numerals or the shape of goods or their packaging.' Since the Act, applications have been made to register the shape of containers (the Jif Lemon squeezy plastic lemon as well as the shape of the Coca-Cola bottle), the shape of goods (Toblerone triangular chocolate), slogans ('Where do you want to go today?', 'Have a break, have a Kit-Kat'), musical marks ('Air on a G String' for Hamlet cigars), sensory marks such as colours (drug manufacturers have successfully registered colour combinations for capsules), smells (the smell of freshly cut grass for tennis balls) and sounds

(MGM's lion's roar for films, three chimes of NBC, and Direct Line Insurance's jingle for insurance services).

Second, marks must be *capable of graphic representation* so that the Trade Mark Register can easily record and search for them and so that they can be advertised. In *Swizzels Matlow Ltd's Trade Mark Application* (1999), an application to register 'a chewy sweet on a stick' was refused on the grounds that the application did not comply with acceptable forms of graphic representation because it did not define what was distinctive about the mark with sufficient precision. Since it was held that it would not be possible to understand the mark precisely without reference to a sample of the goods, the mark was deemed not capable of being represented graphically. In another case, *Libertel Groep BV* v. *Benelux-Merkenbureau* (2003), it was ruled that a sample of a colour does not *per se* constitute a graphic representation since 'a sample of colour may deteriorate with time'. In this case, however, it was further judged 'that deficiency may, depending on the facts, be remedied by adding a colour designation code from an internationally recognised identification code'. In contrast, an application to register 'the smell of freshly cut grass' for tennis balls was held to be sufficient to fulfil the requirement of graphic representation on its own, and the scent was registered as a trade mark. All signs (except those excluded on public interest grounds) are deemed capable *in principle* of distinguishing the goods or services of a particular trader from those of any other trader.

Third, whether or not a sign will actually succeed in being registered depends upon whether it *is capable, in practice, of being distinctive* of a particular trader's goods or services. Distinctiveness is a characteristic that is held to be *achieved in usage* — that is, it is a characteristic deemed to be recognisable by consumers in the marketplace. More precisely, the relevant usage is by the public engaged in the relevant trade or activity, and normally this is held to be the 'average consumer' of the goods in question. A description of the average consumer is provided by the European Court of Justice (ECJ), *Lloyd Schuhfabrik Meyer* v. *Klijsen Handel* (1999). In this case, the 'average consumer' was deemed to be 'reasonably well informed, reasonably observant and circumspect'. According to the Court of Appeal, the task of the court was to inform itself, through evidence, of what the average consumer would know and then to ask the question as to whether he or she would say the mark in question was a badge of origin. Distinctiveness is held to be easier to achieve with an entirely invented word (a strong mark) such as 'Kodak' or 'Exxon', or words or device marks that have no direct meaning in relation to the goods or services concerned, such as Lotus for cars or the Black Horse logo for Lloyds Bank. It is harder to establish with words that are already existing or are essentially descriptive of the product (so-called weak marks). Descriptive names, geographic names or surnames and now single colours are difficult to protect by means of registration because they are words or signs other traders might wish to use when describing their goods or services.

A further notable aspect of the protection afforded by trade mark law is its potential longevity; unlike other forms of intellectual property such as patent and copyright, it has no fixed limit. This is important because of the monopoly of use of marks that trade mark affords, restricting their use by anyone other than the mark owner or licensees. And it is interesting in this respect to note that except in industries such as personal computer software, where the whole product category is only about 25 years old, most big brands are at least 50 to 100 years old. Coca-Cola was launched in 1886, Kodak in 1888, Shell in 1897, Gillette in 1902 and Sony in 1958. Such brands are older not only than the physical plant or equipment used to produce them but also typically than the consumers who use them (Barwise *et al.*, 2000). Yet, as noted above, it is usage that determines the life of the legal protection afforded the mark (in contrast to the statutorily limited protection afforded by other forms of intellectual property such as copyright and patent). In the United Kingdom, a registration becomes vulnerable to cancellation for non-use if there has been no use of the mark, by the proprietor or with his or her consent, for five years from the date the registration was entered on the register, or if use has been suspended for an uninterrupted period of five years or longer. Similarly, in the United States, a declaration has to be filed at the United States Patent and Trademark Office between the fifth and sixth years from the date of registration confirming that the mark has been in continuous use for five years and that it is still in use. If this declaration is not filed, the registration is invalidated.

Registering a trade mark is the first step in the legal recognition and protection of the monopoly use of a mark in relation to particular classes of goods. This monopoly is held to have a twofold purpose: protection of the owner from unfair competition, and protection of the consumer from 'confusion' as to the origin of the goods (although see pp. 108–109). Additionally, in the United Kingdom, and other countries that have a similar legal system based on common law, rights in trade mark can also be acquired through the use made of the mark and those rights can be protected by a legal action known as *passing off*. Essentially, the legal action of passing off is to protect the reputation or goodwill attributed to trade mark *because of its use*. It does not grant an automatic monopoly in a trade mark (as does registration), but gives legal recognition to an existing position. It does not relate only to the unauthorised use of a trade mark, but can also include use of a similar trade 'get-up' (such as packaging), or anything that could be said to 'represent' one person's goods or services as the goods or services of somebody else.

Trade mark as a form of property

Having briefly outlined the terms of current trade mark law, I will now consider some of the more general principles of property law as a way of exploring the legal reasoning that underlies it. One of the most important general points to note in this respect is that, in legal thinking, all forms of property are relational. The legal idea of a right is that it is a two-way process, in that the right generates claims and duties among persons. Rights cannot exist between a person and things because things cannot in law have claims and duties, nor can they be bound by and recognise legal rules. Instead, the appropriate analysis of property, from the legal point of view, is that a right in a thing gives rise to mutual relations between people – that is, to duties and obligations – in respect of *external resources or things*.[2] The organising idea behind property is thus that it is a relationship between persons or subjects in respect of objects or materials (Panesar, 2001: 72); or, to reverse this, the thing itself constitutes the foundation or object of a property right that is a relation between people. Or, to put this yet another way, property law is a means by which a thing is given value (value is added) by establishing relations between people. And in respect of these relations, it is worth noting here that property lawyers often distinguish between two types of right, namely, a right in *rem* and a right in *personam* (ibid.: 12). A right in *rem* is a right in respect of a thing, a *res*. The right is said to 'bind the whole world' in that every subject in the legal system must respect the right. This might be said to be the legal basis of object-ivity. Rights in *personam* bind only specific individuals. So, in respect of the argument being developed here, it might now be asked what kind of a thing can be laid claim to in trade mark law? Or, to put it in the terms above, what value is given – added – to the object, the sign, that is the foundation of trade mark law? And in this process, what relations are established between people?

In law, property is in general terms legally constituted as a dynamic system. That is, it is recognised that there are changes in the subjects and objects of the right and that the legal functions performed by the right of property change with time. Let me outline some of the more important of these changes. Historically, some *subjects* or people have been excluded from having property. Instead, such people have themselves been regarded as objects or material resources in which other persons may have property rights such as ownership. The most infamous example is that of people who were legally deemed to be slaves, who were held to be incapable of having property and instead were the property of their owner. Additionally, until the Married Women's Property Act 1882, a married woman in the United Kingdom had no right to own property (Panesar, 2001: 82). It is also relevant to point out here that subjects of the property relationship need not be human beings but can include the artificially created person (the legal person) that is the corporation. As was noted in Chapter 1, a company has its own separate legal identity and as such can own property in its own right. However, the property relations of corporations are somewhat different from traditional notions of property because of the nature of a corporation. While a corporation in the form of a company limited by shares can both hold and dispose of property in its own right, the corporation itself forms an object or material resource through which revenue is generated. In this respect, the corporation is itself the object of ownership, and its owners are generally those people who supply the capital in the form of shareholders (ibid.: 92).

There have also been historical shifts in the kinds of things that have been the *objects* of property rights. Thus, for centuries the most highly prized object of property in the common-law world was land, with goods having a lesser value. In recent years, however, the importance of both these *tangible* forms of property (land and goods) has been challenged by an emphasis on *intangible* property. This category includes not only debts and shares (many people in the United Kingdom now own mortgages, private pensions and shares), but also different kinds of intellectual property, including copyright and patent as well as trade mark. From the perspective of a corporation, intangibles may include not only intellectual property but also knowledge and know-how, libraries and databases, information and communication systems, research, and so on (sometimes all described as proprietary knowledge). In this respect, 'The expansion in modern times of forms of intangible property means that many commercial entities operating in post-manufacturing industries have intangible property rights greater in value than their tangible property' (Bridge, 1996, quoted in Panesar, 2001: 58). In regard to the growing significance of all these intangible forms of property, it is argued that the nature of value in property no longer lies in its *use value* (as was typically the case with land), but rather in its *exchange value*.[3]

In addition, *the relations between people* established in property law are historically both multiple and changing. In other words, at any one time a proprietary right comprises bundles of mutual relations, rights and obligations between subjects in respect of certain resources or objects (Panesar, 2001: 17). This bundle has been described in numerous ways, but one of the most influential statements is that provided by Hohfeld (1923, cited in Panesar, 2001), who disentangles the following relations: claim rights, privileges, powers and immunities. Of these, perhaps the most enduringly important is the first, for it includes the right to exclude others: 'The aspect of "excludability" is taken by courts as a central requirement before a resource can be admitted into the category of private property' (Panesar, 2001: 12). However, it is this right in particular that is problematic for brand-holders. The *intangible* nature of the sign that is the foundation of trade mark makes it hard to define both on what terms it may be possessed and how others may be excluded (especially since the distinctiveness of a mark is a characteristic that is held to be established in usage).

One route into understanding the legal formulation of intellectual property that may help in this respect is the distinction made in law between *choses in possession* and *choses in action*, for this draws attention to the character of the intangibility of things recognised by the law. Sometimes the distinction is said to be between things that are corporeal and things that are incorporeal.[4] In legal thinking, personal goods are divided into two main types. Where a thing representing personal property is tangible – such as a car, a computer or a book or a pen – it is described as a chose in possession or a chattel, the use of the (French) word *chose* meaning 'a thing'. Where the thing in question is intangible – such as shares in a company, a debt, a copyright or a trade mark in a name – it is described as a chose in action. A chose in possession is a tangible thing that is capable of being in actual possession. A chose in action is a thing that is intangible and is thus incapable of being in actual possession (Panesar, 2001: 57). Money is often classified as both a chose in possession and a chose in action, since it has characteristics of both. On the one hand, a coin is a physical, tangible object and thus a chose in possession. On the other hand, the effective use of money lies not in its mere possession but in its exchange value, and in this regard it is a chose in action.[5]

A further aspect of the legal basis of the distinction between choses in possession and choses in action is related to the question of how such property is protected (Panesar, 2001: 57–60). This is because the distinction is held to relate to how ownership is maintained in tangible and intangible things. As noted above, choses in possession are deemed to be things that are capable of actual possession. What makes a car or a computer mine, from a legal point of view, is that I exercise control over it. Control is only exercised when I have possession of something. In other words, tangible things are choses in possession because it is through possession that ownership is asserted against others. On the other hand, intangible property or choses in action, such as a debt (to pay for the car) or copyright (in a computer software program), cannot be protected by physical protection. The only way in which ownership rights and entitlement to such things can be asserted is said to be by taking action against the wrongdoer. In one case, Judge Channell explained that 'a chose in action is a known legal expression used to describe all personal rights of property which can only be enforced by action and not by taking physical possession'. In an earlier case, Lord Blackburn emphasised that the difference between 'a chose in action and a chose in possession lay between the type of personal property which could be stolen and that which could not be' (all quotations from Panesar, 2001: 57–60). In this respect, trade mark is an example of a property right in an intangible thing; its object is incorporeal, and cannot be actually possessed. As a right in *res*, trade mark binds the whole world, but this legal objectivity refers to *an object that is created in use or its doing*, first at the level of exchange, and then at the level of legal activity. And, as noted earlier and explored further in what follows, this legal activity in turn makes reference to distinctiveness as a characteristic that is itself achieved in usage.

The Trade Marks Act 1994: activity, things and property

Having established some of the legal reasoning that concerns the general category of property, let me go on to consider what is distinctive about trade mark law and how its use may be seen to secure the ownership of brands in the marketplace. This is especially important because it is widely recognised that there has been *an expansion of the terms of use of trade mark in the past fifty years or so*. Indeed, there are a number of writers who argue that the legal support for the monopoly in the use of registered trade marks is, in the context of the contemporary economy, the basis for debilitating commercial monopolies (Lunney, 1999). This chapter will approach the question of who benefits from the terms of the expansion of trade mark law by considering the argument that the claim expressed in intellectual property law is specifically to the embedded nature of (intellectual) activity in the thing (Strathern, 1999). It is hoped that this approach will open up the question of how objectivity is constituted in law; alternatively put, this approach seeks to explore whether and how the law contributes to the objective organisation of interactivity between 'producers' and 'consumers'.

This approach addresses the dependence of trade mark (as one branch of intellectual property law) on labour theory. This is a philosophy developed in the seventeenth and eighteenth centuries, in which it is claimed that individuals have a natural right to own and dispose of private property.[6] Perhaps the best-known exponent of this view is John Locke in his *Two Treatises of Government* of 1690, who bases his justification for private property on the premise that resources are given to mankind (*sic*) by God in common. Thus, the original state of property, in Locke's view, is that it is held in common. But every man has a right to his own person, sometimes described as self-ownership. He also has a right to own his own labour. Finally, in Locke's view, every man has a right to own that which he has mixed with the labour of his own person. Mixing one's labour with the common resources that God has given to mankind extracts that which is held in common into private ownership. This philosophy, while immensely influential in legal and political thought, has led to many questions: what is the relationship of labour to the value added to the thing in question? Even if labour can be owned and such labour is mixed with (common) resources, why should it automatically mean that the resource becomes the private property of the labourer? Why should the mixing of labour with a resource provide any private entitlement at all? Furthermore, if, as Locke argues, only activities that improve the resources are constitutive of property, how are such improvements to be recognised? Such questions have an obvious relevance to the operation of trade mark law. As is argued in Chapters 2, 3 and 4, the logo is a sign of the brand, where the brand is a set of relations between products, established in but exceeding the activities of both 'producers' and 'consumers'. Whose labour, then, should be recognised as adding value to the sign that is the object of an intellectual property claim? On what basis may improvements be judged as innovation, creativity or invention? Is it appropriate that any sign be recognised as private property at all? If so, how?

Let me try to outline the specificity and significance of the law's attempt to answer some of these questions by discussing the law of trade mark in rather more detail. First, consider the current legal definition of trade mark again: 'any sign capable of being represented graphically which is capable of distinguishing the goods or services of one undertaking from those of other undertakings' (s. 1(1)). The notion of sign at issue will be considered here via a discussion of the semiotics outlined in Chapter 4 (Peirce 1978; Deleuze, 1986, 1989). As noted there, according to Peirce, the image is not a unified or closed whole, but rather an ensemble or set of logical relations that are in a state of continual transformation or development. Another way of saying this is that sign and its object are not immediately given entities but 'abstract elements of a sign continuum' (Rochberg-Halton, 1986: 86). From this perspective, the law is implicated in the mediation of things in so far as it can be shown to have a role in the 'development of the sign'. And the argument to be outlined here will suggest that the law is indeed so implicated with respect to both the axes of signification described in Chapter 4. These are the horizontal axis of association – that is, an axis of contrast, contiguity and opposition – and the vertical one of (product) differentiation and (brand) integration.

Consider here the series of changes in the law that are a part of the TMA 1994 and some of the judicial responses to this Act. First, whereas previously a logo could be protected as a trade mark only if it had already been recognised to be distinctive by the public, the TMA of 1994 makes the involvement of the public in the setting up of a trade mark irrelevant. In the terms of the Act, trade marks need now only be registered to be legally enforceable – that is, registration need not now be preceded by public recognition of the brand (although renewal of registration does require usage, as noted on p. 101). The previous criterion of the centrality of use (and thus of consumer recognition and acceptance of distinctiveness) as a condition of legal recognition has been replaced in TMA 1994 with the simple fact of registration. This change provides a more secure legal basis than used to exist from which the economic power of large firms may make good that registration through the production of brand awareness in the practices of marketing (see Chapter 4). This is thus an important shift in the legal regulation of producer–consumer relations. It moves trade marks from an already limited legal existence in the public domain further towards ownership by private corporations. Indeed, in some respects it seems that the public ownership of common resources presumed by Locke is here rejected. Certainly the shift extends the brand owner's independence of consumers in securing legal ownership of the brand, an independence that had previously been limited by the earlier legislation's emphasis on the necessity of prior consumer recognition for the acceptance of a legal claim to the ownership of trade marks.

Second, at the same time that a trade mark may come to be established without prior consumer recognition, a trade mark may now be infringed, by a use of the sign that is protected even when it is not trade mark use. The 1938 Act gave the proprietor of a registered trade mark the exclusive right to use the mark, and trade mark use was required for it to be infringed. However, in the rewording of this proviso in the 1994 Act, the exclusive rights are held to be infringed by use of a sign without consent. This raised the question whether this change in wording to refer to use of a sign, as opposed to a trade mark, was significant. The case of *Arsenal Football Club plc* v. *Reed* (2002, ECJ) suggests that it is. In this case, it was held that trade mark use is not necessary for infringement, only a use prejudicing the trade mark as an indicator of origin. Here, then, at the same time that consumer use is no longer deemed necessary for registration, the use of the sign may be held to infringe a trade mark even when that use – as, in this case, as a badge of allegiance – is not trade mark use. This is, to say the least, an uneven representation of use to protect a trade mark.

Third, the TMA 1994 enables brand owners to assert a monopoly on the use not simply of particular names and slogans, but also of specific colours, shapes, smells, sounds, gestures or movements, and catchphrases, as well as two-dimensional logos and three-dimensional shapes. However, here it should be noted that there may be limitations placed on the signs to be used as trade marks in relation to public interest. So, for example, it has recently been ruled that there is a public interest in 'not unduly restricting the availability of colours available for use' in the marketplace (*Libertel Groep BV* v. *Benelux-Merkenbureau* (2003)). Similarly, while the shape of goods may themselves be registered as a sign, as in the case of the triangular chocolate bar Toblerone, this shape must contain some addition or 'capricious alteration' that makes it capable of distinguishing those goods from the same sort of goods sold by someone else. So, for example, in *Philips* v. *Remington* (1999) it was held that a three-dimensional shape of a three-headed rotary shaver with the heads arranged in an equilateral triangle was not capable of distinguishing the goods of one trader from another. Although Philips had had an effective monopoly of three-headed shavers for many years (supported by patent), this did not mean that the shape was distinctive in a trade sense. Philips still had to establish that the shape had features that would distinguish it from those of a competitor who put similar goods on the market.

Fourth, the phrasing of the marks that may be registered in the TMA 1994 is effectively an open-ended list, subject only to the provisos mentioned above. To some, the open-endedness of the definition of what may constitute the object of a trade mark registration represents legal support for the appropriation of signs that had previously been in common, unrestricted use into private ownership. Others argue that traders have anyway had a *de facto* monopoly of many signs through the common law protection afforded by passing off.[7]

Fifth, the TMA includes the removal of the prohibition on 'trafficking' in trade marks contained in the 1938 Act, and thus facilitates multi-class applications. The earlier Act had forbidden trade mark proprietors to traffic in their marks. In effect, this Act prevented merchandisers from registering famous names or characters as trade marks if their intention was to deal in marks primarily as commodities *in their own right*, rather than to identify or promote merchandise in which they were interested in trading. As Jane Gaines notes, the lifting of this restriction on the licensing of marks seems to indicate an internal reversal within trade mark law: 'While unfair competition law is based on the prohibition against palming off one's goods as the goods of another, licensing itself is essentially a "passing off"' (1991: 214).[8]

Sixth, there has also been a growing judicial acceptance – partial and uneven, but recognisable nonetheless – of more expansive trade mark rights over the past twenty or so years. In very general terms, this expansion comprises a movement away from a 'confusion' definition of infringement (as to the origin of the product) towards a broader 'dilution' definition, which precludes all unauthorised uses that would lessen (or take advantage of) the mark's distinctiveness (Davis, 2001). Thus, it used to be the case that trademark infringement would only be found where the use of a protected mark by someone (X) other than its owner (Y) was likely to cause consumers to be *confused* as to the origin of the product to which the mark was attached. The issue was whether consumers would think that X's product actually came from Y. Now it is increasingly being suggested – with varying degrees of success – that if X's use of Y's signs on its product causes consumers to be reminded of Y on seeing X's product, even while knowing that X and Y are distinct traders, infringement has occurred. In other words, *creating associations between products is becoming established as the exclusive prerogative of the trade mark owner*; associations created by other producers can be legally prevented if they *dilute* the first mark. (The very use of the term 'dilution' seems to indicate an acknowledgement of the flows of products and signs at issue.)

This shift in interpretation is linked to the question of how the law should respond to recent changes in the commercial role of trade marks in the market. On the one hand, the role of the trade mark as a guarantor of (minimum) quality or standards is arguably less crucial to a wide range of goods and services now than it was in the past. One impetus for early trade mark legislation was to enable the consumer to choose between products of a certain quality that carried a well-known mark and others of lesser or unknown quality. However, consumer legislation has ensured that in many countries the public can expect a certain minimum quality for a wide range of goods and services, whether a mark attaches to them or not. Instead, it is held – in marketing at least – that the competition between goods and services has come to reside more and more in what is called their publicity value, reputation or brand image. Indeed, this is explicitly what is increasingly at issue in legal decision-making in the Benelux countries.[9] On the other hand, changes in the organisation of production mean that the origin of the thing that is the foundation of the property right is itself increasingly uncertain. For example, the ownership of many well-known brands is concentrated in a relatively few companies, many of which operate across international borders, while it has been reckoned that just three companies account for the ownership of nearly one-third of all branded products sold in UK supermarkets (Davis, 2001: 205). A trade mark X on a soft drink may thus mean that it is produced not by X Soft Drinks Ltd but by its brand owner, a large multinational, which may also produce a number of competing brands, as well as the supermarket's 'own-brand' product. Conversely, there are a few brands whose ownership is divided among a number of companies. So, for example, the Benson and Hedges cigarette brand is owned by three companies: Gallagher, BAT and Philip Morris, each owning the brand in different parts of the world (G. Lury, 1998: 128). The implications of brand identity for the quality of branded products are thus not easily established by the average consumer, no matter if he or she be reasonably well informed, reasonably observant and circumspect in legal terms. In respect of these economic changes, then, it seems that the role of the trade mark in protecting the consumer from confusion as to the origin of the mark is increasingly inadequate or outmoded. The dispute over the expansion of trade mark law outlined above concerns whether or how the terms of consumer protection should be redefined.

The likelihood of association

A consideration of a number of cases that relate to ambiguous wording in a section of the 1994 Act that specifies grounds for the opposition of a trade mark registration (or founding an infringement action) provides some indication of what is involved here. The ground in question is: 'identical marks on similar goods and services, with the proviso that there exists a likelihood of confusion on the part of the public which includes the likelihood of association with the earlier mark' (s. 5(1)). This wording was new to the TMA 1994 and comes from Article (1)(b) of the European TM Directive, which sought to 'harmonise' trade mark law across the EU. It is generally accepted that 'likelihood of confusion' in the proviso means the likelihood that the public will be confused as to the origin of the mark. However, some EC member states, especially those represented by the Benelux court, argue that the addition of the words 'including a likelihood of association' to the proviso extends the protection given to trade marks beyond their function as indicators of origin. They argue that it now includes protection for the commercial value, or reputation, of marks that might be *diluted by association* with another mark *even when the public is not confused as to origin*. As already noted, this shift in the criteria can be considered in relation to the two axes of signification introduced in Chapter 4 (Deleuze, 1986, 1989; Rodowick, 1997). Aspects of this shift in relation to the horizontal axis – those relating to likelihood of association – will be considered first here, followed by those relating to the vertical axis – that is, those concerning the degree of similarity between the mark and the sign and the goods and the services.

One of the first UK cases to consider the meaning of the new proviso outlined above was *Wagamama* v. *City Centre Restaurants* (1995). The plaintiff was the proprietor of the mark 'Wagamama' for restaurant services and operated a London restaurant under that name. The defendant operated an Indian restaurant under the name 'Raja Mama'. The plaintiff sued for infringement, arguing infringement as to trade origin and likelihood of association. Laddie J accepted that there was a likelihood of confusion but rejected the argument that the likelihood of association imported the non-origin concept of dilution into UK law. Instead, he took the view that 'likelihood of association' derived from previous case law by which marks are 'associated in the sense that one is an extension of the other or that they are derived from the same source'. In this ruling, then, likelihood of association was 'contained' within the classic English legal concept of 'likelihood of confusion'. This decision was criticised by those who supported an anti-dilution approach to trade mark such as the one recognised in Benelux law as asserted in the case *Claeryn/Klarein* (Benelux Court of Justice, 1975). Claeryn was a well-known alcoholic drink and Klarein a toilet cleaner. There was no argument that the public would believe the two products originated from the same source. What the drinks maker argued was that if the 'Klarein' mark continued to be used, the public would associate the two products, and the reputation of the 'Claeryn' mark and therefore its value would suffer. The Benelux court accepted that there was a likelihood of association, although not a likelihood of confusion as to source, and the drinks-maker won the case.

The ECJ was called upon to decide whether the broad Benelux or the narrow UK interpretation of 'likelihood of association' would prevail under the European TM Directive in the case of *Sabel* v. *Puma* (1998). Puma was the registered proprietor of two German trade marks comprising bounding puma and leaping puma devices, registered in respect of jewellery and leather goods. Puma opposed the registration of Sabel's sign of a bounding cheetah device with the name 'Sabel' for jewellery. The German Supreme Court decided that the marks were not sufficiently similar to give rise to likelihood of confusion as to origin, but that the similarity of the 'semantic' content of the marks might give rise to a likelihood of association. When this ruling was tested at the higher court of the ECJ, it was decided that the likelihood of association was not sufficient grounds for Puma to oppose registration of the Sabel mark. However, while this case may be seen as supporting the narrow (English) interpretation of the proviso, the terms of the court's decision indicate something not quite so straightforward. On the one hand, the European court ruled that a likelihood of association was merely one element of a likelihood of confusion as to origin, not a separate ground for opposition. On the other hand, it also ruled that likelihood of association must be appreciated 'globally', taking into account various factors:

> The global appreciation of the visual, aural or conceptual similarity of the marks in question must be based on *the overall impression* given by the marks, bearing in mind, in particular, their distinctive and dominant component. The wording of Art 4 (1)(b) of the Directive – 'there exists a likelihood of confusion on the part of the public . . .' – shows that the perception of marks in the mind of the average consumer of the type of goods or services in question plays a decisive role in the likelihood of confusion. The average consumer normally perceives a mark *as a whole* and does not proceed to analyse its various details. In that perspective, the more distinctive the earlier mark, the greater the likelihood of confusion. It is therefore not impossible that the conceptual similarity resulting from

the fact that two marks use images with analogous semantic content may give rise to a likelihood of confusion where the earlier mark has a particularly distinctive character, either *per se* or because of the reputation it enjoys with the public.

(Cornish, 1999: 493; emphasis added)

So, while this ruling suggests that the likelihood of association is not a separate factor in finding conflict, it asserts that the likelihood of association helps to define the scope of the likelihood of confusion. Thus, it is argued that where two marks have an 'analogous semantic content', there may be likelihood of confusion. It is further argued that the more distinctive the earlier mark, the greater will be the likelihood of confusion, and therefore marks with a highly distinctive character, either *per se* or because of their recognition in the market, enjoy broader protection than marks with a less distinctive character. This is a broadening of the grounds of conflict, which now include the mark 'as a whole' – that is, the distinctiveness of the earlier mark, its reputation and the likelihood that the public might associate the two marks. In this way, judgements on the distinctiveness of a sign may be seen to take increasing account of what Deleuze calls the horizontal axis of signification, that of association. In the particular case of *Sabel*, however, the ECJ held that neither of the marks was particularly distinctive, and their use did not give rise to a likelihood of confusion.

The degree of similarity between the mark and the sign and the goods and the services

The ruling for a 'global appreciation' also makes relevant to the case for infringement of trade mark *the degree of similarity between the mark and the sign and the goods and the services* to any judgement of distinctiveness. This ruling thus brings into legal reckoning the vertical basis of signification described by Deleuze, that of differentiation and integration. In doing so, it appears to over-rule earlier practice. In *British Sugar* (1996), Jacob J suggested that a discrete three-stage approach should be taken to applying this section of trade mark law, in which judgements as to the mark and its object are held distinct. First, ask whether the marks are the same or similar. Next, ask whether the goods are the same or similar. Finally, ask whether the proviso applies and there is a likelihood of confusion including a likelihood of association between the two marks. If the (sequential) answers to all three questions are positive, Jacob J opined, then there will be conflict. However, the ECJ ruling in the *Sabel* case suggests that rather than applying a stage test (in which each question may be answered independently of how the others are answered), it is now considered desirable to take a 'global approach' to the interpretation of this section of the Directive. In other words, the answer to any of the three questions posed by Jacob J may depend on how the other two are answered. In another case, *Canon* (1999), the ECJ summarised this new approach in the following terms:

> A global assessment of the likelihood of confusion implies some interdependence between the relevant factors, and in particular a similarity between the trade marks and between these goods and services. Accordingly, a lesser degree of similarity between these goods and services may be offset by a greater degree of similarity between the marks and vice versa. It follows that . . . registration of a trade mark may have to be refused, despite a lesser degree of similarity between the goods or services covered, where the marks are very similar and the earlier mark, in particular its reputation, is highly distinctive.
>
> (Cornish, 1999: 494)

And in respect of this global approach, in which the similarity of the marks and that of the goods and services may be set off against each other, the shifting grounds for establishing whether or not goods or services are similar are also important.[10]

Once again, previously existing practice was based on answers to a three-part questioning, first set out in *Jellinek* (1946). First, what are the nature and composition of the goods? Second, what is the respective use of the articles? Third, what are the trade channels through which the commodities are bought and sold? However, in the case *British Sugar* (1986), Jacob J asked further questions in addition to these three.[11] In the case of self-service consumer items (as were the goods in question), he asked, where in practice are they found or likely to be found in supermarkets, and, in particular, are they likely to be found on the same or different shelves? What is the extent to which the respective goods and services are competitive, taking into account how the trade classifies the goods? And here he even considered the packaging in which the product is presented to be relevant: 'The product comes in a jam jar because it is like a jam. . . . Supermarkets regard the product as a spread. The jam jar invites use as a spread.' He concludes by identifying the following six factors as relevant in considering whether a mark is similar or not:

a   the respective uses of the respective goods or services;
b   the respective users of the respective goods or services;
c   the physical nature of the goods or acts of service;

d   the respective trade channels through which the goods or services reach the market;

e   in the case of self-serve items, where in practice they are respectively found or likely to be found in supermarkets and in particular whether they are, or are likely to be, found on the same or similar shelves;

f   the extent to which the respective goods or services are competitive. This inquiry may take into account how those in trade classify goods, for instance whether market research companies, who of course act for industry, put the goods or services in the same or different sectors.

(Cornish, 1999: 475)

Moreover, in another case it was held that a further factor in a judgement of distinctiveness relates to whether the goods are expensive or for a specialist market. In these cases, it has been held, purchasers will take more care and are therefore less likely to find similar marks confusing. Thus, 'Lancer' was allowed for mass-market cars despite opposition from the manufacturers of the up-market 'Lancia', since the risk of confusion 'was unlikely to survive the mechanism of purchase' (*Lancer TM* (1987)).

A moving image

To sum up so far: In the case of choses in possession, it is through possession that ownership is asserted against others. In the case of choses in action, entitlement to ownership of the thing at issue is asserted by taking action against the wrongdoer. The 'action' that is relevant here is guided by judgements as to the distinctiveness of a mark. But, as is apparent from the discussion above, the action of the law relating to the distinctiveness of trade mark is not consistent. The exercise of finding whether two marks are confusingly similar has been described by the courts as an art rather than a science, to which, according to Laddie J in *Wagamama* (1995), 'the judge brings his own, perhaps idiosyncratic pronunciation and view or understanding of them'. Nevertheless, it seems clear that the circumstances in which consumers may be found to suffer confusion as to the origin of the object have been widened. And there is certainly some support for the view that there is a shift from protection arising from confusion as to origin to protection against dilution even if, in English rulings, the shift is not formulated in precisely these terms. This may be seen in terms of an involvement of the law in the development of the sign, specifically in respect of the horizontal axis of signification described earlier, that of association. Furthermore, it would seem that the law is willing to recognise and provide protection for goods that are marked by a sign whose distinctiveness is not intrinsic to the mark as such but may be established in the relation between signs and the goods that they mark. This is an expansion of trade mark law in relation to the vertical process of signification. Thus, the distinctiveness of the sign is legally recognised to be perceived by the consumer in a process of global appreciation – that is, in the perception of the relations between the sign and the mark and the goods and services established in 'the course of trade'. Furthermore, this 'course' is recognised in law to be a dynamic process in which the activity that is the basis of protection is not clearly fixed in relation to a discrete origin. Or to put this another way, the activity of the course of trade that is the basis of the claim to the particular property rights at issue cannot be broken down by the law into discrete stages; rather the converse. The very distinctiveness of the goods themselves is held to be in part a function of the channels – in which is included packaging (such as jars) and the shelving in supermarkets – via which they are distributed. In these respects, the law may be seen to acknowledge a process of production in which the thing that is the object of trade mark law is never simply identical with itself but is transformed as it is brought to market.[12]

In short, in the legal reasoning described here, the thing that is the object of the claim is a sign whose distinctiveness cannot be clearly separated from the goods to which a mark – the graphic representation of the sign – is attached. Furthermore, this object is not a discrete entity whose nature may be fixed or attributed to a clearly identifiable point of origin, but some-thing that is constituted in the course of trade. And the course of trade is understood as an activity of bringing something to market. This is the activity (or labour) in which the objectivity of the thing is not fixed, but rather is distributed or dynamic. To put this another way, in the shifts described here, the thing that is the foundation of property rights is recognised to be realised in a process or activity that occurs in time through the structuring of the market; this is the specific nature of its (intangible) objectivity. In relation to the shifts described above, then, the law may be seen to be acknowledging that marketing is of increasing importance to the economy and that the thing-in-process provides itself (as) an incentive for innovation, and as such is a medium of competition. In these ways, the law provides support for the exclusive and extensive ownership and exploitation of the brand as an abstract, intangible and dynamic thing.

Brands as assets

This section will show how this understanding of the trade mark as a very particular form of property is recognised, contested and exploited in the economy. That is, it will show that the intangible or incorporeal thing that is the foundation of trade mark law is at the heart of a number of contemporary forms of exchange. Consider the case of trade mark licensing. This is the practice of allowing others to use your trade marks on approved goods or services under terms that allow you to control the quality of the goods or services covered by the licence (and, as noted on p. 108, the scope of this practice was radically extended by TMA 1994).[13] In its most common form, trade mark licensing is the licensing of third parties to produce or offer to supply more or less the same goods as those produced by the trade mark owner. But while there is a long tradition of licensing of technological know-how and patents in industry, licensing of trade marks is only now being systematically developed. Many companies have begun routinely to make such agreements not only with third parties, but also with their own subsidiaries. Thus, these companies own all intellectual property centrally and charge subsidiaries for use. For example, though many of the brands acquired as part of the take-over of Rowntree by Nestlé are sold only in Britain (for example, 'Quality Street', 'After Eight'), they are owned by the Swiss company and licensed back to a British subsidiary. It is argued by marketers and others that making a financial charge for the use of a trade mark focuses the user (whether they be a subsidiary or not) on the value of the asset and the need both to protect and to exploit that value.[14] Higher royalty rates are now being demanded than was the case before, and stricter conditions to ensure the proper use and maintenance of trade marks – both in legal and in marketing terms – are also evident.

The past twenty or thirty years has also seen the rapid growth of franchising[15] as a business strategy. Franchised business now accounts for over 38 per cent of all retail sales in the United States and originates 12 per cent of the gross national product (Caves and Murphy, 2003: 82). Franchising is a

> distinctive form of capital formation; one which permits flexible accumulation but eschews flexible specialization. For the franchisee it offers entrepreneurship in a package, ambition-by-numbers, capitalism in kit form; for the franchiser it gives access to capital without ceding control, reconciles integrated administration with entrepreneurial motivation.
>
> (Perry, 1998: 51)

Examples of brands developed through the use of franchising include McDonald's (Ritzer, 1993; Royle, 2000), Holiday Inn, Interflora, Dyno-Rod drain and pipe cleaning, Prontaprint printing and copying shops, Hertz rental cars, Clarks shoe shops and the global airline BA. The ex-CEO of BA, Robert Ayling, writes:

> Franchising has also proved an effective way of developing our business. Franchising at British Airways dates back to 1993 and is central to our growth strategy. We tend to franchise where we don't have the right size

of aircraft, or expertise in a particular market, or legal rights to fly. For example, we cannot fly from Johannesburg to Durban for these reasons, so Connair flies it as a franchise.

. . . Our franchising agreement allows other airlines to use British Airways' intellectual property – logo, style, trademark and service standards – provided they deliver product consistently to our specifications.

(1999: 43–44)

As indicated here, franchising typically involves the granting not only of rights to use trade marks as discussed earlier, but also of rights to use the business system developed by the licensor, typically in exchange for a royalty or turnover-related payment.[16] In this respect, it involves the sharing between firms of a number of intangible assets, only one of which is the trade mark. The arrangements may cover not only the look and design of the business, but also staff training, specialised accountancy and business control systems, criteria for staff selection, and so on.

A key issue in franchising is the relation between franchisor and franchisee. This is because the characteristics of the intangible assets that are shared between them – the trade mark and related intellectual property – are 'defined and maintained by its mode of use' (Caves and Murphy, 2003: 83). In other words, in economic practice, as in the legal understanding of trade mark as a chose in action, it is use that defines the objectivity of the intangible asset at issue. And it is interesting to note here that although franchises are sometimes run as a loose confederation of independent operators, it is not uncommon, as in the case of McDonald's, for the franchises to function as 'little more than subsidiaries of the corporation' (Royle, 2000: 13, 35–55). In other words, the relation between franchisor and franchisee can 'just as easily represent a strengthening as much as a weakening of corporate control' (ibid.: 54). This strengthening of control typically operates through the regulation of the brand. A UK franchisee of McDonald's comments:

[T]he one thing I've learnt in the last two years, is that the brand is everything, they won't let you do anything without it being checked, tested and quality tested so many times . . . having a McDonald's franchise there is a frustration factor . . . changes that are made company-wise you have to go along with, they are foisted upon you, you have no say in what happens . . . we are an extension of the company.

(Quoted in Royle, 2000: 45)

In the case of McDonald's (an example of what is called a 'format franchise'), franchisees are economically dependent on the corporation as a consequence of extremely rigid and detailed rules and procedures, a paternalistic management style and what Royle terms 'recruited acquiescence'.[17] However, their legal 'independence' allows many of the corporation's activities to slip through a variety of regulatory loopholes. In short, the separation between McDonald's and its franchise is 'a legal rather than an economic distinction' (Royle, 2000: 197), enabling the corporation to exercise control, and accrue licence fees, while restricting liability.

This tendency – for the exertion of economic control in conditions that minimise corporate risk and accountability – is described by Naomi Klein (2000) as a commercial race towards weightlessness. It is taken to its limit in the case of those companies that have been established on or are being developed through the exploitation of trademark licensing arrangements alone. Thus, for example, the fashion clothing company Tommy Hilfiger is run entirely through licensing deals. Hilfiger commissions all its products from a group of other companies: Jockey International makes Hilfiger underwear, Pepe Jeans London Hilfiger jeans, Oxford Industries makes Tommy shirts and the Stride Rite Corporation makes its footwear (ibid.). Companies such as Hilfiger, and to a lesser extent Ralph Lauren, Calvin Klein and others, are thus able to acquire virtual (or 'weightless') production capacities through an extensive network of licensing agreements. These agreements function on the basis of an exchange between the designer, who provides the product design and permission to use the brand name, and the licensee, who pays to make, distribute and sometimes advertise the branded product on the designer's behalf. As their reward for the deal, the designers obtain a specific proportion of sales (in the case of the Ralph Lauren Corporation, that cut is 6 per cent – Caminiti, 1998) as well as guaranteed minimum payments each season. The licensee obtains the exclusive right to manufacture and distribute for a brand that has an established reputation and appeal among consumers (Moore, 2000: 269).

Such licensing arrangements are not necessarily made with only one licensee. To use the example of Ralph Lauren again, more than thirty companies are licensed to manufacture, distribute and advertise his ranges of products, which include jeanswear, underwear, jewellery, cutlery (flatware) and furniture in over one hundred countries (Moore, 2000: 268–270). Many of Lauren's licensees are well-established brands in their own right. They include Rockport/Reebok, which manufactures the Ralph Lauren footwear ranges; Westpoint Stevens, which makes Ralph Lauren sheets, towels and bedding, while Clairol, the international cosmetics conglomerate, holds the licence for the production and distribution of Ralph Lauren perfumes world-wide. The partnership with Clairol has been especially lucrative for the Ralph Lauren Corp., and in 1997 earned the company in excess of $20 million in brand payments alone (Caminiti, 1998, quoted in Moore, 2000).

Even the responsibility for funding the continuing advertising support of the brand does not always remain with the brand or designer's company. Instead, it may be transferred to licence partners. A senior executive responsible for licensee relations in his organisation explains the transfer of financial responsibility in the following way:

> The licensees are initially attracted to the company because we have a strong brand. They commit to production, and distribution and they start to realise that the success they enjoy through us depends upon the continued success of the brand. So we take advantage of that dependence and shift the responsibility of maintaining and supporting the brand, by that I mean in the form of advertising costs, to them.
>
> (Quoted in Moore, 2000: 270)

As an example of this shift in responsibility, the advertising budget of $20 million for the Polo jeans brand was paid for entirely by Sun Apparel, the licensee responsible for the manufacture, distribution and promotion of the jeans brand world-wide (Caminiti, 1998, quoted in Moore, 2000).[18] Sun Apparel's financial support of the Polo brand is by no means unique within the sector. Indeed, one company that participated in a survey conducted by Moore (2000) indicated that all its brand and promotional costs were met by its licensee partners. Nevertheless, while the design companies mentioned delegate the responsibility for manufacturing and distributing diffusion brands to their licensee partners, they nevertheless retain control over all aspects of designing, manufacturing and distributing their couture and ready-to-wear ranges. These collections are not as financially significant as the diffusion or lifestyle ranges. Arguably, however, they are the most important in terms of the development of the overall brand 'image' (see Chapter 4), since these are the garments that are featured in their twice-yearly fashion shows, and receive extensive media coverage. In these and other ways, the control of brand image gives brand owners a defining influence over licensing, and many of the economic benefits accruing from the organisation of the brand in terms of production for increasing returns (see Chapter 3).

From the late 1980s onwards, the brand also becomes conspicuous in company mergers and acquisitions. This use of the brand as a recognised commercial asset is closely linked to the emergence of formal accountancy practices of brand valuation and the recognition of brand equity that occurred in the late 1980s. A study of acquisitions in the 1980s showed that whereas in 1981 net tangible assets represented 82 per cent of the amount bid for companies, by 1987 this had fallen to just 30 per cent (Blackett, 1998: 89). This growth in the commercial importance of intangible assets became a public issue when, in 1988, Nestlé paid £2.5 billion (more than five times the book value) to win control of the Rowntree group, while Philip Morris purchased Kraft for $12.6 billion, six times what the company was worth on paper. In the same year, Interbrand (a branding consultancy that is now a part of Omnicom Group Inc.[19]), in collaboration with the London Business School, conducted the first 'whole-portfolio' valuation for the UK foods group Rank Hovis McDougall (RHM). In 1989, the London Stock Exchange endorsed the concept of brand valuation as used by RHM, and a number of major branded goods companies now formally recognise the value of brands as intangible assets on their balance sheets.[20] In the United Kingdom, these include Cadbury Schweppes, Grand Metropolitan, Guinness, Ladbrokes and United Biscuits; in France, Pernod Ricard and Group Danone; while in Australia and New Zealand, companies include Pacific Dunlop, News International and Lion Nathan.

The brand consultancy Interbrand works on the principle that the value of a brand, like that of any other economic asset, is the worth *now* of the benefits of *future* ownership (Blackett, 1998: 91).[21] It argues that in order to calculate brand value it is necessary to identify clearly:

> the actual benefits of future ownership; that is, the current and future earnings or cash flows of the brand;
> their security and predictability and, therefore, the multiple (of profits) or discount rate (to cash flows) which can with confidence be applied.
>
> (Blackett, 1998: 91–92)

Interbrand provides criteria for the assessment of both brand strength[22] and the discount rate or the multiple to apply to brand-related profits, and argues that these criteria can be applied in a consistent, logical and verifiable manner. It produces tables of the world's most valuable brands, most of which are American, on an annual basis. Thus, for example, in 1999 the top ten companies were all American, with Nokia (Finland) making it to 11th place, Mercedes (Germany) to 12th and Nestlé (Switzerland) to 13th. Coca-Cola, the most valuable brand, was estimated to be worth $84 billion (59 per cent of the stated company value of $142 billion). In 2003, Coca-Cola was still top, Nokia had risen to sixth place, and Mercedes to tenth, while Nestlé had fallen to 21st. US brands claimed 62 places in the top 100, including eight of the top ten spots. There was no UK-owned brand in the top 20 in 1998, while in 2003 the top British brand was HSBC at 37th. However, it is still not possible to recognise the value of brands on balance sheets in the United States and many other places. There is also only a very limited acceptance of the usefulness of brand accounting within many companies. Nevertheless, it is increasingly possible for companies to treat the brand as they do any other form of valuable asset. Thus, companies dispose of unwanted brands in much the same way as they dispose of a subsidiary, and acquire others to repair deficiencies in their brand portfolios – as, for example, was the case with the Unilever acquisition of Cheseborough Ponds and Ford's purchase of Jaguar. Once brand value is recognised, it also becomes possible to mortgage or lease brands and thus to use them as a form of security.

The growth of the company Virgin provides an example of the radical use of the brand as a financial asset, and demonstrates further possible links between the use of the brand as a financial asset and the legal constitution of trade mark as an intellectual property right. The CEO, Richard Branson, writes:

> We are in essence an unusual venture capital organization: a branded one. Whereas most venture capitalists are a financial resource, backing management teams and their ideas, we offer a powerful branding and management resource. We are also well placed to get any additional financial backing that may be required. As part of the deal we control how the brand – which we now know to be our greatest asset – is used. We therefore retain at minimum 51 per cent control of most Virgin branded businesses and are highly selective about what we invest in. Nine out of ten projects we look at are potentially very profitable but if they don't fit with our values we reject them. . . .
>
> (1999: 235)

Initially a record label, the Virgin company now comprises a portfolio of companies providing goods and services in a diversity of product and service markets. The company's origins in the music industry are important to Branson, giving him experience in a business in which rights to properties are often shared through complex arrangements (Lury, 1993). Thus, he claims that it is as a consequence of the company's origin in the music industry that 'we have the kind of management mind-set that regards partnership with other companies as a perfectly natural way of doing business. . . . We are a federation of businesses' (Branson, 1999: 235–236).

The flexibility of the Virgin brand is not constrained by product category. As Branson puts it, 'we've never been constrained by the "What business are we in?" question' (1999: 232). This is a consequence of the exploitation of a core competence: the ability to manage high growth through alliances, joint ventures and outsourcing. The diversified group is said to be bound together by five core values – quality, value for money, competitiveness, innovation and fun – which comprise the brand. The idea, Branson says, is to build brands not around products but around reputation. The great Asian names imply quality, price and innovation rather than a specific item. I call these 'attribute' brands: They do not relate directly to one product – such as a Mars bar or a Coca-Cola – but instead to a set of values.

(Quoted in N. Klein, 2000: 24)

While the wholesale adoption of the Virgin model is rare, it is associated with a more widespread transformation in the organisation of production. This involves a shift in the locus of control such that companies that might once have understood themselves as manufacturing companies come to see themselves as marketing companies. For example, as noted in Chapter 3, Nike does not itself manufacture the goods that bear its name: manufacture is sub-contracted to factories in shifting locations in the Far East. As is true of Virgin, what is important to the success of the company is the development, mainte-nance and exploitation of rights to use the company trademarks and associated logos. Nevertheless, Nike, like many other companies, retains a great deal of control of certain aspects of production, not only providing designs, but speci-fying materials, requiring standards of production and enforcing certain kinds of quality control, while not actually owning production capabilities itself. (Of course, many of the political campaigns targeted at Nike have sought to make it take responsibility not only for the standards of products being produced, but also for the human and environmental conditions in which these products are produced; see N. Klein, 2000.) But while many companies continue to seek to control much of the production process (even if they do not own their own manufacturing plants or service outlets), this is not normally true in Virgin's case. Branson writes:

As in the music business, third parties have always been responsible for much of the operation. Only the customer-facing activities [in Virgin air-lines] are Virgin branded or trained. Our cost base is therefore far lower than our main competitors' on most routes.

(1999: 230)

Or once again drawing parallels with the music industry:

Our culture is one of corporate artists: challenging conventions is proving to be one of the best ways to bring about success. Our approach to man-aging each business is based on our roots. Instead of musicians, the artists Virgin now manages are the individual companies and, of course, the Virgin brand. Virgin Management is fully involved with launching new companies, reviewing the opportunity, setting up the business, and providing a creative team of managers who are seconded to new Virgin companies for as long as they are needed. Fledgling Virgin ventures thus acquire the trademark management style plus unique skills and experience from all parts of the group. After the business has been set up, however, it is the responsibility of the individual company's management.

(1999: 237–238)

The result is what Branson calls a virtual brand that is 'regenerated rather than extended in the conventional sense, by each business we become involved in' (ibid.: 235). This is a radical statement of the use of a brand to manage a process of non-linear production across conventional trade categories. Growth is here a consequence not simply of brand extension, but of regeneration. This is the multiplication of brand origins, or, perhaps better, the management of a network of relations in which each new origin has the potential to provide the basis for further growth. It is, as Branson says, a *trade mark management style* (for a discussion of trade mark style in the art world, see C. Lury 2002).

The law and things: object trials

Taken together, these changes indicate that there has been a shift in the terms of protection offered to brand owners by trade mark legislation and that this shift supports developments in the ways in which brands are exploited commercially. As the earlier discussion of the terms of the legal recognition of distinctiveness indicates, the protection afforded to the trade mark owner is not simply a claim to some discrete or fixed 'thing'. Instead, it is a claim to something that emerges in the relation between a sign, a mark and goods and services, and in a process of being brought to the market. Moreover, as the discussion of commercial practice indicates, this is a legally mediated objectivity that is not only potentially exploitable as the site of product innovation, but also a means of corporate growth, through both brand extension (McDonald's) and brand regeneration (Virgin). The terms of the security of ownership afforded the mark owner by trade mark law have commercial significance in relation to the internal organisation of companies *and* to co-operative and competitive relations between companies. They facilitate the use of trade mark in such a way as to establish networks and alliances within and between firms in ways that support particular forms of capital accumulation. As such, trade mark is an increasingly important means by which capital may not only build monopolies but also have investments in the ownership of innovation (Strathern, 1999). In these respects, then, trade mark law does more than protect the mark owner from unfair forms of competition. It makes it possible for mark owners to exploit new forms of production and exchange, to establish and lay claim to property rights in new forms of objectivity – that is, it protects and enables forms of production and exchange that are non-linear. But this is not all. An important, but not yet discussed aspect of the legal support for the management of a non-linear or global process of production concerns the law's representation of the activities of the public or the consumer. As was noted earlier, usage by the public is central to legal thinking in respect of trade mark, yet in what follows it will be suggested that the activities of consumers are recognised in partial and uneven ways. The consequence, as Jane Gaines notes, is that trade mark law, like other intellectual property law, cuts networks up, producing 'protected and unprotected, exclusive and nonexclusive zones' (1991: 145).

So far, it has been suggested that the activity embedded in the thing that is the object of trade mark law comprises the innovative (but not necessarily inventive) processes in which some-thing is brought to market. But the legal representation of this activity is uneven. It acknowledges the activities of many of those involved in the qualification–requalification of products, including market researchers, but only minimally acknowledges the activities occurring after sale. In this regard, consider a ruling relating to the opposition of the name 'Rysta' as a mark to indicate that a company had repaired secondhand stockings by an invisible mending process (*Aristoc* v. *Rysta*, 1945). Of three grounds for opposition, one was that this was not in fact a proposed use of the mark as a trade mark at all (Trade Marks Act 1938). In accepting this argument, Viscount Maugham notes that in an earlier Act (the Trade Marks Act 1905), the purpose of the mark is stated to be 'indicating that they are the goods of the proprietor of such trade mark by virtue of manufacture, selection, certification, dealing with, or offering for sale'. He continues that while the relevant section of the 1938 Act is much vaguer – merely stating that the purpose of the mark is to indicate '"a connection in the course of trade" between the goods and the proprietor of the mark' – it seems to him 'beyond doubt' that hitherto a registered trade mark has the purpose of indicating the origin of the good – that is, as he puts it, 'either manufacture or some other dealing with the goods in the process of manufacture or in the course of business before they are offered for sale to the public' (Cornish, 1999: 464). It is this 'before' that indicates the partiality of the legal representation of the course of trade, since it implies that the process of bringing something to market is brought to culmination or fixed at the moment of sale. To put this another way, while in later cases the distinctiveness of the object before sale is not fixed at any particular stage or moment in time, but established in dynamic relations between stages (in the 'course of trade'), such dynamism is in this instance halted at the moment of sale. Activity after sale is here recognised to be discrete (separable both from other stages of activity and from the thing itself). And this view has not since been substantially revised. The implication is that such post-sale activity does not contribute to the improvement of the object or resource in Lockean terms; it is insufficiently object-ive – or object-ifying – for the law in this respect.

Consider again the case of *British Sugar* v. *James Robertson* (1996), in which Jacob J seeks to answer the question as to whether a product is a jam or a 'dessert sauce or syrup'. British Sugar produced a large number of sugar-related products under the general mark 'Silver Spoon'. One of these was a syrup topping for ice cream and other desserts, which it marketed as 'Silver Spoon Treat' in toffee and other flavours. It also (somewhat surprisingly, given the weakness of the mark) was able to register the word 'treat' as a trade mark for dessert sauce and syrups. British Sugar brought a case for infringement against James Robertson, the well-known jam manufacturer, for its product 'Robertson's Toffee Treat'. In considering whether the Robertson product did indeed fall within the specification of goods for which the mark is registered (spreads or toppings), Jacob J notes that Robertson's itself describes the relevant product as a dessert sauce or syrup. Thus, the small print on the back of the jar says, 'Toffee Treat is delicious at breakfast, with desserts or as a snack anytime. Spread Toffee Treat on bread, toast or biscuits, spoon it over yoghurt or ice-cream or use as filling for cakes' (quoted in Cornish, 1999: 471). Jacob J continues in his representation of the plaintiff's case:

> So, say British Sugar, the product can not only be used on a dessert, but Robertson's positively suggest this. Thus, even if the product has other uses, it is, *inter alia*, used on desserts. . . . It does not matter if . . . other uses are much commoner: the fact that the product can be used as a dessert sauce means it is one.
>
> (Quoted in Cornish, 1999: 471)

However, Jacob J disagrees with this view: 'I reject this argument.' A number of reasons are given for this rejection. As noted earlier, he argues that

> Supermarkets regard the product as a spread. The jam jar invites use as a spread. When it comes to construing a word used in a trade mark specification, one is concerned with how the product is, as a practical matter, regarded for the purposes of trade. After all a trade mark specification is concerned with use in trade. The Robertson product is not, for the purpose of trade, a dessert sauce.
>
> (Quoted in Cornish, 1999: 471)

Additionally, however, Jacob J does consider use (as the six criteria outlined on pp. 113–114 suggest he should). Thus, he introduces the fact that the use of the spread with dessert is likely to be slight. Here he cites an estimate that: 'all potential uses of the product, other than as a spread, amounted to less than five per cent of the volume' (quoted in Cornish, 1999: 471). Most pointedly for the argument being made here, however, he further argues that while even jam can also be used as a dessert, and 'everyone knows and sometimes does that', no one would describe jam as a 'dessert sauce' in 'ordinary parlance'. In short, Jacob J thinks that the use of 'treat' causes the plaintiff no harm, because 'by and large one [jam] is not in practice a substitute for the other [sauce]' (quoted in Cornish, 1999: 471). That some-thing has the potential to be used as would be another product does not, in this ruling, mean that it is the other product *or even that it is similar enough to it to be a substitute for it*. But substitutability in the actual practice of more or less everyone is not the same trial of substitutability that is adjudicated by marketing. In the qualification trials of marketing, it is precisely the (recursive) recognition of the *possible* uses of something (what some people sometimes but not always do, or even what some people could possibly do, but usually do not) that produces the integrated object, the brand. In short, the trial of object-ivity in the law courts does not produce the same some-thing that is produced in the trials of marketing.

This discrepancy between object-ivity in the law and in marketing is revealing for what it suggests about their respective representation of consumer activities. It might be seen to suggest that marketing provides a more adequate (a more just) representation of the activities of the consumer than the law. But this is not so. On the one hand, marketers explicitly acknowledge the value of consumer activities in the building of brands ('Effectively, a brand is nothing but a network of associations in the consumer's mind' (Andrew, 1998: 190)[23]). On the other hand, trade mark holders are advised by marketers to be wary of acknowledging the activities of consumers as object-ive. Consider, for example, the following 'rule' given by marketers to trade mark owners as to correct usage of trade marks:

> A trade mark is an adjective. It is not a noun and it is not a verb.[24] It should always be used in print as an adjective qualifying a noun or noun phrase. The noun or noun phrase which the trade mark adjective must qualify is of course the generic name for the product.
>
> (Blackett, 1998: 60–61)

This rule is deemed to be necessary by marketers since the property rights acquired by registration of a trade mark can be lost in those exceptional cases in which consumer activities are legally held to be objectifying. In a judgment often referred to as genericide, it is legally established that if a trade mark becomes the generic name for the thing itself, then the trade mark owner loses exclusive rights to the mark (Gaines, 1991; Coombe, 1998). Examples of words that started off their lives as trade marks but now have lost their status as private property include gramophone, zip, tabloid and escalator. Other marks, while still registered, are frequently thought of by the public as being common names, for example Biro, Thermos, Cellophane and Xerox. In these and other cases, then, trade mark owners must continually watch to ensure that brand and genre remain distinct if they wish to continue to assert property rights. In the terms of the genericide ruling, it seems that the law is willing to recognise the thing that is the object of a property right as brought into being in consumer activity (although only when it is common or generic activity – that is, what everybody does). But with this ruling in mind, marketers insist that what they produce is merely an adjective, a qualification of something that exists in its own right, independently of the trials of either the law or marketing.

In sum, the legal recognition of the activity of the consumer in the definition of the distinctiveness of the trade mark is partial and uneven. In this respect, the law contributes to the operation of the brand as interface (see Chapter 3). As noted earlier, the performance of the interface of the brand both connects 'producers' and 'consumers' and removes or separates them from each other. In other words, while it is the basis of two-way exchanges between producers and consumers, informing how consumers relate to producers and how producers relate to consumers, the exchanges mediated by the interface of the brand are partial and asymmetrical. On the one hand, it seems that the law is unwilling to extend recognition of the activity embedded in a thing to consumers unless that activity is a common or generic use of something. In this respect, it seems that the law sides with marketers who have elaborated techniques to produce a situation where 'the initiative is with the shelves, rather than with the shopper' (Bowlby, 2000: 32, quoted in Arvidsson, forthcoming). Where consumers do assert their initiative – so as, for example, to use a product in an atypical way – the law recognises this as a mere may-be. On the other hand, in those cases where consumer activity may be understood as being so common as to be generic, its object-ive significance is recognised by the law. In anticipation of such situations, marketers decline to assert the objectifying capacities of even their own representation of consumer activities.

Coda

The law's contribution to the organisation of the brand thus appears to stem from the selective legal interpretation of the relation between activity or labour and the value of the intangible thing that is the object of the property claim. It recognises the mark holder's right to protection in terms of distinctiveness in such a way as to promote the ownership of an investment in innovation (whether it is inventive or not), while denying the capacity to innovate to consumers. In doing so, the law may be seen not only as promoting and inhibiting exchange between producers and consumers, but, most importantly, as informing the asymmetry of this exchange through its own particular notion of object-ivity. In this respect, trade mark law is one of the mechanisms by which the consumer's ability to exercise choice – in anything more than a restricted sense of selection from pre-given options – is now more than ever under the control of global corporations. It limits the terms of interactivity, reinforcing the coercive predictability of the interaction the brand affords, rather than extending the margins of its indeterminacy.

6 Interactivity

Face-to-profile communication

Interactive computer media perfectly fits this trend to externalize and objec-
tify mind's operations. The very principle of hyperlinking, which forms the
basis of much of interactive media, objectifies the process of association often
taken to be central to human thinking. Mental processes of reflection,
problem solving, recall, and association are externalized, equated with
following a link, moving to a new page, choosing a new image, or a new
scene. . . . Put differently, in what can be read as an updated version of
French philosopher Louis Althusser's concept of 'interpellation,' we are asked
to mistake the structure of somebody else's mind for our own.

(Manovich, 2001: 61)

Introduction

Karin Knorr Cetina (2000) provides a provocative argument as to why sociologists need to take objects seriously today. She argues that the way in which
we relate to objects is changing profoundly, and identifies a number of
processes that contribute to this change, both subjective and objective (of
which only the latter will be discussed in any detail here). First, Knorr Cetina
suggests that there has been an enormous increase in the volume of non-
human things in the social world – of technological objects, consumer goods
and scientific things. Second, she argues that many objects break away from
the received definition of fixed things. She suggests that they can be defined
almost as the obverse of this: that objects are now characterised by an indefiniteness of being. In short, objects now lack (conventional) object-ivity; they
are instead characterised by a lack of completeness of being and a non-identity
with themselves. Considering the example of scientific objects, Knorr Cetina
shows that objects such as the gene lie at the centre of a process of investigation (see also Fraser, forthcoming). Objects, she says, are characteristically
open, question-generating and in the process of being defined. They are

processes and projections rather than definite things. Third, she suggests that relations between subjects and objects are now so important that we live in what she calls a post-social era.

Focusing on scientific and technological objects, consumer goods and exchange commodities, Knorr Cetina argues that contemporary objects are characterised by a changing, unfolding character; things are now 'as much defined by what they are not as by what they are' (2000: 528). Her suggestion is that more and more objects exist not only as things-to-be-used but also as things-to-be-related-to and things-to-be-transformed. Objects undergo continual processes of development and investigation; they appear on the market in continually changing updates, versions and variations. They have a dual structure: they are simultaneously things-to-be-used and things-in-a-process-of-transformation:

> Computers and computer programs are typical examples; they appear on the market in continually changing 'updates' (progressively debugged issues of the same product) and 'versions' (items marked for their differences from earlier varieties). These objects are both present (ready-to-be-used) and absent (subject to further research).
>
> (2000: 528)

A significant proportion of the objects she describes are technologies, but what she says also applies to technologically prepared and upgraded goods. In this sense, foods, even fruit and vegetables, are as much an example of this tendency, she says, as are television sets and software programs; they are produced (grown) in continually updated varieties and sold in different versions. Fashion goods provide another example, undergoing continuous transformation, organised by the dynamic of model and series (Baudrillard, 1997), in which a model gives rise to a series of variations, which in turn spins off a new model. Objects of design – chairs, toasters and egg-cups – are continually redesigned too; their fixedness is a matter of moments of stability in a sequence of changes and it is always in danger of disappearing. This dual structure is a consequence of a referential nexus of objects, 'the phenomenon that one object refers to another and this one to a third, in an unending series of referrals' (Knorr Cetina, 2000: 529). So, for example, the consumer objects which we (think that we) want in order to complete our being always refer to further objects in an unending series. (This is another way of thinking about how it is that relations between differentiated products make up a more abstract object such as the brand.)

A further level to the indefiniteness of the objects Knorr Cetina describes is that there is always more to them than we are likely to discover in everyday use. The computer is once again the example here: its potential capacity is much greater than most of us require, greater than most of us can even understand. In this sense, computers are expanding environments of realisation. The unfinishedness of many contemporary objects, Knorr Cetina suggests, makes increasing relational demands on us; they are unfolding structures of absences which call on us as subjects to relate to them. Indeed, it is for this reason, she suggests, that sociology needs to address what she calls post-social relations, relations between objects and objects, and objects and subjects, not only subjects and subjects.

This is a persuasive argument for the sociological significance of object relations today – that is, of what might be called *the increasing relationality of objects*. And this book has argued that the brand is an example of an (abstract) object that calls upon us to relate to it; to interact with it. To the relativity of objects produced by money, the brand introduces and elaborates relationality. It compulsively includes or implicates us in ways that are not always straightforward and are deliberately designed to be open-ended. But to accept Knorr Cetina's argument is not to say that relational objects are new in some absolute sense, only that the conditions required for their recognition have only recently made their appearance. This is to say, it is the way in which subjects relate to objects – and objects relate to objects – that is changing, not some essential aspect of objectivity. It is to argue that object relations have increasingly become a concern beyond the restricted fields of science and technology. In the case of the brand, the relations in which it partakes are the concern of what has been called soft capitalism (Thrift, 1997) and what might – by analogy – be called soft science (that is, economics is supplemented by design and marketing). But the knowledge relations in which the brand partakes are not confined to laboratories or even to business schools (Latour and Woolgar, 1986; Thrift, forthcoming); its object-ivity is rather a matter of – and for – an economy of everyday life; it is a matter of *interactivity*.

Interactivity: 'you may'

In his discussion of 'Political Machines' (2001), Andrew Barry argues that interactivity has come to be a dominant model of how objects can be used to produce subjects. He suggests that interactivity is becoming a model for the exercise of political power that does not take a disciplinary form. For example, in contradistinction to the disciplinary technology associated with the injunction 'You must', he suggests that interactive technology – of which, so it is suggested here, brands are an example – is coming to be associated with the injunction 'You may'. He notes that in an interactive model, subjects 'are not disciplined, they are allowed' (ibid.: 129). The negative implication, as Barry sees it, is that at the same time that an experimental self is called into being (one who may play with object-ive possibilities), the space for learning from the other is reduced. Here he draws on the thinking of Slavoj Zizek (1997), who suggests that interactivity is more appropriately understood as interpassivity, since the user of an interactive machine allows the machine to be active on the user's behalf, so displacing any activity (or creative passivity) of his or her own. The activity of the machine is a projection of the user's activity, but is largely predictable, pre-selected and highly circumscribed. As a consequence, 'instead of referring to mutual influence that might be peripheral and trivial, [interactivity] now refers to a highly structured form of mutual fatefulness' (Goffman, 1961: 35).

What might it mean, then, to argue that the brand is an object of inter-activity? In Chapter 4, it was suggested that the brand is made visible in a face, but this face is not that of someone engaged in face-to-face interaction, but one face of an inter-face, the surface of communication of a new media object (Manovich, 2001). Perhaps one way to address the interactivity of the brand is to see the face of the brand as speaking to – as targeted at – not another face, but a profile. As Callon *et al.*, describes the economy of qualities, 'All in all, what is being produced is a progressive "profiling" of products that, through successive adjustment and iteration, ends up profiling both the demand and the consumer' (2002: 205).

A logo that illustrates face-to-profile communication is that of Apple Macintosh, which welcomes the user of one of its computers on being switched on with a graphic image that is simultaneously a frontal portrait of a face and the profile of another.[1] This logo represents the brand as looking out at (watching) the user and locates the user within the space of the screen in the same (real) time. In this graphic image, the positions of object and subject are simultaneously separated and conjoined, represented as the whole and a part of each other, and the perspectives of subject and object are simultaneously rendered reciprocal and tangential to each other.

But what exactly is a profile? It is a technique that emerges at the intersection of the history of methods of visualising data and the history of portraiture. In an account that draws attention to this intersection, Joachim Krausse argues that

> [t]he silhouette is the diagram of a portrait. It reduces the quantity of information of the singular phenomenon to the characteristic profile of a planar figure which – and this is what is new – can be visually compared with other figures. The individual only becomes 'character' with the introduction of standards. And it is only when there is a spectrum of individuation that the struggle focusing on standards begins. It is just a small step from distinction to discrimination.
>
> (1998: 15)

The profile in turn may be seen as a development of the silhouette. In contemporary uses, the profile is a model or figure that organises multiple sources of information to scan for matching or exceptional cases, and is able to target individuals for specialised messages. While it is most popularly associated with the tracking down of particular kinds of criminals,[2] it is a routine procedure in many arenas of social life, producing not only probable transgressors but also probable consumers (Elmer, 2000: 68; Elmer, forthcoming; Poster, 2001). In marketing and advertising, profiling makes use of information from a wide range of sources, including, for example, online and offline purchase data, supermarket loyalty cards, surveys, sweepstakes and contest entries, financial records, property records, census records, motor vehicle data, credit card transactions, phone records, product warranty cards, subscription records and public records. Techniques of profiling are constantly being updated and are increasingly automated. They may operate without the knowledge of those to whom the information collected refers. So, for example, agent-based computer modelling has begun to be used to simulate markets and profile consumers, while Hewlett-Packard Labs in Palo Alto, California, has developed a technique for finding whether or not any set of individuals have the same preferences without revealing what they are. Similar techniques exist in the case of software agents such as cookies, affective computing and similar interfaces that take a more active role in assisting the user than the standard Graphical User Interface (GUI). By tracking the user, these interfaces acquire information that they use to 'help' the user with his or her tasks and automate them; in this process, a profile of the user is established.

A number of points may be made here. Most importantly, in these developments the profile is not simply an indicator of a (social) reality; it is also a device for regulating – intervening in – that reality. For example, profiles contribute to the emergence of what Greg Elmer (forthcoming) describes as a pervasive default culture, by which he means the systematic incorporation of technological choices in the absence of consumer responses. Such default settings, he suggests, almost always entrench economic and political interests, as, for example, in the case of the bundling of Microsoft's Web browser.

Loyalty: 'you could and you should'

An example of the management of brand interactivity as face-to-profile communication is the loyalty card, of which at least one is to be found in about 85 per cent of UK households (Shabi, 2003: 15). The Tesco Clubcard has 10 million active households; Nectar has signed up 11 million; and the Boots Advantage scheme claims 15 million members. Such schemes reward their members for shopping loyally: Tesco, for example, gives you a point worth a penny for every pound you spend, which you receive once you reach 150 points. You can spend these in stores or redeem them against 'freetime' offers such as hotel tokens. In the United States, a two-tier pricing system operates in some stores; if you do not have a loyalty card, you pay more.

But what do the stores get from this? A number of things: they 'consolidate' how much consumers spend in one store (the launch of a card will give sales a 1–4 per cent sales 'uplift'); but also, just as importantly, their use provides information that has commercial value:

> Edwina Dunn, CEO of Dunnhumby, data analysts for Tesco, says, 'You can find people interested in cooking from scratch, or people who shop with distinct flavours in mind, or where convenience is key. We are trying to track lifestyles in terms of what is in the basket.'
>
> (ibid.: 15)

Such information can be used to develop new products, be linked to special promotions, either in store or via selected mail-outs; or sold on to manufacturers.

> The ideal, says Rick Ferguson at Colloquy magazine ('the voice of the loyalty marketing industry'), is to move your customers along a relationship chain, 'from casual shoppers and disloyal consumers to real brand loyalists, where they get stuck in what we call a "spin cycle" of shopping frequently and responding to offers'. That spin cycle, he adds, is 'the ultimate level of profitability'. Retailers get us to that point by analysing the loyalty card database to determine who has the potential to become a better shopper.
>
> (ibid.: 17)

The Nectar card scheme involves a number of firms, including Sainsbury's, Barclaycard, BP, Debenhams, Vodafone, Adams, Thresher and Ford, that do not share each other's database information, but do share the analysis of it, carried out by Nectar card operators Loyalty Management UK.

> The company's CEO, Rob Gierkink, says that, 'without question', the combined effect is more powerful, and he goes on to give an illuminating example of how. Sainsbury's very best customers, he says, tend to be families, who can be spotted in other Nectar stores by, for example, high mobile phone or petrol usage. 'Now we can take that information and project it across the rest of our data-base. We can see what looks like a big family, but who may not be going to Sainsbury's. For the first time, retailers can say not just, "Who are my best customers?" but, "Who look

like they could really be really good customers?"' Stores and other Nectar members can try to attract these potential high-spend customers by mailing them tempting offers.

(ibid.: 17)

While data protection laws restrict how firms may pass on the information they collect, they must provide information if requested by the law courts. So, for example, in the United States:

> In one instance, a man's card-tracked purchase of expensive wine was used to show that he could afford to pay more alimony. In another, a supermarket proposed to use till receipts to prove that a man who sued after tripping over a yogurt spill in its store was an alcoholic.
>
>   . . . After the September 11 attacks, reports Albrecht [director of the US-based Consumers Against Supermarket Privacy Invasion and Numbering, or CASPIAN (nocards.org)], 'Federal agents reviewed the shopper card records of the men involved to create a profile of ethnic tastes and supermarket shopping patterns associated with terrorism.'

(ibid.: 19)

In considering a series of related developments, Manovich (2003) points out that we live at a time when computer and network technologies are more and more actively entering real physical spaces, and that such technologies are used more and more to deliver data to, and extract data from, physical space. He provides examples of three inter-related kinds of technologies by which this is occurring. First, video and other types of surveillance technologies translate physical space and its dwellers into data. Second, cell-space technologies work in the opposite direction: delivering data to the mobile space dwellers. Cell-space is physical space 'filled' with data that can be retrieved by a user using a personal communication device. Some data may come from global networks such as the Internet; some may be embedded in objects located in the space around the user. Publicly located computer/display displays may present the same visible information to passers-by. These displays constitute the third way in which space is 'augmented'.

The brand may be seen as a further example of this third kind of technology. It is a public display (of sorts) that delivers information to the consumer (about products, services and events) and feeds back information about the consumer to the brand owner (in conjunction with other information provided by product bar codes, retail information, market research and so on). In this perspective, the brand interface is a device for the creation of meta-data or 'data about data'. It is what enables us to ' "see" and retrieve data, move it from place to place, compress and expand it, connect data with other data, and so on' (Manovich, 2003). The logo is a kind of computer software agent[3] designed to automate the search for relevant information in the saturated information of the contemporary economy. Of course, Manovich acknowledges that physical space was always augmented by images, graphics and type, but substituting all these by electronic (informational) displays makes it possible to present dynamic images, to mix images, graphics and type and to change the content at any time. But these three kinds of technologies very much belong together, he suggests. Together, they make the physical space into a data-space, extracting data from it (surveillance) or augmenting it with data (cell-space, computer displays to assist the viewer). In short, delivering information to users in space and extracting information about these users are closely connected in the workings of the interface, face-to-profile communication. This makes the distinction between surveillance and assistance (or, as Elmer puts it, punishment and reward) in interactivity hard to sustain.

In the management of the delivery and extraction of information about a population, whether with the aim of surveillance or assistance, the state has historically played a significant role. Thus, the regulation and specification of product information has for a long time been an important aspect of state intervention in the market. In most countries, governments require products to be described in particular ways at the point of sale. Food products, for example, are required by law to be described in terms of their constituents. But recent controversies over BSE, genetically modified food and dioxins have pushed food safety up the consumer agenda at both a national level, so that the UK's Food and Standards Agency is beginning to be more interventionist, as is the EU, which is developing a system of regional food regulation. Such bodies struggle to find ways of dealing with indeterminate or open-ended objects. The European Food Safety Authority, established in 2002, is responsible for handling food scares, and is introducing the so-called precautionary principle into food laws, obliging regulators to take action to mitigate the possibilities of food-related dangers even where there is scientific uncertainty (Austin, 2003). What is at issue here is whether and how the very nature of scientific 'proof' can be changed (Dratwa, cited in Barry, 2002) so as legitimately to acknowledge uncertainty while still providing object-ive evidence that may inform decisions on how to act (Narration, 2002).

In the United States, there is typically greater reliance on the law than on governmental regulation in relation to issues of governance and product liability. In a recent case, in January 2003, a judge dismissed a claim brought by two teenagers against McDonald's for causing their obesity. Judge Robert W. Sweet, of the New York Southern District Court, dismissed the allegations, citing lack of evidence. Overall, he took the same approach as the English high court in the McDonald's 2002 scalding coffee case: if consumers know the risks associated with a product and the producer has made full disclosure of those risks, they cannot blame the producer when they actually happen. But he also identified the central question as 'where the line be drawn between an individual's own responsibility to take care of herself, and society's respons-ibility to ensure that others shield her' (quoted in Austin, 2003: 9), and gave the plaintiffs time and leave to re-file. He advised them to 'flesh out' their amended complaint with an argument not mentioned in the original case con-cerning the food additives and flavourants that go into hamburgers, chips and milkshakes. This, he said, might 'establish that the dangers of McDonald's products were not commonly well known and therefore that McDonald's had a duty towards its customers', as well as potentially exposing deficiencies in the company's defence and making causation easier to prove (ibid.: 9).

Talking back

A further factor in the organisation of interactivity is of course whether and how consumers organise themselves to talk back. But consumer organisation in relation to the brand is not and cannot be a simple matter. One of the points made in this book is that while brands rely upon the participation of consumers, they place severe limits on interactions with them.[4] Sometimes indeed it may seem that all that consumers can do is buy or not buy (branded) products. But this is not so. Typically, consumer organisations have aided the consumer's decision-making by providing comparative information within product cat-egories about price and quality, although the latter has been measured in rather limited, mechanical ways, typically to do with the evaluation of a product's function and efficiency. In the United Kingdom, the consumer organisation and magazine *Which?* has historically been an example of this kind of approach. At the same time, consumer campaigns have adopted both more and less carefully targeted campaigns to some effect. Campaigns have been organised in relation to manufacturing place of origin (for example, the boycott of goods from South Africa during apartheid) and the labour practices of specific companies (against Nestlé, Nike and McDonald's, for example). There have also been initiatives to form alliances between (particular groups of) producers and consumers, as in the long-standing case of the Co-operative movement in the United Kingdom. There are also more recent attempts by some consumer organisations to move beyond evaluation of products in terms of price and efficiency, and to address the process of production in broader terms. So, for example, the appointment of a new chief executive of the National Consumer Council in 2003 was linked to a new emphasis on the rights of poor households: 'So much of the consumer agenda looks jaded, with its focus on value for money and equipment instead of inclusion and fairness. . . . There is a need for reinventing the consumer approach' (Mayo, quoted in Benjamin, 2003: 4). At the same time, there are an increasing number of organisations and movements, such as Fairtrade, Adbusters, green consumption, ethical consumption and Local Exchange Trading Systems, that challenge corporate control to a greater or lesser extent and offer alternative models of exchange (see Williams, 2000b for a useful overview of such activity; Barry, 2003).

The case of Fairtrade is especially interesting here, because it functions as a brand itself in many respects (see fairtrade.org.uk; ptree.co.uk; pan-uk.org; ethicalconsumer.org). The Fairtrade Foundation, a charitable organisation, does not produce goods, but promotes the use of a Fairtrade mark or label (this, like many other logos, is a graphic representation of a person) for prod- ucts that meet standards of fair trade. It was set up by CAFOD, Christian Aid, New Consumer, Oxfam, Traidcraft Exchange and the World Development Movement, which were later joined by the Women's Institute (Britain's largest women's organisation). Sales of fair trade foods have grown rapidly in recent years. Fairtrade brands now account for 14 per cent of the total UK roast and ground coffee market, and there are more and more products avail- able under this label: sugar, wine, honey, fruits, juices, snacks and biscuits, chilli peppers and meat as well as tea, coffee and bananas. The Co-op, Safeway and Sainsbury's supermarkets have even started their own Fairtrade lines, while Starbucks and Costa Coffee also have Fairtrade sub-brands. World-wide sales of Fairtrade products are thought to be close to £300 million a year (Vidal, 2003: 8). The director of the Fairtrade Foundation says:

> As globalisation happened, people understood more where their food was coming from and were really shocked to discover the conditions of the people growing it. . . . Trade became a major issue in the 1990s. Seattle [and the World Trade Organization] underlined the importance of what was happening on the other side of the world. The development charities have now put trade at the centre of their work.
>
> . . . Fairtrade is the only standard that brings producers and consumers together. . . . It enables consumers to express their preferences for a dif- ferent system of trade and gives power back to the producers instead of just imposing on them standards that salve consciences here. It still has the potential to grow significantly.
>
> (Lamb, quoted in Vidal, 2003: 8)

But such campaigns face many problems. In a discussion of how the Foun- dation might move into the field of fashion clothing, the executive director says:

> It's a very complex supply chain . . . and it would be impossible to imple-
> ment fair trade at every stage immediately. We will start where the 'high
> value added' takes place, the bits where the most value is added in terms
> of work. That's where the farmer grows the cotton and when workers
> manufacture the garment.
>
> (Quoted in Porter, 2003: 56)

Even if the focus is restricted in this way, the problems are immense, because
of the ways in which global flows of people, capital, products and ideas are
currently organised. 'America's 25,000 cotton farmers receive three times
more in subsidies than the entire US aid budget for the whole of Africa's 500
million people' (Katherine Hamnett, quoted in Davis, 2003: 16). There are,
however, a number of companies that claim to make 'stylish "sweat-shop-free"
clothing', such as American Apparel, SweatX, People Tree and Ethical
Threads. So, for example, People Tree is a £2 million business in more than
20 countries, and produces garments and jewellery from ten countries across
Asia, Africa and Latin America. In the United Kingdom, the Co-op has
recently agreed to sell People Tree organic cotton T-shirts through 58 of its
outlets. The company's mission statement is as follows: 'People Tree's collection is made with organic cotton and handwoven fabrics to promote natural
farming that is safe to the environment and safe to the wearer, and create
much-needed income in rural areas' (www.ptree.co.uk). American Apparel
stores plan to have photo galleries and video screens showing documentary
footage of Third World sweatshops, while its magazine advertisements use the
slogan 'F**k the brands that are f**king the people' (Carrell, 2003: 3). The
impetus behind Fairtrade and other linked movements is for what are sometimes described as socially responsible goods.

   Of course, workers' rights organisations have for a long time protested
about scandals involving Third World textile firms, which affect many major
global brands. The focus for campaigns include fatal factory fires in India,
lock-outs of staff in Indonesia, and violence against trade union activists in
Thailand and Guatemala. A Thai supplier to Levi's, Nike and Adidas recently
closed down its factory owing employees $400,000 in back-pay. Workers
claimed they were forced to work through the night and were drugged to
keep them awake. Gap, Calvin Klein and Tommy Hilfiger are among 26 US
clothing and sports firms that have agreed to create a $20 million compensa-
tion fund to settle a lawsuit by sweatshop workers for 23 garment companies
on Saipan, an island near Guam in the Pacific (Carrell, 2003: 3). Associated
political campaigns have recently acquired a heightened visibility, notably
including an ongoing series of anti-globalisation protests (N. Klein, 2000;
Monbiot, 2003). There have been significant demonstrations at the meetings

of the World Trade Organization (WTO), a coalition of nations dedicated to promoting 'free' trade, notably in Seattle in 1999 and then at subsequent meetings, and these have contributed to further protests and demonstrations.

Following this initial demonstration, over a thousand non-governmental organisations (NGOs) formed a coalition criticising the activities of multi-national companies and calling for an end to the WTO's programme to cut trade tariffs and open up markets. Their protests are a response to the developing global regime of property rights, which supports the logic of flows in which brands move. It is suggested that the WTO is unfairly dominated by a few nations and represents the interest of big corporations and that its disputes system allows for devastating sanctions if trade rules are broken (Monbiot, 2003). For example, the United States and other wealthy countries have used the GATT (General Agreement on Tariffs and Trade) negotiations to try to link trading agreements with the extent to which other countries control counterfeiting and enforce intellectual property rights. The World Intellectual Property Organization (WIPO), part of the United Nations, is active in strengthening intellectual property laws around the world and ensuring that they are enforced; and the European Union, as described on p. 110, has established a new trademark system to embrace the whole of the EU. It is also suggested that the WTO undermines international agreements on the environment and undercuts the sovereignty of countries on issues as diverse as food safety and labour standards.

Perhaps one of the most famous political assaults on brands in the United Kingdom is McLibel. This is the name given to a long-running protest, trial and publicity campaign concerning McDonald's beginning in the mid-1980s. Details of this story are to be found on the Internet; indeed, a noteworthy aspect of this demonstration − which describes itself as a campaign for environmental and social justice issues − is that it led to the construction of a Web site in 1996: www.McSpotlight.org. This site (constructed by the McInformation Network, a network of volunteers working from 16 countries) describes itself as 'the biggest, loudest, most red, most read Anti-McDonald's extravaganza the world has ever seen', although it also aims to provide information about other multinational corporations as well.

A number of points may be made in relation to this and other anti-brand campaigns. First, there is a clear recognition that it is the brand's visibility that makes it especially vulnerable to objection (so, for example, the McSpotlight site claims, 'McDonald's were chosen [as a symbol] because . . . everyone's heard of them'). Second, it is apparent that the distribution of different kinds of information plays a key role in the organisation (or dis-assembly and re-assembly) of the brand. Information is vital not only to protests against corporate activities − the McSpotlight campaign further explains its decision to focus on McDonald's on the grounds that 'there's stacks of in-depth information available about them' – but also to corporate responses to such protests. Thus McDonald's itself insists that the company has been among the first in their field to provide information to their consumers. In relation to issues of food quality, for example, the company assert that they recognise 'a responsibility to help our many customers make *an informed choice* when they eat in our restaurants' (www.McDonalds.co.uk, 20 June 2004, emphasis added). In this regard, brands may be seen to make use of – and in part be constituted by – the political info-technologies of transparency, monitoring and consultation that Andrew Barry (2004) describes as characteristic of many other contemporary political objects or events. Third, it seems that the open-endedness of the brand may contribute to an indeterminate politics or a politics of indeterminacy. So, for example, the McLibel case led to a landmark legal decision in relation to the role of witnesses. At one stage of the trial, the judge had ruled that certain parts of the defence (including a section on rainforests) were to be struck out on the grounds that the witness statements gathered by the defendants did not provide sufficient evidence to support those areas. But the Court of Appeal restored all parts of the defence struck out by the judge. This was on the basis that the defendants were entitled to draw not only on their own witnesses' statements, but also on what they might reasonably expect to discover under (the then not yet completed) cross-examination of the company's witnesses and an examination of as yet unknown (to the defendants) McDonald's documents. This ruling appears to recognise the open-endedness of the potential uses of information in the constitution of the brand. Or, as the McSpotlight Web site puts it, 'the nature of [McDonald's] business means loads of contemporary issues are relevant'.

Distributed demonstrations

It is not only when consumers are (more or less) organised or (more or less) rational that they are able to be effective (or, perhaps better, that their actions have an effect) in challenging or transforming brands, however. For example, rumour has been shown to be an effective form of counterpublicity in relation to the brand, 'provoking alternative forms of authorship and new sources of authority' (Coombe, 1998: 161), and the use of logos in graffiti and other identity marks may also function in the same way. Rosemary Coombe gives a number of examples, including one in which a rumour, circulating from 1978 until the late 1980s, linked the Procter and Gamble company (the largest US corporation producing cleaning and food products) to Satanism. In these rumours, occult significance was attached to the man-in-the-moon logo used on most of its products. This corporate insignia, which originated in 1851, was said to be the mark of the devil. It was claimed that when you turned the logo to a mirror, the curlicues in the man's beard became 666, the sign of the Anti-christ. The anti-rumour campaign cost millions of dollars: Procter and Gamble hired private investigators, instituted lawsuits against rivals who were alleged to be spreading the story, and established a toll-free hotline to respond to the twelve to fifteen thousand monthly calls the company was receiving from concerned consumers. But in 1985 the company admitted defeat and removed the 134-year-old trade mark from its products, a decision described by marketers as 'a rare case of a giant company succumbing to a bizarre and untraceable rumor' (quoted in Coombe, 1998: 146). Drawing on Homi Bhabha, Coombe argues for the effectiveness of rumour in challenging the terms of the brand interface precisely because of its ability to weave stories around *the disjunctive present or the not-there of distributed production*. She argues that the power of rumor is precisely that it is elusive and transitive, anony-mous and without origin: 'Traveling anonymously, without clear meaning, authority, or direction, rumors colonize the media in much the same way that commercial trademarks do, subversively undermining the benign invisibility of the trademark's corporate sponsor while maintaining the consumer's own lack of authorial voice' (ibid.: 163). Sanford Kwinter similarly describes rumour in terms of a threefold structure: propagation by means of immediate and localised interactions; the slow and gradual invasion of a territory over time; and its indeterminacy, especially with regard to its sources (2001: 126). Whereas brands belong to everyone and are possessed by someone (typically a company), rumours belong to no one and are possessed by everyone.

The effectiveness of rumour, grafitti and other kinds of distributed protests such as McLibel is in part attributable to the indeterminate objectivity of the brand (see Barry, 2003 for a discussion of ethical assemblages). One factor here – as the McSpotlight Web site illustrates – is the use of the Internet to circulate information about the timing and character of protests between dif-ferent groups and individuals in an uncertain but effective network. The circu-lation of the following email is symptomatic here:

From: "Personalize, NIKE iD" nikeid_personalize@nike.com
To: "Jonah H. Peretti" <peretti@media.mit.edu>
Subject: RE: Your NIKE iD order o16468000

Your NIKE iD order was cancelled for one or more of the following reasons:

1)   Your Personal iD contains another party's trademark or other intellectual property
2)   Your Personal iD contains the name of an athlete or team we do not have the legal right to use

3)　Your Personal iD was left blank. Did you not want any personalization?

4)　Your Personal iD contains profanity or inappropriate slang, and besides, your mother would slap us.

If you wish to reorder your NIKE iD product with a new personalization please visit us again at www.nike.com

Thank you, NIKE iD

From: "Jonah H. Peretti" <peretti@media.mit.edu>
To: "Personalize, NIKE iD" nikeid_personalize@nike.com
Subject: RE: Your NIKE iD order o16468000

Greetings,

My order was canceled but my personal NIKE iD does not violate any of the criteria outlined in your message. The Personal iD on my custom ZOOM XC USA running shoes was the word "sweatshop".

Sweatshop is not:
1.　another party's trademark,
2.　the name of an athlete,
3.　blank, or
4.　profanity.

I chose the iD because I wanted to remember the toil and labor of the children that made my shoes. Could you please ship them to me immediately.

Thanks and Happy New Year, Jonah Peretti

From: "Personalize, NIKE iD" nikeid_personalize@nike.com
To: "Jonah H. Peretti" <peretti@media.mit.edu>
Subject: RE: Your NIKE iD order o16468000

Dear NIKE iD Customer,

Your NIKE iD order was cancelled because the iD you have chosen contains, as stated in the previous e-mail correspondence, "inappropriate slang". If you wish to reorder your NIKE iD product with a new personalization please visit us again at nike.com

Thank you, NIKE iD

From: "Jonah H. Peretti" <peretti@media.mit.edu>
To: "Personalize, NIKE iD" nikeid_personalize@nike.com

Subject: RE: Your NIKE iD order o16468000

Dear NIKE iD,

Thank you for your quick response to my inquiry about my custom ZOOM XC USA running shoes. Although I commend you for your prompt customer service, I disagree with the claim that my personal iD was inappropriate slang. After consulting Webster's Dictionary, I discovered that "sweatshop" is in fact part of standard English, and not slang.

The word means: "a shop or factory in which workers are employed for long hours at low wages and under unhealthy conditions" and its origin dates from 1892. So my personal iD does meet the criteria detailed in your first email.

Your web site advertises that the NIKE iD program is "about freedom to choose and freedom to express who you are." I share Nike's love of freedom and personal expression. The site also says that "If you want it done right . . . build it yourself." I was thrilled to be able to build my own shoes, and my personal iD was offered as a small token of appreciation for the sweatshop workers poised to help me realize my vision. I hope that you will value my freedom of expression and reconsider your decision to reject my order.

Thank you, Jonah Peretti

From: "Personalize, NIKE iD" nikeid_personalize@nike.com
To: "Jonah H. Peretti" <peretti@media.mit.edu>
Subject: RE: Your NIKE iD order o16468000

Dear NIKE iD Customer,

Regarding the rules for personalization it also states on the NIKE iD web site that "Nike reserves the right to cancel any personal iD up to 24 hours after it has been submitted". In addition, it further explains: "While we honor most personal iDs, we cannot honor every one. Some may be (or contain) other's trademarks, or the names of certain professional sports teams, athletes or celebrities that Nike does not have the right to use. Others may contain material that we consider inappropriate or simply do not want to place on our products. Unfortunately, at times this obliges us to decline personal iDs that may otherwise seem unobjectionable. In any event, we will let you know if we decline your personal iD, and we will offer you the chance to submit another." With these rules in mind, we cannot accept your order as submitted. If you wish to reorder your NIKE iD product with a new personalization please visit us again at www.nike.com

Thank you, NIKE iD

From: "Jonah H. Peretti" <peretti@media.mit.edu>
To: "Personalize, NIKE iD" nikeid_personalize@nike.com
Subject: RE: Your NIKE iD order o16468000

Dear NIKE iD,

Thank you for the time and energy you have spent on my request. I have decided to order the shoes with a different iD, but I would like to make one small request. Could you please send me a color snapshot of the ten-year-old Vietnamese girl who makes my shoes?

Thanks,
Jonah Peretti

<no response>

As one forwarder writes:

. . . this will now go round the world much farther and faster than any of the adverts they paid Michael Jordan more than the entire wage packet of all their sweatshop workers in the world to do. . .

I normally avoid making a plea to pass on these things, but this time I say: JUST DO IT

The character of distributed demonstrations can be understood in relation to the difference between strategies and tactics (de Certeau, 1998; Kwinter, 2001). Strategy proceeds by projecting, fixing and consolidating; it describes in order to oppose; it comprises distinct things and 'proper' places, 'proper' names. Tactics, on the other hand, do not have a proper place, but rely upon emergence, eruptions, changes, to produce adversarial effects within the domain of power, yet without actually opposing or confronting it as such. They proceed not by global oppositions but by local interventions; by describing what should be as well as what is; they are provocations, interventions in the margins of indeterminacy. As Kwinter puts it, 'Tactics are never autonomous but always contingent. It depends on the very conditions – power – that it both lacks and seeks to subvert' (2001: 123). They function so as to produce an assembly, a combinatorial process, or perhaps, more acutely, a form of 'free indirect speech' (ibid.: 126), of passing things on and off. They are concerned with establishing a new scale of thresholds and effects, with the production of socially responsive and responsible objects.

And in considering tactics, it may be useful to consider what Agnes Heller identifies as everyday thinking ([1970] 1984) as part of which she describes as a number of general 'schemes of conduct and knowledge'. According to Heller, these include pragmatism, probability, imitation, analogy, over-generalisation and 'the rough treatment of the singular case' (ibid.: 165–182). Such everyday schemes of knowledge may be contrasted with the schemes of knowledge involved in the design of the brand. So, for example, Heller argues that 'everything we do on the level of everyday life is based on probability'. This everyday notion of probability is however to be distinguished both from the probabilistic (statistical) calculations that produce the brand, and from the 'possible'. On the one hand, the 'objective basis of action based on probability is provided by habit and repetition' (ibid.: 168); it can 'extend from action based on nothing more than impulse, to action based on moral reflection or on calculation', or indeed, to action based on 'belief' (ibid.: 170). On the other, for Heller, 'Action undertaken for no better reason than it is *possible* is not a reliable guide in the business of everyday living: it lands us in too many catastrophes of everyday life' (ibid.: 168).

There is a recognition here of the multiple temporalities at work in everyday life. What is also important, then, is Heller's further claim that the overriding characteristic of everyday life is that it is heterogeneous, tied as it is to an assortment of partial functions that are often irrelevant or antagonistic to one another. So, for example, it is argued that the pragmatic character of everyday thought means not only that everyday thought is a preparatory step towards the realisation of some practical purpose, but also that this thought process does not easily become detached from the task to be performed. This is because it is meaningful in relation to the proposed aim and to nothing else. Hence, for Heller, everyday knowledge remains an embedded, heterogeneous amalgam, and cannot ultimately be incorporated.

This heterogeneity does not, of course, exclude the possibility of more or less coherent or planned spheres of action in everyday life: rather, it is their precondition. Significantly, Heller describes such possibilities in terms of a process of 'emergence', the creation and re-creation of 'the generic', by which she means activity that is a part of general human praxis. One way of developing this recognition in legal thought is provided by Rochelle Dreyfuss's suggestion that if the use of a mark is the most economical way to refer to a set of connotations, it should be permitted as an example of 'generic expressivity' (1990, cited by Coombe, 1998). In this formulation, Dreyfuss seeks to secure legal recognition of the radical heterogeneity of categories of objects in use. She aims to provide a mechanism by which the multiplicity of things in use may be recognised and the present limited legal recognition of consumer activity opened up to the diverse probabilities of everyday life. Whether and how the potential of everyday life thinking to increase the possibilities of action may be recognised and elaborated is, however, still an open question.

One implication of the argument developed here, however, is that it is inappropriate to try to specify what it is to be human without reference to the inhuman. It is unrealistic to identify the everyday as a pure and unified principle of (social) life, of inexhaustible vitality, with ineradicable capacities for resistance and renewal, underpinning everything else. Such an assumption is not of course necessarily integral to the advocacy of the everyday, the ordinary or the generic (or even of the cultural) as a site of radical transformation. But perhaps such an advocacy needs to be strengthened by an explicit affirmation of their relation to a complex heterogeneity of subjects and objects. So, for example, in place of the Minotaur of everyday life, which he considers an abstract kind of monster, Steven Crook (1998) proposes a more monstrous, because a more heterogeneous, analysis of social life. This would involve a concern not simply with human practices, but with humans, artefacts and non-humans, with what Knorr Cetina describes as a post-social world.

Coda

A key issue in debates on interactivity – across different sites of information technology – is whether it is a process that can shift the framework that began the exchange between the parties in the first place (Morse, 1996; Mackenzie, 2002). And in this respect, what is important to remember about the brand is that it is not simply a machine for the production and consumption of information; it retains a margin of indeterminacy. It is a transducer of information where transduction is 'a process whereby a disparity or difference is topologically and temporally restructured across some interface. [Transduction] mediates different organizations of energy' (Mackenzie, 2002: 25). Or to put this the other way around, information supplies determination to the brand; it informs the brand or 'imparts a form to it, or at least that part of it that remains open to determination' (ibid.: 26).[5] However, while this implies that the organisation of the mediation of supply and demand as interactivity may function to produce the brand as either (more or less) closed or (more or less) open in principle, it remains the case that the brand is more often closed than open in practice.

7   The objectivity of the brand

Interactivity and the limits of rationality

> For the thing we are looking for is not a human thing, nor is it an inhuman thing. It offers, rather, a continuous passage, a commerce, an interchange, between what humans inscribe in it and what it prescribes to humans. It translates the one into the other. This thing is the nonhuman version of people, it is the human version of things, twice displaced. What should it be called? Neither object nor subject. An instituted object, quasi-object, quasi-subject, a thing that possesses body and soul indissociably.
>
> (Latour, 1996)

Introduction

Sociologists have not normally concerned themselves with objects – except in the Durkheimian sense that social facts be treated as such. Material culture was for a long time left mainly to anthropologists; physical artefacts were typically treated as part of that domain of anthropology that merges with archaeology and ethnology. But the agenda has shifted in recent years, particularly as studies of popular culture, design and consumer culture have come to the fore (for example, Forty, 1986; Norman, 1988; Hebdige, 1988; Miller, 1997; Featherstone, 1991; du Gay *et al.*, 1997; Dant, 1999; Attfield, 2000; Molotch, 2003). There has, moreover, been considerable interest in the materiality of culture and its mediation in the culture industries (Adorno and Horkheimer, 1982; Adorno, 1991; Appadurai, 1986, 1996; Kopytoff, 1986; Thomas, 1991; Lury, 1993; Lash and Urry, 1994, forthcoming; McRobbie, 1998, 1999; Poster, 2001; Manovich, 2001; Lash, 2002). Alongside this, there is a renewed interest in materialism, especially in Italian political thought (Hardt and Negri, 2000). Perhaps most insistently, however, there have been writings within the sociology of science and technology and elsewhere which problematise the roles of objects, quasi-objects, factishes and hybrids (Latour and Woolgar, 1986; Latour, 1987; Knorr Cetina, 1997,

2000; Law, 1984, 2002; Feenberg, 1991, 1999; Michael, 2000; Barry, 2001). In addition, a number of feminist theorists have sought to address the question of ontological politics through a reconsideration of matter in science and technology (Haraway, 1997, 2000; Mol, 1999, 2002; Kerin, 1999; Wilson, 1998; Vitellone, 2003a, b; Fraser, 2002, 2003). These developments can be seen in the context of a move within contemporary sociology to reconsider the social in such a way as to include the natural and the artificial or techno-logical (Urry, 2000). And the aim here – as part of what might be called a sociology of objects or things (Frow, 2001; Slater, 2002a, b) – is also to open up the domain of the social, to move beyond discussions of the social exclus-ively in terms of the (human) subject. Thus, this book started from the premise that objects matter; that they orient communication, frame time and space, and co-ordinate social action (Goffman, 1961, 1971; Appadurai, 1986; Miller, 1987; Latour, 1996; Knorr Cetina, 2000); in short, that objects (co-)produce the social.

The approach adopted has been to identify some of the distinctive features of contemporary objectivity by focusing on one of the objects – the brand – by which economic activity is currently produced. In this respect, the book has argued that the brand is an object of an informational economy (Castells, 1996; Barry, 2001; Lash, 2002; Mackenzie, 2002). This argument derives from the view that contemporary knowledge processes are heavily centred on objects, and that such objects have specifically designed properties that may be investigated (although they are not fully determined at the moment of design). As Karin Knorr Cetina puts it,

> A knowledge society is not simply a society of more experts, of techno-logical infra- and information structures, and of specialist rather than par-ticipant interpretations. It means that knowledge cultures have spilled and woven their tissue into society, the whole set of processes, experiences and relationships that wait on knowledge and unfold with its articulation. This 'dehiscence' of knowledge, the discharge of knowledge relations into society, is what needs to be rendered as a problem to be solved in a soci-ological (rather than economic) account of knowledge societies. . . . We need to trace the ways in which knowledge has become constitutive of social relations.
>
> (1997: 9–10)

The presumption has been that the object of the brand is defined by know-ledge practices: those it partakes of and those that take place within it (Kwinter, 2001: 14). These knowledge practices are not confined to labora-tories, studios or even to business schools (Latour and Woolgar, 1986;

Alpers, 1998; Thrift, forthcoming); rather, they are constitutive of social relations. They extend into – or rather they implicate – the everyday world. Rather than seeing the object of the brand as fixed, closed or inert, the aim has been to see it as 'a procedure, a recipe, and [as] coextensive with a course of [inter]action' (Latour, 1996: 83). So, the brand has been described here in terms of processes of objectification, such as, for example, the design and promotion of object-ives, the staging of product qualification trials (of standardisation and differentiation) and the adjudication and evaluation of object-ivity or object effects (Callon, 1998b, 1999; Callon *et al.*, 2002). But the book has also described the brand as an object that is potentially open, indeterminate and never identical with itself. It is these potential characteristics that make of the brand a compelling object of sociological concern.

The book has argued that the brand is an object not simply of knowledge but of information. As Andrew Barry argues, information is not simply raw scientific data; it is linked to practices of government and self-government; it has regulatory effects. 'Its existence is thought to imply a transformation in the conduct of those who are, or who should be, informed. . . . It is a moral as well as a technical concept' (Barry, 2001: 153). The focus has been on the brand as an object of information in this double sense: it is an object that is both *constituted in* and *constitutive of* information. It is both a response to the embedding of the logics of information in the economy and a diagram of production of further information for the economy. Barry describes the implicatedness of information in objects such as the brand very well; he writes:

> [I]nformation cannot be understood either as a realistic representation of an external world, nor merely as a social construction. It is more than just a social construction because the object which is represented plays its part in the production of information. . . . At the same time, scientific information is both more and less than a realistic representation of the world, because to produce information demands a practical and technical intervention in the world which necessarily abstracts the object from the complexity of its environment. In this view, information can be true in the sense it can be accurate, but it cannot be True, if by Truth we mean a representation of an essence which exists independently of a more or less standardised and socially sanctioned set of practices of measurement and experiment. The production of scientific information does not mirror the world as it is, but forges something new, with more or less inventive consequences. It multiples realities.
>
> (ibid.: 154–155)

What has been at issue in this book is the increasing role of embedded logics of information in the organisation of the economy (Thrift, 1998), and the ways in which the embedding of these logics provides a new set of conditions in which object-ivity trials may be conducted. The aim has been to describe some of these trials, to consider their object-ive effects – that is, to consider their ability to object-ify (and subject-ify). Following this, the approach adopted here is that the brand is not a construction invented in an effort to describe reality. Instead, the argument is that brands are objects that multiply realities, with 'more or less inventive consequences'. They are objects that are

> progressively enforced by the joint movement of the economy and eco-
> nomics . . . [they are objects that] perform behaviours and therefore have
> the obduracy of the real; yet in turn [these objects] are performed by
> these behaviours and therefore have the contingency of an artefact.
>
> (Callon, 1998b: 46–47)

An object of the artificial sciences

The case for the artefactualism of the brand (Franklin *et al.*, 2000) has been developed in this book by arguing that the brand is an object of the artificial sciences (Simon, [1969] 1981), in this case the sciences of economics, market-ing and design. From this perspective, one of the most significant character-istics of the brand is that it is an object that is designed so that it may be otherwise; that is, that it may be quite other – in particular ways – than it is. As Mark Poster describes the Internet, while the brand 'is a machine, a thing in the world, an object extended in space, it is nonetheless underdetermined' (2001: 13).[1] The 'is' of the brand is also its 'may-be'; in its being – its objec-tivity – it has the potential to be otherwise, to become. Or, as it has been described earlier, the brand is an example of transitivity, of the introduction of possibility into the thing (Massumi, 2002). Such an object does not tend towards full determination or closure; rather, it exists in a state of in-determination, a situation of (un)control. This is what makes it an increasingly important object-ive of contemporary capitalism. But to describe the brand as an object into which possibility has been introduced is not to imply that the brand is, or even may be, any-thing. The indeterminacy of the objectivity of the brand is not absolute; uncontrol is not the same as lack of control. There is instead limited possibility designed into the brand; or, as Callon would put it, the brand is a 'kind of lock-in'. That is, the brand is not an unfortunately dete-riorated objectification of perfect flexibility, but rather the objectification of a manageable flexibility, of indeterminacy within limits.

> Once organized and hence locked-in, the market becomes calculable by the agents. Once the work of standardization (at least partial) of calculating tools is well on its way, each agency is in a position not only to calculate her decision but also, by construction, to include, at least partially, in her calculations the calculations of the other agencies.
>
> (Callon, 1998b: 50)

Or, as Herbert Simon might put it, the brand as artefact is of the order of a 'necessity that rises above the contingencies'.

Simon argues that the necessities of an artefact stem from 'the inabilities of the behavioural system to adapt perfectly to its environment'. They are a consequence of what he calls 'the limits of rationality' ([1969] 1981: x). This influential formulation has sometimes been taken to imply that such limits may and should be overcome. And much contemporary economics is concerned with pushing back the limits of rationality in the economy – that is, with extending the reach of rationality and multiplying its calculations, with increasing flexibility, speeding things up, and making more and more elements of the production process the object of calculation. For example, several branches of applied economics, including operations research and organisations theory, assist companies to achieve an ever-greater (procedural) rationality. Operations research provides algorithms for handling difficult multivariate decision problems, sometimes involving uncertainty. The simplex method for linear programming, queuing theory and linear decision rules for inventory control and production are important algorithms of this kind. Similarly, recent developments in management accounting make use of a wide range of non-financial measures, including set-up times, inventory levels, defect and rework rates, material and product velocity, to make the future predictable. Accounting tools have also been developed to frame market time by allowing for calculations of equivalence between events occurring at different dates (Callon, 1998b; Miller, 1998). These and numerous other procedures are widely used in business decision-making today as part of an economic performance measurement industry (Meyer, 1994; Thrift, 2000). As Callon says,

> the tools are constantly reconfigured to take into account in more and more detail a set of entities and relationships which were hitherto excluded from the framework of calculation. The framing becomes more refined, richer, delving into the complexity of relationships, and in so doing it authorizes decisions which are more and more calculated or (to use the commonly-accepted word) more and more rational.
>
> (1998b: 24)

But uncertainty, complexity and (in)operationality continue to limit the application, usefulness and efficacy of the frames of operations research techniques and rational procedures. They continue to limit the joint movement of economics and the economy. In this context, the brand affords an alternative response to the limits or boundedness of rationality, one that does not seek to go beyond, overcome or remove limits, but rather reconfigures the very notion of a limit. In doing so, it re-introduces value into economic rationality or calculation. Or to put this another way, the brand offers the potential for the economy to be managed as an open rather than as a closed system (Kwinter, 1998; De Landa, 1996).[2]

This potential openness may – in the light of the reliance of the brand on information – be understood in terms of information theory.[3] On the one hand, the brand may be organised so as to respond to its environment in ways determined by its self-organisation. In this regard, the brand is not merely self-organising but autopoietic, or self-making. In such cases, however, the brand is informationally closed (it is bound by the limits of rationality); the brand is not open to its environment. Instead, the environment merely triggers changes determined by the brand's own structural properties, as implemented through reproducible techniques. In these situations, the brand is a more or less closed object. The brand is produced in the mutually constitutive interactions between its components rather than in communication with its environment or context. But on the other hand, the self-organisation of the brand may sometimes happen in such a way that it does not merely function to reproduce itself, but is able to be informed by its environment and produce (itself as) something different, something in differentiation. In such cases, the brand may be said to be more or less open to its environment, although the information fed back (or fed forward) into production does not have direct or straightforwardly predictable effects. What is suggested here is that in these cases the brand involves a modification of understandings of limits and inside–outside relationships. In these situations, the brand contributes to 'the disappearance of the outside, and of outsideness, as part of new spatializations and iconographies of social interaction' (Shields, 2003: 49). It may thus be seen as an example of the building up of capital through the occupation of what Massumi calls the 'inside limit of the relational' (2002: 88); as such, the brand is an example of 'the powering-up – or powering-away – of potential'. It is an object of both *pouvoir* and *puissance*.

An object of the interface

In respect of this potential, the notion of the interface (Chapter 3) is central to the argument proposed in this book. So let me try to describe its functioning one more time, this time via the account of economics as a performative discipline provided by Michel Callon (1998b). In this rich description, Callon develops a case for the importance of the process of framing (and its counterpart, overflowing) to the joint performance of economics and the economy. Adapting the term 'the frame' from the work of micro-sociologist Erving Goffman (1961, 1971) and applying it in the field of economics and the economy, Callon writes:

> Framing is an operation used to define agents (an individual person or a group of persons) who are clearly distinct and dissociated from one another. It also allows for the definition of objects, goods and merchandise which are perfectly identifiable and can be separated not only from other goods, but also from the actors involved, for example in their conception, production, circulation or use. It is owing to this framing that the market can exist and that distinct agents and distinct goods can be brought into play. Without this framing the states of the world can not be described and listed, and consequently, the effects of the different conceivable actions can not be anticipated.
>
> (1998b: 17)

As this suggests, framing is important to Callon in that it enables the economy (and society) to be seen as a social network, or, as Callon prefers to describe it, an agency-network. But the activity of economic framing also has (at least) three specific effects for him, namely, the disentangling of goods, the creation of calculative agencies, and the identification of externalities, all of which are integral to the production of a market economy. The term 'frame' certainly has an advantage over that of 'limit' in that it enables the separation of the inside and outside of something (such as the economy) to be seen less as a fixed boundary and more as an operation, a process or technique of partitioning, bracketing or reducing. But it has been argued here that what produces the brand as an artefact (or what produces the particular abstract object-ivity or artefactuality of the brand) is the functioning of a particular kind of interactional frame, namely the frame as interface. In exploring the significance of this claim, the understandings of the frame developed in studies of the media have been adapted and applied to the brand, an artefact of the economy.

The organisation of the brand in terms of an interface between two worlds – the world of its own internal requirements and the world in which it is inside – has implications for all three frame effects described by Callon. Consider first how Callon describes the importance of marketing in the process by which framing may be done. He takes the example of the marketing mix (Chapter 2), suggesting that the implementation of this concept 'substitutes a quadruple reality – the fundamental 4Ps – for a product considered as an indivisible entity'. As he puts it, 'a product is a Price, it is the object of a Promotion, it is a Place where it is available and, lastly, it is the target of a Product strategy' (1998b: 26). He continues:

> The product is thus a multidimensional reality, an entanglement of properties that the marketing mix disentangles. The [marketing mix] thus facilitates a more detailed analysis of buying decisions, as well as the preferences which they express or reveal. The seller, instead of settling for a rough calculation, has an instrument which enables him, by varying each of the four dimensions, to distinguish in detail all the relations involved and to calculate each one independently. The framing of decisions proves to be greatly enhanced, as it is by the use of econometrics mobilized by marketing management. The latter makes it possible to construct sub-populations of consumers and to link them to certain characteristics of products.
>
> (1998b: 28–29)

This analysis draws attention to the information-intensive relationality of the product, the ways in which relations of marketing knowledge extend into and beyond the product, and the ways in which the product is made manipulable or manageable as a multi-dimensional reality through the introduction of (marketing) information. But a crucial dynamic of the framing of the market is missed if the focus is only on how the attributes of a particular product or service are disentangled and multiplied. This book has argued that it is the management of *relations between (multi-dimensional) products* that has come to constitute a new abstract object or artefact, the brand. In particular, it was argued that the organisation, co-ordination and integration of probabilistic, global and transductive relations between products are what comprise the brand. In this approach, the management of the brand *as a set of relations between products* simultaneously enables the differentiation and disentanglement of specific products or services (for exchange) and sustains the emergent objectivity of the integrated brand as a dynamic yet indivisible entity.

Second, Callon argues that it is the management of the interval in time between giving and counter-giving that is the basis of a differentiation of calculative agencies in terms of interestedness and disinterestedness. As he puts it,

> The emergence of a calculative agency, says Bourdieu, depends on a time frame. Either the return gift is in the frame, and the agency is calculative, or it is beyond the frame and she is not. In the first instance the decision takes into account the return gift, in the second, it ignores it. This taking

into account depends only on the framing, the tracing of a boundary between relationships and events which are internalized and included in a decision or, by contrast, externalized and excluded from it. . . . Framing demarcates in regards to the network of relationships, those which are taken into account and those which are ignored.

(1998b: 14)

What has been argued here, though, is that the brand is an organisation of relations between products that holds open, intervenes in or configures the interval in time between giving and counter-giving, what was described as the response time of interactivity. This co-ordination of the response interval is a consequence of the indeterminacy of the brand – its ability to be informed by constructions of the consumer. It is what enables the brand not simply to *mark* time, but also to *make* time as flow (as, for example, the logics of consistency or sameness, fashion, collection and event described in Chapter 3). This organisation of the logic of flows is made visible in the personalisation or facialisation of the logo (Chapter 4).

Third, Callon notes that the work of framing is never done; that when, after having identified some externalities, the agents decide to reframe them, to internalise the externalities, other externalities appear. In short, there are always relations that defy framing, and framing is impossible to take to conclusion. It has been argued here that in the case of the brand, the functioning of techniques of feedback and feed-forward is such that the presumed (neo-classical) unity of time and place of the market is suspended and disrupted. Indeed, the market is to be understood not as a series of interactions, but in terms of interactivity. As a set of relations between products, a meta-temporal entity, the brand is able to incorporate the internalisation of what might have been (so, for example, previously unconsidered constructions of consumers and their preferences may be retrospectively internalised) and of what may yet be (as yet unknown preferences are anticipated). In other words, marketing is not simply an add-on to a (linear) process of production, but rather, radically reconfigures its temporality, contributing to the emergence of a non-linear process of production. The focus here was not so much on the role of marketing in the iterative co-ordination of relations between the production process and its environment. Rather, it was on the production of an object that is 'the systematic stock-piling for future use of the possible actions relating to a thing, systematically thought-out on the general level of abstraction' (Massumi, 2002: 94). It was argued that what is significant is both that the abstraction of the brand functions as a storehouse of action and that what is stored for future use is mere may-be or possible object effects. To sum up, it is the dynamic framing of the market in terms of an interface that performs the brand as a very specific kind of object: an abstract, dynamic and indeterminate object, what has been called here a complex object.

An object of mediation

One way in which the indeterminate objectivity of the brand is produced is through the role of marketing in the organisation of what was called distributed or consuming production (Chapter 2). It was argued that the brand emerges from attempts to address and manage precisely those aspects of relations between buyers and sellers that are not governed by price through the use of information about the consumer in processes of product differentiation. This is understood by marketers in terms of a management of brands through the appropriation of consumer engagement, sense of purpose or experience in product development (Mitchell, 2001; Grant, 1999; Pine and Gilmore, 1999). One implication of this looping activity is that the brand is 'neither altogether a cause nor altogether a consequence, not completely a means nor completely an end' (Latour, 1996) – that is, the brand is an object of mediation. This is another way of putting the argument that the brand is a new media object (Manovich, 2001; and see Chapter 1).

Let me illustrate the significance of the notion of medium by once again comparing the brand with money in establishing the substitutability of products (or services). Consider this statement of the limits of rationality by neoclassical economist Friedrich von Hayek in his essay 'The use of knowledge in society' (1945). He begins by asking, 'What is the problem we wish to solve when we try to construct a rational economic order?' and continues:

> On certain familiar assumptions the answer is simple enough. *If* we possess all the relevant information, *if* we can start out from a given system of preferences, and *if* we command complete knowledge of available means, the problem which remains is purely one of logic . . . the marginal rates of substitution between any two commodities or factors must be the same in all their different uses.

But he insists that this is 'emphatically *not* the economic problem which society faces'; this is because

> the 'data' from which the economic calculus starts are never for the whole society 'given' to a single mind which could work out the implications, and *can never be so given*.
>   . . . the knowledge of the circumstances of which we must make use never exists in concentrated or integrated form, but solely as the dispersed

bits of incomplete and frequently contradictory knowledge which all the separate individuals possess. The economic problem of society is thus not merely a problem of how to allocate 'given' resources – if 'given' is taken to mean given to a single mind which deliberately solves the problem set by these 'data'. It is rather a problem of how to secure the best use of resources known to any of the members of society, for ends of relative importance only these individuals know. Or, to put it briefly, it is a problem of utilization of knowledge not given to anyone in its totality.

(1945: 526–527; emphasis added)

Given what he describes as the unavoidable limits of rationality (the impossibility of any 'single mind' ever acquiring total knowledge), he advocates price as the best mechanism for establishing the substitutability of products. That is, he advocates price as the best mechanism or means for establishing the market equivalence between products in a dynamic situation in which knowledge is distributed, and can ever be given to anyone in its totality. This is because price is a message that reduces and localises informational requirements. The brand, it has been argued here, is an alternative solution to this problem; it too is a mechanism for communicating information, but it provides an alternative calculus to price by which the substitutability of products may be established. It is not a means or transparent mechanism (although see pp. 161–163 for a discussion of changing understandings of transparency): rather, it is a medium: that is, it can register – even anticipate – change through the opening it offers onto qualitative differentiation.

The argument has been that it is in relation to the medium of the brand that the qualification–requalification trials of product standardisation and differentiation are increasingly conducted. The qualification trials of marketing, for example, model the production of qualities as the actual presentations of lived relations (Massumi, 2002: 221) in probabilistic, global and transductive relations between 'producers' and 'consumers'. As a consequence, the quantitative equivalence or substitutability of products that is established through the operation of price as an economic calculus, or currency, is supplemented by the qualitative differentiations of the brand. It is able to act as an alternative social currency for the adjustment of supply and demand because it translates – or better, because it transduces (Mackenzie, 2002). The brand emerges as an alternative calculus – a new media object – in what is increasingly a media economy (or an economy of mediation). It is a privileged medium of translation, both a mediation of things and a thingification of media (Lury, in press; Lash and Lury, forthcoming). It is not simply an object of the media, or simply a media processor; rather, it is a media synthesiser and media manipulator (Manovich, 2001).

As a new media object, the brand is also a potential medium of innovation. As Latour puts it, 'The idea of mediation or event enables [us] to retain the only two characteristics of action which are useful – i.e. the emergence of novelty together with the impossibility of *ex nihlio* creation' (1996). It is this capacity for innovation that is one the properties that makes the brand a key asset in the contemporary economy. However, these innovations may be anti-inventive as well as inventive (Barry, 2001). In practice, while exerting a profound influence on the social and political organisation of production, the mediation of the brand does not often extend the possibilities for action for either rival producers or consumers, but rather closes them down. On the one hand, the brand 'expresses a global ability to sense and be affected, qualitatively, for change. It injects a measure of objective uncontrol, a margin of eventfulness, a liveliness' into the processes of production (Massumi, 2002: 225), through, for example, the use of the product as marketing tool. On the other hand, it tends often only to make possibilities – mere may-bes – more anticipatable, tying object and subject together in what are often coercively predictable ways. In this sense, the brand may be seen as an object that dominates through its ability to include, and not only to exclude (Baudrillard, 1997). Moreover, while the brand has the potential to bring 'an understanding of the outside, of society, economy and customer, to the inside of the organization and to make it the foundation for strategy and policy' (Drucker, quoted in Mitchell, 2001: 77), this potential is not often realised. In practice, brands are more often closed than open. The situation remains much as it did when marketing expert Theodor Levitt called for a marketing revolution in 1960:

> When it comes to the marketing concept today, a solid stone wall often seems to separate word and deed. In spite of the best intentions and energetic efforts of many highly able people, the effective implementation of the marketing concept has generally eluded them.
>
> (Quoted in Mitchell, 2001: 77)

In other words, many brands do not operate as interfaces; instead, they function like a wall or shield, insulating the production process from its environment. Furthermore, the brand has a further potential disadvantage: it – and its capacity for innovation – may be the object of exclusive property claims (see Chapter 5). As protected by the law of trade mark, the brand is both a medium of innovation (both inventive and anti-inventive) and a pre-emptive barrier (a limit) against innovation by others. Indeed, it is because of the potential that it offers for the establishment of monopolies that Hayek (while advocating the use of multiple currencies) did not approve of the development of brands.

An object of interactivity

Like Goffman and Callon, Bruno Latour (1996) considers the activity of framing to be integral to social life. However, he suggests that the frame is the device whereby complex sociality is made merely complicated. In drawing a comparison between primate and human sociality, he makes a distinction between the complex and the complicated:

> 'Complex' will signify the simultaneous presence in all interactions of a great number of variables, which cannot be treated discretely. 'Complicated' will mean the successive presence of discrete variables, which can be treated one by one, and folded into one another in the form of a black box.

In regard to primate sociality, he suggests that each actor's every action is interfered with by others. And since succeeding in one's aims is mediated by continual negotiation, this can be described in terms of complexity – that is to say, in terms of the obligation to take into account a large number of variables at the same time. This, he suggests, describes primate sociality that occurs in the progressive composition of dyadic interactions, without any totalising or structurating effects. He writes:

> Each action is mediated by the action of partners, but to effect this mediation, it is necessary that every actor composes for themselves the totality in which they are situated – a variable totality whose solidity must be reverified each and every time through new trails. . . . Complex social life becomes the shared property of all primates.

But whereas for monkeys, interaction constructs social life step by step, for humans it is, says Latour, never more than a residual category. This is because for an interaction to take place, one must first reduce the relationship so that it does not mobilise all social life – with which it would otherwise end up being co-extensive.[4] This is to make a claim that in order to grasp interaction, 'we need to be able to timeshift, dislocate, make lopsided and delegate the present interaction, so as to make it rest provisionally on something else, while waiting to take it up again':

> It is only through isolating it by a frame that the agent can interact with another agent, face to face, leaving out the rest of their history as well as their other partners. The very existence of an interaction presupposes a reduction, a prior partitioning.

What prevents human interaction from proliferating outside and from being interfered with inside by all the other partners is the frame, which Latour variously describes as a two-way membrane, an operator of reduction, a set of partitions, umbrellas or fire-breaks. All of these devices permit passage from a situation that is complex to one that is merely complicated. But as Latour also acknowledges, while neither individual action nor structure is thinkable without the work of rendering local, nor are they possible without the work of making global. And it is in respect to both sets of processes – localising and globalising – that objects make human interaction possible: 'Neither individual action nor structure are thinkable without the work of rendering local – through channeling, partition, focussing, reduction – and without the work of rendering global – through instrumentation, compilation, punctualization, amplification.' The significance of objects for Latour, then, is that they make possible a move from a complex social life to a complicated one. Yet the brand as it has been described in this book is precisely an object that enables a complex human sociality – that is, it is an object that makes possible human interaction in which a large number of variables are taken into account at the same time. While the brand is, as Latour would say, a black box (in which the object is defined by its input and output functions alone), it is a black box with a screen or an interface. Alternatively put, the suggestion is that the brand is an instance of 'managed complexity', rather than the 'enforced complexity' of primate social life (Manzini, 1989), and perhaps this is only another way of talking about what Knorr Cetina describes as the post-social.

Indeed, the implication of the argument presented here is that the effects of the interface of the black box of the brand need to be considered carefully. In her ethnographic study of the use of computers, *Life on the Screen*, Sherry Turkle describes the interactivity afforded by the computer interface in terms of a changed understanding of *transparency*. This changed understanding is associated by Turkle with the use of the Macintosh's iconic computer interface in particular, but is also, so she argues, 'part of a larger cultural shift' (1996: 42). It is a transparency in which a system, rather than encouraging its users to 'look beyond the magic to the mechanism', as was true of the early IBM PCs, tells its users 'to stay on the surface'. She writes:

In a culture of simulation, when people say that something is transparent, they mean that they can easily see *how* to make it work. They don't necessarily mean that they know *why* it is working in terms of any underlying process.

(ibid.: 42; emphasis added)

The iconic style of the Macintosh, she argues, does 'nothing to suggest how [its] underlying structure could be known'; instead, it is 'visible only through its effects' (ibid.: 23). In place of the assumption that 'an object is transparent if it lets the way it works be seen through its physical structure' (ibid.: 79), this transparency is 'somewhat paradoxically . . . enabled by complexity and opacity' (ibid.: 42). The ethical and political implications of this shift are ambivalent (see, for example, Brown and Michael, 2002). On the one hand, this new understanding of transparency may encourage an acceptance of opacity and lead to a willingness to abdicate authority; on the other hand, it can 'confront us with the dependency on opaque simulations we accept in the real world' (Turkle, 1996: 71). This confrontation can feed into either 'simu-lation resignation' or 'simulation denial'. Both kinds of responses are only too understandable in relation to brands when 'companies adopt corporate codes of conduct that seem to be much more to do with protecting corporate repu-tations and attracting customers and better recruits than they are to do with the pay and conditions of workers' (Royle, 2000: 9).[5] But Turkle believes that the new notion of transparency she identifies can also pose a challenge 'to develop a more sophisticated social criticism' (1996: 71).

The suggestion outlined here is that a key concern in the development of any such 'sophisticated' criticism must be whether it is possible to shift the framework that organises the exchange between the parties (Morse, 1998; Mackenzie, 2002). In this respect, it is important to remember that the brand is not simply a machine for the production or consumption of information; it retains margins of indeterminacy, and the activities of consumers can extend these margins (see Chapter 6). In this respect, the extension of the scope of witnessing in law brought about by the McLibel case, the introduction of the use of the precautionary principle in government regulation of standards and the proposal for legal support for trade marks as marks of generic expressivity are all significant. However, while organised interactivity may transform the object of the brand, the extent of that transformation is in practice severely limited. This is because any transformation is dependent not only on the degree to which the processes that organise the brand have a capacity to main-tain a margin of indeterminacy, but also on the willingness of those involved in organising that capacity to act upon the information they receive. This willing-ness is currently severely limited, and as a consequence the brand is more often closed than open. The law contributes to the closed objectivity of the brand by regulating the use of the sign that is protected as a trade mark and enabling its private ownership. Marketing acknowledges the role of the activ-ities of the consumer in the emergence of the brand, but is ultimately unwill-ing to defend that role as object-ive. Perhaps most importantly, the qualitative differentiation of the medium of the brand is ultimately constrained by the pursuit of profit. The potentiality of the brand is, then, in many respects, complicatedly predictable rather than truly interactive.

Coda

Describing the societies in which we live is a general Euro-American project, so Marilyn Strathern (2002) observes. She further notes that the interest of economists is that their descriptions are meant to help us act; even if their knowledge is not predictive, it is meant to stimulate future policy or market behaviour. Such knowledge is typically pursued through frames in which action is interested, persons and goods are disentangled, and the measurement of externalities is made possible. This is one type of description, she says, a type that makes use of information about the world that purifies it, that transforms its dimensions into calculable measurements. But the object-ivity of the brand is produced through the frame of the interface. Its mode of description is different, not quite so pure; it contains within itself not only a descriptive ('this is') but also an imperative ('this should') (Simon, [1969] 1981). As such, it is an example of what Strathern describes as a second type of description, in which

> [t]he normative guideline, the ethical principle, has already jumped from description to action; it pre-empts the connection. The anticipation of action is as much a condition of the description, we might say, as a consequence of it. . . . Action is already implied.
>
> (2002: 263)

To put this another way, while the brand may be totalising, it is not a total fact (Mauss, 1976); it cannot be given in its entirety to a single mind at any single point in time. The nature of the objectivity of the brand is that it is not and can never be completed. This is both the source of the value of the brand as an object of contemporary capitalism (it is a thing into which possibility has been introduced), and what makes it open to other concerns. I want to conclude by suggesting that sociologists need to be able to address the object of the brand – and others like it – in terms not only of the descriptive but also, as Simon puts it, of the imperative. This would involve sociologists contributing to the implication of social activity in object-ivity without yet becoming complicit in objectivity as a fixed thing. It would involve the multiplication of partial, impure and unfinished solutions to the complex problem of creating a rational economic order.

Notes

1 Just do what? The brand as new media object

1 This quotation was chosen for me by Deirdre Boden, a great colleague and friend, who died in 2001. I would like to acknowledge her encouragement and guidance in the early stages of this project.

2 In Chapter 4, the ways in which the logo organises the ratio(nality) of time and space through the manipulation of qualities will be described in more detail.

3 Money in its perfected or increasingly abstracted form, Simmel argues, is *an absolute means* because it is completely teleologically determined and is not 'influenced by any determination from a different series' ([1907] 1990: 211). As Gertrude Stein put it, 'Whether you like it or whether you do not money is money and that is all there is about it' (1936, quoted in Zelizer, 1998: 59).

4 Zelizer argues that modern consumer society has in any case turned 'the spending of money not only into a central economic practice, but a dynamic, cultural and social activity. . . . This is the irony: while the state and the law worked to obtain a single national currency, people actively created all sorts of monetary distinctions. Outside the world of printing and minting, however, people spent less energy on the adoption of different objects as currencies than on the creation of distinctions among the uses and meanings of existing currencies – that is, on earmarking' (1998: 59). In this perspective, brands may be seen as a form of corporate earmarking: while not controlled by the state, brands are a kind of privately owned currency. They are attempts by firms to create their own worlds of distinction (and in this respect operate rather like a passport as well as a currency). Other examples of this tendency include the electronically mediated forms of money being developed by banks, universities, transport companies, utilities and commercial firms such as Club Med (ibid.: 65).

5 For Lev Manovich, from whom the term 'new media object' is adapted, it is important to understand the wide-ranging implications of the contemporary intersection of two previously separate histories: those of media and the computer. He writes, 'Media and computer – Daguerre's daguerreotype and Babbage's Analytical Engine, The Lumière Cinématographie and Hollerith's tabulator – merge into one. . . . This meeting changes the identity of both media and the computer itself' (2001: 25). He refuses to fix the definition of new media objects by describing one (or more) particular object(s), but rather suggests that what is indicated by the

term is the computerisation of culture. New media objects may thus, for Manovich be understood in terms of a set of general principles. Specifically, they may be described in numbers – that is, by means of numerical representation; as modular – that is, they comprise discrete samples or parts; as highly automated; as variable – that is, they are not fixed once and for all, but can exist in different versions; and as able to transcode – that is, able to translate something into another format.

6 There are a number of philosophers whose use of the notion of 'frame' is also relevant, including Heidegger (1977). Here, I will merely introduce the understanding of the action of the frame implicit in Bergson: 'To obtain this conversion from the virtual to the actual, it would be necessary, not to throw light on the object, but on the contrary, to obscure some of its aspects, to diminish it by the greater part of itself, so that the remainder, instead of being encased in its surroundings as a *thing*, should detach itself from them as a *picture*. . . . There is nothing positive here, nothing added to the image, nothing new. The objects merely abandon something of their real action in order to manifest their virtual influence of the living being upon them' (Bergson, 1991: 36–37).

7 An analogy may be drawn here with the currency derivatives described by Lee and LiPuma as speculative instruments. Like the brand, they operate at a meta-temporal level. However, their framing activity, although relying on the volatility of the underlying security, is organised in terms of a fixed temporal interval in which they are exercisable (2002: 204). This is the frame as 'hedge', a punctuation of the temporality implicit in the underlying assets. As Lee and LiPuma note, the Black–Scholes equations provide the standard method for pricing the relations between risk and temporality that underpin trading in currency derivatives. The brand makes use of no such standardising method of calculating risk.

8 Simmel notes that salt, cattle, tobacco and grain have all been simple means of exchange, their use typically being determined by individual interest. The use of jewellery as a medium of exchange, however, marks a new development for Simmel in so far as 'it indicates *a relation between individuals*: people adorn themselves for others' ([1907] 1990: 176; emphasis added). 'Exchange, as the purest sociological occurrence, the most complete form of interaction, finds its appropriate representation in the material of jewelry, the significance of which for its owner is only indirect, namely as a relation to other people' (ibid.: 177). He notes that adornment is a social need for relationality, and that certain kinds of ornament are reserved for particular social positions; so, for example, in medieval France, gold was not permitted to be worn by people below a certain rank. He goes on to suggest, however, that money is better able to serve as an absolute intermediary or means of exchange between products, although only, he says, if coinage is raised above its qualitative characteristics as a metal (such as gold).

9 See Howard Caygill's (1998) discussion of the notion of experience in the work of Walter Benjamin for some sense of what is lost in the presentation of colours as discrete and discontinuous.

10 The company has three defining characteristics: it has its own legal personality (see Chapter 5), it can issue tradable shares to any number of investors, and those investors have limited liability (Micklethwait and Wooldridge, 2003).

11 The IMF has itself commissioned a series of promotional advertisements broadcast on CNN and other cross-national channels, perhaps the first stages of establishing itself as a brand.

12 Conversely, television may be described as a machine designed, not to sell products to people, but as a market to advertisers.

13 My brother, Adam Lury, brought my attention to a cartoon by James Stevenson in which a man looks out of a picture window, and is surprised to see the TV logo CNN in the lower right corner.

14 However, the process of association cannot always be contained, and the Nike brand image may also include an association for some consumers with exploitation and sweat-shops.

15 Lee and LiPuma say, 'Members of capitalist economies almost invariably think of "the market" as a third-person collective agent, to which first-person agents, such as "We the investors", respond but do not necessarily identify with. The covert asymmetries of agentive verbal ascriptions reflect this relationship. Thus, "the market" can act, indicate, warn, hesitate, climb and fall, but is not usually able to take second-order verbs such as reflect, assume, guilt, or take responsibility in the ways that a national people might' (2002: 196).

2 Marketing as a performative discipline and the emergence of the brand

1 As noted in Chapter 1, although I will consistently speak about the brand, there are many different types of brands and multiple branding processes at issue here.

2 This is not to say that brands cannot be said to exist before this: as other chapters will discuss, some form of branding may be said to have existed for almost five thousand years.

3 This account of the history of Starbucks draws closely on the account provided by Koehn (2001).

4 Bourdieu (1993: 15) provides a schematic categorisation of symbolic agents in which he argues that 'the field of cultural production is structured, in the broadest sense, by an opposition between two sub-fields: the field of restricted production and the field of large-scale production. [In the former] the stakes of competition between agents are largely symbolic, involving prestige, consecration of artistic celebrity. Economic profit is normally disavowed . . . and the hierarchy of authority is based on different forms of symbolic profit e.g. a profit of disinterestedness, or the profit one has on seeing oneself (or being seen) as one who is not searching for profit.'

5 The following account draws closely on Arvidsson (forthcoming).

6 As Arvidsson notes, this scepticism is upheld in the marketing industry itself. He notes that Julie Lannon and Peter Cooper, who were marketers themselves, claim that the main attraction of such linear sequential models, like DAGMAR (Developing Advertising Goods for Measured Advertising Results), was that they 'lend themselves so readily to measurement'. In other words, these models were attractive because they generated the data that legitimated existing institutional arrangements. 'Procedures like this are highly useful in the maintenance of organizational systems, despite the fact they reflect a world reality (in contrast with an organizational reality) that few would recognize' (Lannon and Cooper, 1983: 197, 198, quoted in Arvidsson, forthcoming).

3 The interface of the brand: complex objects, interactivity and partial solutions

1 Manovich has made a compelling case for the use of categories from computer science as categories of new media theory; he develops the examples of 'interface', 'database' and programming among others (2001: 48).

2 Simon argues that painting, architecture, planning and engineering, as well as economics, are artificial systems.

3 This is an explanation of the brand by reference to purpose or function. But it is not meant to imply either that this purpose or function is natural or beyond question, or that it is not the site of conflict. Simon argues that the underlying principles at issue here are those of rationality, and much of his work is concerned to address what he calls the limits of rationality. This concern — and in particular whether limits are understood as something to be overcome — will be addressed more explicitly in Chapters 5, 6 and 7.

4 This can — and will — be compared to the use of looping processes that characterise new media objects (Manovich, 2001; and see Chapters 4 and 6).

5 Another example is the slogan for the Starbucks sub-brand Fairtrade coffee: 'Coffee that cares: commitment to origins'. As the publicity leaflet puts it, '"Commitment to origins" means we're committed to paying and treating suppliers fairly, to respecting and sustaining the global environment, to contributing to local communities, and most of all, to being a partner rather than just a purchaser of coffee.'

6 Although this mode of innovation does not derive from innovation in the production process, it may of course require it.

7 The Onitsuka Tiger corporation was founded by Japanese entrepreneur Kihachiro Onitsuka, but later changed its name to ASICS Tiger corporation and is now a $2.5 billion company world-wide.

8 The manufacture of Nike products in shifting locations in the Pacific Rim is a consequence of the continuing cheap and plentiful labour and the developed network of raw materials and parts suppliers in this region. The exploitation of cheap labour is not unique to Nike, but Nike has been among the most commercially adept, and the least shamefaced, in its reliance upon a very powerless labour force.

9 This is a strategy that enables brand exclusivity to be reconciled with wide availability.

10 Hayek is one of the most influential exponents of economic liberalism.

11 Hardt and Negri (2000) describe the relations between producers and consumers in the Fordist era as being mute.

12 The Swatch Group Ltd, acquired Groupe Horologe Breguet from Investcorp SA in 1999. This company was one of the oldest timepiece manufacturers in the world and now produces high-quality hand-assembled timepieces situated in the highest price segment of the 'haut-de-gamme' watch market.

13 Marina Warner notes, 'From the 1880s onwards, the goddess of victory ratified innumerable claims, commercial as well as political. Nike/Victoria appears on trademarks, cigar labels, as a stamp of quality, a guarantee of authenticity. A cipher, she speaks to us — mutely but all the time and insistently — of winning through against the odds, and perpetrates the illusion that triumph is ours' (1987: 143).

14 This attempt to displace the temporality of fashion might usefully be juxtaposed with that of a company such as Gap, whose changes in products are so regular and routine that the brand is best described not in terms of fashion but rather as routine, ubiquitous, everyday or generic. This strategy – of the staple rather than the spectacle – has its problems too.

15 Take as an example here the rise of what is called 'concurrent design' across many spheres of production (Julier, 2000). This approach to design and manufacture was intended to supersede the previously existing linear system of product development, whereby departments or divisions within a firm worked according to a chain of command. Instead, teams comprising members from different departments work simultaneously on the development of products, continuously exchanging information and the results of development. Of crucial importance in this process is the use of computer aided design packages that enable the speedy exchange of complex design information among the members of the development team. But even more significantly, concurrent design also brings together the so-called above-the-line elements of production – packaging, advertising and promotion – with the below-the-line elements – the engineering of an object, the design of tooling for its manufacture, and so on (ibid.: 25). In this respect, concurrent design contributes to the bringing closer together of a cycle of production and consumption.

16 In practice, there are stagnant pools as well as white-water rapids in the flow of information, dangers as well as 'advantages' of path dependency in complex systems (Urry, 2003). The case of the UK retailer Marks and Spencer is an example here: its recent market failure was widely ascribed to an institutionalised inability to respond to a changing market environment. Similarly, on being asked about the recent downturn in the performance of McDonald's, a commentator remarks, 'As a brand, McDonald's has been one of the most incredible success stories in history. . . . But there are so many chinks in the armour now, nothing short of reinventing the brand will save it over the long term' (Williams, quoted in Donegan and Webster, 2002: 20). Whether selling salads will be sufficient is uncertain.

17 The adoption of the principle of store-clustering by Starbucks discussed in Chapter 2 is another example.

4 Logos: from relations to relationships

1 It is thus rather appealing to consider competition between brands as tournaments of value, as implied by Appadurai (1986).

2 Semiotics is sometimes contrasted with semiology, a linguistic approach to the study of signs associated with Ferdinand de Saussure (1983).

3 Peirce writes, 'The Sign can only represent the Object and tell about it. It cannot furnish acquaintance with or recognition of that object; for that is what is meant . . . by the Object of a Sign; namely, that with which it presupposes an acquaintance in order to convey some further information concerning it' (1978: 100).

4 Rodowick writes, 'Peirce's semiotic founds itself on the Image as . . . "phanerons", defined as a fundamental appearing. Peirce argues for a "descriptive science of reality" or a semiotic realism wherein mind and matter exist on a continuum and have the same substantive identity' (1997: 39).

5 It is interesting to note just how many logos makes use of eyes, hands, faces and other figures which function as metonymies of an absent human subject or animal (Mollerup, 1997). Most frequent, however, is the use of a name: '[The] differentiation of corporate ownership is rarely represented in the public sphere of the commercial marketplace. Brand names that incorporate the names of individuals are far more common on the packages and in the advertising of goods that consumers encounter. Ownership is much more easily conceptualized in individual terms, and the prevalence of patriarchs in consumer culture (Colonel Sanders, Orville Redenbacher, "Mr. Christie", Frank Perdue, Dave Thomas) legitimates a misrecognition of personal control over the manufacture and distribution of goods' (Coombe, 1998: 160; see also Berlant, 1993).

6 The discussion of the colour of experience in the work of Walter Benjamin by Howard Caygill (1998) has much to offer a more detailed consideration of the role of qualities in the organisation of perception.

7 Another way of putting this is that 'uniqueness and novelty [are] qualitative rather than . . . subjective' (Rochberg-Halton, 1986: 68).

8 Peirce writes, '[T]hat the quality of red depends on anybody actually seeing it, so that red things are no longer red in the dark, is a denial of common sense. I ask the conceptualist, do you really mean to say that red bodies are no longer capable of transmitting the light at the lower end of the spectrum? . . . You forget perhaps that a realist fully admits that a sense-quality is only a possibility of sensation; but he thinks a possibility remains a possibility when it is not actual. The sensation is requisite for its apprehension; but no sensation nor sense-faculty is requisite for the possibility which is the being of the quality. Let us not put the cart before the horse, nor the evolved actuality before the possibility as if the latter involved what it only evolves' (1978: 85–86).

9 According to Rodowick, Deleuze derives these two axes specifically from Bergson (Rodowick, 1997: 10).

10 This account of Williams's use of the notion of flow recognises that Williams does not make the distinction that Deleuze draws between the rational and the irrational interval (1986, 1989; see also Rodowick, 1997). This is a distinction between the interval that produces association and the interval as interstice or cut. Deleuze draws this distinction most clearly in a discussion of a Jean-Luc Godard film, *Je t'aime je t'aime*. He writes, 'The so-called classical cinema works above all through linkage of images, and subordinates cuts to this linkage. On the mathematical analogy, the cuts which divide up two series of images are rational, in the sense that they constitute either the final image of the first series, or the first image of the second. This is the case of the "dissolve" in its various forms. . . . Now, modern cinema can communicate with the old, and the distinction between the two can be very relative. However, it will be defined ideally by a reversal where the image is unlinked and the cut begins to have an importance in itself. The cut, or interstice, between two series of images no longer forms part of either of the two series: it is the equivalent of an irrational cut, which determines the non-commensurable relations between images. . . . the images are certainly not abandoned to chance, but there are only relinkages subject to the cut, not cuts subject to the linkage. . . . There is thus no longer association through metaphor and metonymy, but relinkage on the literal image; there is no longer linkage of associated images, but only relinkages of independent images. Instead of one image after

the other, there is one image *plus* another, and each shot is deframed in relation to the framing of the following shot' (1989: 213–214). The usefulness of this distinction in relation to cinema is clear. However, as Deleuze notes, it is a relative distinction, and the assumption here is that it cannot be drawn as a matter of principle in relation to the logo (that is, the logo is not always or necessarily differentiated by either a rational or an irrational interval).

11 The (abstract) personalisation of objects – even of abstract objects such as capital – is not of course new, but is characteristic of many forms of exchange (Simmel, [1907] 1990; Taussig, 1999; Deleuze and Guattari, 1999).

12 John Frow describes this process from a different perspective: '[B]rands and brand advertising seek, by means of the specular circularity of applied market research, to invoke a *recognition*-effect in consumers: in Kapferer's words (1992: 2), whereas "a product's price measures its monetary value . . . its brand identifies the product and reveals the facets of its differences: functional value, pleasure value, and symbolic value as a reflection of the buyer's self-image". This matrix of values thus forms an Imaginary, in the sense that it projects an identity which, reflecting neither the product nor the parent corporation, is modeled on the effect of the unity of a person, and provokes a mirroring identification on the part of the consumers of the brand image. . . . In Laplanche and Pontalis's (1973: 210) precise definition, the brand Imaginary "is characterised by the prevalence of the relation to the image of the counterpart (*le semblable*)"; it is that process of imaginary identification which is the source of the brand's "non-rational hold over the buying behavior of the consumer"' (2002: 68).

13 As Deleuze and Guattari point out, 'information theory takes as its point of departure a homogeneous set of ready-made signifying messages that are already functioning as elements in biunivocal relationships, or the elements of which are biunivocally organized between messages. Second, the picking of a combination depends on a certain number of subjective choices that increase proportionally to the number of elements. But the problem is that all of this biunivocalization and binarization (which is not just the result of an increase in calculating skills, as some say) assumes the deployment of a wall or screen, the installation of a central computing hole without which no message would be discernible and no choice could be implemented' (1999: 179).

14 Other examples of abstract signs include the Mercedes star, the three rhombuses of Mitsubishi, the Bass red triangle and the Orange orange square.

15 From the perspective in which time is conceived as something real, this is more than an analogy. Kwinter writes, '[T]he clock appeared in culture, initially as a form of pure rationality and as a pure function, at once invisible and inseparable from the continuum of bodies, behaviours, building-apparatuses, and the social life that they carved up. If an independent clock mechanism was abstracted later from this empirical arrangement of elements . . . , it was only to affect the body/architecture continuum in an ever deeper and more generalized way. For example, the clock was soon transposed from the monastery to the town marketplace (from the domain of private faith to that of commerce, an invisible but active connection that Western capitalism has never sought to sever); and when the modern clockface was invented, it allowed time to be dissociated ever further from human events, at once spatially projected in vision and displayed in a marvelously rationalized form' (2001: 17). He continues his analysis by suggesting

that Bentham's Panopticon may be seen as a similar temporal device, expressing 'a total and abiding vision that a society produced for itself – a vision that never came to be incarnated in the building in question but that was inserted rather into the social body all the more effectively and surreptitiously at a level, or a number of levels, at which architectural objects in the classical sense simply do not appear' (ibid.: 18).

16 Conversely, commodities have been described as 'faceless brands – products or services that achieve their primary functional aim but do so without any distinctive characteristics or identifiable differences' (Barwise *et al.*, 2000: 75).

17 This account of shifters draws closely on the presentation in Rodowick (2001). In furthering the consideration of the rationality of the brand, it is worth drawing attention to Rodowick's point that for Hegel and much of contemporary thought, 'The sensate "this" (*das sinnliche*) that we aim for does not belong to language: it is inexpressible and therefore neither true nor rational' (2001: 7).

18 As Don Ihde notes, the dynamism of the frame, page or screen of viewing is fundamental here (see also Deleuze, 1986, 1989; Sobchack, 1992; and Manovich, 2001). Historically, in relation to the frame, window or screen a series of transformations in visibility have been made possible, including changes in the field within which the object is seen (Ihde, 1995: 149), most obviously a delimiting or editing of the field. Additionally, frames may also involve techniques of magnification and reduction – of both object and subject, and of their movements – so that relative motion may also be magnified or reduced. In these ways, apparent distance between object and subject is transformed in particular and perhaps unexpected ways. Thus, for example, seeing through lenses diminishes depth – the object field is flattened. This is particularly dramatic in the case of television, in which, in contrast to linear perspectival space, the size of the figure in the background remains the same as that of the figure in the foreground. Furthermore, the magnification of minute motion by a frame in the mediated situation may also magnify aspects of time not likely to be noted in ordinary contexts. Ordinary time-space is technologically deconstructed and reconstructed in a bricolage of image space-time. In the case of cinematographic-like technologies, time reversals, flashbacks, special effects and discontinuities have been raised to a high technical art (ibid.).

5 The brand as a property form of relationality

1 The chapter relies on a number of legal texts, notably Panesar (2001), Davis (2001) and Torremans (2001).

2 In this sense, the law supports a view of subjects and objects as external to one another and thus as essentially distinct.

3 Exchange value is not exclusively the prerogative of the market but is also a feature of state–subject relations. Moreover, there have been a number of debates that seek to extend the objects that may form the foundation of a property right. Thus, Reich (1964, cited in Panesar, 2001) argues for the need to recognise how a person's wealth has changed historically. He emphasises how governments have become a major source of wealth for people (for example, welfare benefits, pensions, licences and so on), supplementing or even displacing more conventional forms of wealth. Reich argues that these forms of wealth should be accorded the

same degree of protection as traditional forms of wealth such as lands and goods. His arguments do not fit well with traditional property thinking, though. On the one hand, the right to exclude others traditionally empowers the holder of a property right with a right to exclude the whole world from interference with the right that is vested in him or her. In contrast, claims to a welfare benefit often entitle a claimant who satisfies the criteria with a right not to be excluded from enjoyment thereof rather than a general right in *rem*. As a consequence, welfare benefits are conventionally thought to constitute a form of common property rather than a form of private property (Panesar, 2001: 96–99).

4 The argument that has been developed in this book is that the brand is incorporeal or intangible but not immaterial.

5 As this example indicates, in legal thinking the concept of exchange is held to be intangible (Panesar, 2001: 59).

6 In *Two Treatises of Government* (1690, cited in Macpherson, 1978), John Locke argues that the right to private property is one of the natural rights of an individual and consequently protected by natural law. The right is natural in the sense not that every individual was born with a right to property, but in that it is acquired through conduct that is natural to man. Private property rights are acquired by natural, moral and rational conduct which individuals left to their own devices would perform. As such, private property is acquired separately and does not arise through the prescriptive law of the state. The role of government is to protect the right of property along with other rights such as the right to life or liberty.

7 The fundamental difference between trade mark and passing off is that in passing off there is no property in the relevant name or other indica, as there is in a registered trade mark. Instead, passing off protects the claimant's ownership of his goodwill or reputation, which may be damaged by the defendant's misrepresentation. Nonetheless, brand owners had frequently made recourse to passing off to protect identifying insignia that trade marks would not.

8 She goes on to note that the unlimited transference, so fundamental to licensing, was anticipated and aptly described by a provision in the 1938 Trade Marks Act against 'trafficking in trade mark'. Here it was held that licensing helps companies dispose of reputation 'as though it were a marketable commodity'. It is this 1938 provision that was removed in the 1994 Act.

9 To this extent, then, there is a convergence between the law of trade mark and that of passing off, although of course there still remain a number of important differences. Goodwill is personal (not private) property, and it is the claimant's goodwill that is the property right protected by passing off action. So, for example, Lord Diplock comments, 'A passing off action is remedy for the invasion of a right in property not in the mark, name or get-up improperly used, but in the business or goodwill likely to be injured by the misrepresentation made by the passing off of one person's goods as the goods of another." But while goodwill can be assigned or licensed, it cannot be separated from the business that generated it. By contrast, trade marks are able to be assigned and licensed by their proprietors separately from the business to which they attach, so long as they do not become deceptive.

10 Of course, within the production process there are disputes over which stage is most important. Take the following example: 'San Francisco designer Primo

Angeli has devised a branding concept he calls the "RapidAccess" process. This process inverts the traditional model of product development: it creates the package first, then asks for it to be filled with a product to match. In a brochure promoting the process, Angeli writes that his objective is to increase the odds that the customer will buy the product. "Since the package is the product, why not turn things around? Why not develop finished looking packages with highly competitive brands and product names. Test and qualify them with consumers. Then turn the most effective packages over to R&D. Ask them to make a product that fits the pre-tested, pre-approved package."

Angeli has successfully applied this method to products for the Continental Baking Company, Miller Brewing Company and Just Desserts' (Novosedlik, 1995: 38).

11 Although, as noted above, Jacob J also argued that it was necessary to take a stage approach in assessing the distinctiveness of a mark.

12 It is worth noting here that Jacob J specifically mentions the role of marketing in describing the course and remarks that, 'of course', it acts for industry.

13 In particular, commercial activities in the fields of leisure and entertainment have made much greater use of this possibility in recent years.

14 This practice often has tax advantages for the parent company.

15 In his study of McDonald's, Royle writes, 'According to Felstead (1993), the origin of the word franchise dates back to the Middle Ages. In Norman England, barons were granted territories by the King in return for the payment of royalties and "provided they met many other requests made by the Monarch" (Felstead, 1993: 39). The original meaning of the word comes from the French "affranchair", meaning releasing "from servitude or restraint". However, as Felstead (1991) argues, the modern franchise is absolutely not about release "from restraint or servitude"' (2000: 36).

16 There has been a shift in the past twenty or so years in Europe and the United States from what is sometimes referred to as 'first-generation' franchising, in which the franchisee acquires the identity of the franchisor through the trade mark but conducts business as an independent distributor, to 'format' franchising. In the latter, it is not just a trade mark but a whole way of doing business – a business format – that is supplied to the franchisee (Felstead, 1993; Hoy and Stanworth, 2003).

17 Royle writes, 'In most European countries, as in the United States and elsewhere, the average age of the McDonald's workforce is young. In the UK, for example, approximately two-thirds of the workforce are under 21. . . . In Germany and Austria, very few under-18s are employed, largely because their employment is strictly regulated by national legislation. In addition, a large proportion of these workforces consists of foreign workers, particularly *Aussiedler* economic migrants from Eastern Europe. . . . The findings suggest that all of these workers have something in common; they are unlikely to resist or effectively oppose managerial control. McDonald's is able to take advantage of the weak and marginalised sectors of the labour market, what we have termed *recruited acquiescence*' (2000: 198).

18 On the other hand, the law supports the right of the trade mark owner to restrict the movement of goods. The supermarket chain Tesco obtained genuine Levi 501 jeans from suppliers outside the European Economic Area (EEA) and sold them in

its UK stores at roughly half the price of jeans sold in authorised Levi stores. Levi Strauss had always refused to sell jeans to Tesco, in part because the sale of Levi jeans alongside groceries was held to undermine the image of the brand. Levi Strauss therefore commenced proceedings in the UK high court, claiming that the import into and subsequent sale of jeans within the EEA constituted an infringement of its trade mark rights. The judgment was that the mark holder – Levi Straus in this case – must give explicit consent to importation before it can be considered that it has renounced its rights. Implied consent cannot be inferred merely from silence on the part of the trade mark proprietor. This judgment thus gives mark holders increased control over the distribution of their goods in Europe and in maintaining the reputation of their brands.

19   Interbrand is itself a brand, with the tag-line 'Creating and managing brand value™'.

20   There are a number of parties who have an interest in the valuation of brands, including chief executives (wanting to unlock shareholder value), bankers (wanting to establish an agreed value for brands as part of their security), brand managers (wanting to develop and extend the equity of their brands), advertising agencies (wanting to demonstrate that a reduction of ad-spend can reduce the value of a brand), marketing directors (wanting to demonstrate the benefits of their management of brand portfolios), accountants (wanting business) and finance directors (establishing royalty rates) (Simpson, quoted in G. Lury, 1998: 118).

21   This is a further point in support of the argument made in Chapter 3 that the brand contributes to the organisation of the temporality of the market.

22   The model of brand strength in the Interbrand valuation model has seven components: stability of market in which the brand performs (10 per cent); stability or longevity of brand itself (15 per cent); market leadership (25 per cent); long-term profit trend (10 per cent); consistent investment and support (10 per cent); geographic spread (25 per cent); and legal protection under trademark and copyright law (10 per cent).

23   Another commonly cited marketing definition of a brand is 'a collection of perceptions in the mind of the consumer' (www.buildingbrands.com/definitions). As one Coca-Cola executive puts it, 'If Coca-Cola were to lose all of its production-related assets in a disaster, the company would [survive]. By contrast, if all consumers were to have a sudden lapse of memory and forget everything related to Coca-Cola the company would go out of business' (quoted in Barwise *et al.*, 2000: 75).

24   Significantly, a number of brand holders – such as Phil Knight of Nike – have begun to argue that their brands should be understood not as nouns, but as verbs. In these formulations, brand holders recognise the commercial value of the open-endedness of the brand.

6   Interactivity: face-to-profile communication

1   This logo may be seen as one example of what Deleuze and Guattari describe as the mixed semiotic of Western culture: 'In developing the concept of faciality, Deleuze and Guattari oppose the frontal face of the despotic regime and the profile of the passional regime, concluding that in the West especially the two regimes tend to

combine in a mixed semiotic that brings together the facializing operations of despotic signification and passional subjectification' (Bogue, 2003: 107).

2 In this respect, it is interesting to compare Galton's use of composite photography (in which photographs of the members of a family or a particular social 'type', such as criminals, are overlaid to create a single image) with the use of a composite portrait of the users of Betty Crocker products in the brand logo.

3 Examples include 'BUZZwatch which "distills and tracks trends, themes, and topics within collections of texts across time" . . . ; Letizia, "a user interface agent that assists a user browsing the World Wide Web by . . . scouting ahead from the user's current position to find Web pages of possible interest" and Footprints, which "uses information left by other people to help you find your way around"' (Manovich, 2001: 35).

4 As Manovich says in relation to computer games, 'computers can pretend to be intelligent only by tricking us into using a very small part of who we are when we communicate with others' (2001: 34).

5 As Mackenzie outlines, the notion of transduction is taken from the work of Simondon, a theorist who sought to reinterpret cybernetic theories of information and technology according to transduction, and at the same time sought to develop a richer notion of information.

7 The objectivity of the brand: interactivity and the limits of rationality

1 Mark Poster outlines what he means by underdetermination in the following terms: 'Not only are [underdetermined] objects formed by distinct practices, discourses and institutional frames, each of which participates in and exemplifies the contradictions of capitalism and the nation-state, but they are also open to practice; they do not direct agents into clear paths; they solicit instead social construction and cultural creation' (2001: 17).

2 Kwinter argues that what he calls bio-logic began with 'the nineteenth century's science of heat (thermodynamics) as the study of inelectable transitions (cold to hot, order to disorder, difference to homogeneity) and the theory of evolution (the homogeneous and simple to the differentiated and complex' (1998: 40). He says, 'It marks the transition where communication, control and pattern formation – in a single phrase, relationships of information – take over in an organized substrate from relationships of energy' (ibid.: 40). Summarising the implications of Ilya Prigogine's more recent work on thermodynamics, Manuel De Landa writes, 'If one allows energy to flow in and out of a system, the number and type of possible historical outcomes greatly increases. Instead of a unique and simple equilibrium, we now have multiple ones of varying complexity (static, periodic, and chaotic attractors); and moreover, when a system switches from one to another form of stability (at so-called bifurcation), minor fluctuations can be crucial in deciding the actual form of the outcome' (1996: 181–182).

3 The following description draws closely on Katherine Hayles's (1999) account of shifts in understandings of information in the post-Second World War period.

4 Perhaps this is only another way of saying, as Simmel does, that 'man [*sic*] is an indirect being' ([1907] 1990: 211).

5 Many of the codes developed by businesses that are widely considered to be

pioneers in social responsibility (for example, Levi's) make no reference to international standards, liveable wages or other International Labour Organisation (ILO) instruments. Similarly, Reebok's code contains only a general reference to international human rights standards, and many codes differ from and even contradict international labour principles. For example, whereas some affirm the right to collective bargaining, others (for example, Toyota) only allude to respect between labour and management, and others still (for example, Caterpillar and Sara Lee Knit Products) actually favour the elimination of trade union activities (Royle, 2000: 9).

Bibliography

Aaker, D. A. (1996) *Building Strong Brands*, New York: Free Press.

Abercrombie, N. and Longhurst, B. (1998) *Audiences: A Sociological Theory of Performance and Imagination*, London: Sage.

Adkins, L. (1995) *Gendered Work*, Milton Keynes, UK: Open University Press.

Adkins, L. (2000) 'Objects of innovation: post-occupational reflexivity and re-traditionalizations of gender', in S. Ahmed, J. Kilby, C. Lury, M. McNeil, and B. Skeggs (eds) *Transformations: Thinking Through Feminism*, New York: Routledge.

Adkins, L. (2002) *Revisions: Gender and Sexuality in Late Modernity*, Buckingham, UK: Open University Press.

Adkins, L. and Lury, C. (1999) 'The labour of identity: performing identities, performing economies', *Economy and Society*, 28(4): 598–614.

Adorno, T. (1991) *The Culture Industry: Selected Essays on Mass Culture*, London: Routledge.

Adorno, T. and Horkheimer, M. (1982) *Dialectic of Enlightenment*, New York: Continuum.

Allen, J. (1980) 'The film viewer as consumer', *Quarterly Review of Film Studies*, 5(4): 481–499.

Alpers, S. (1998) 'The studio, the laboratory, and the vexations of art', in C. A. Jones and P. Galison (eds) *Picturing Science, Producing Art*, London: Routledge, pp. 401–417.

Andrew, D. (1998) 'Brand revitalisation and extension', in S. Hart and J. Murphy (eds) *Brands: The New Wealth Creators*, London: Macmillan, pp. 184–195.

Appadurai, A. (ed.) (1986) *The Social Life of Things: Commodities in Cultural Perspective*, Cambridge: Cambridge University Press.

Appadurai, A. (1996) *Modernity at Large: Cultural Dimensions of Globalization*, Minneapolis: University of Minnesota Press.

Appadurai, A. (2002) 'Deep democracy: urban governmentality and the horizon of politics', *Public Culture*, 14(1): 21–48.

Armstrong, S. (1996) 'Pop goes the red', *MediaGuardian* (London), 1 April, p. 9.

Arvidsson, A. (forthcoming) 'The labour of consumption. The power of brands', *Journal of Consumer Culture*.

Attfield, J. (2000) *Wild Things: The Material Culture of Everyday Life*, Oxford: Berg.

Austin, A. (2003) 'Lawsuits put food firms on menu', *The Times. Law* (London), 25 March, p. 9.

Ayling, R. (1999) 'British Airways: brand leadership results from being true to our long-term vision', in F. Gilmore (ed.) *Brand Warriors: Corporate Leaders Share Their Winning Strategies*, London: HarperCollins Business, pp. 37–48.

Barron, A. (2002) 'Copyright, art and objecthood', in D. McClean and K. Schubert (eds) *Dear Images: Art, Copyright and Culture*, London: Ridinghouse and ICA, pp. 277–309.

Barry, A. (2001) *Political Machines: Governing a Technological Society*, London: Athlone Press.

Barry, A. (2002) 'Political innovation and scientific uncertainty: a comment on the precautionary principle', paper prepared for EASST meeting, York.

Barry, A. (2003) 'The ethical business', unpublished paper.

Barry, A. (2004) 'On transparency: oil, economy and democracy in Azerbaijan and Georgia', Inside and Outside Markets Workshop, Paris, 31 May–1 June.

Barry, A. and Slater, D. (eds) (2002) Special Issue 'The Technological Economy', *Economy and Society*, 31(2), May.

Barwise, P., Dunham, A. and Ritson, M. (2000) 'Ties that bind: consumers and businesses', in J. Pavitt (ed.) *Brand.new*, London: V&A Publications, pp. 70–97.

Baudrillard, J. (1994) *Simulacra and Simulation*, Ann Arbor: University of Michigan Press.

Baudrillard, J. (1997) *The System of Objects*, trans. J. Benedict, London: Verso.

Bellos, A. (2001a) 'Ronaldo faces jail over his Nike deal', *Guardian* (London), 11 January.

Bellos, A. (2001b) 'What happened to the beautiful game?', *Guardian* (London), 14 January.

Bellos, A. (2001c) 'How Nike bought Brazil', *Guardian* (London), 9 July.

Benjamin, A. (2003) 'Fair fighter', *Guardian Society* (London), 19 March, p. 4.

Bennett, T. and Woolacott, J. (1987) *Bond and Beyond: Career of a Popular Hero*, London: Routledge and Kegan Paul.

Bergson, H. (1991) *Matter and Memory*, New York: Zone Books.

Berlant, L. (1993) 'National brands/national body: *Imitation of Life*', in B. Robbins (ed.) *The Phantom Public Sphere*, Minneapolis: Minnesota Press, pp. 173–208.

Bibby, D. (2003) 'Brand as metaphor', www.brandchannel.com (accessed 18 January 2003).

Blackett, T. (1998) *Trademarks*, London: Macmillan Business and Interbrand.

Bogue, R. (2003) *Deleuze on Music, Painting, and the Arts*, London: Routledge.

Bolter, J. D. and Grusin, R. (1999) *Remediation: Understanding New Media*, Cambridge, MA: MIT Press.

Borger, J. (2000) 'This leading American business guru claims these trainers could spell the end of capitalism: can he be serious?', *Guardian* (London), 29 September, pp. 4–5.

Bourdieu, P. (1977) *Outline of a Theory of Practice*, Cambridge: Cambridge University Press.

Bourdieu, P. (1983) *The Field of Cultural Production: Essays on Art and Literature*, New York: Columbia University Press.

Bourdieu, P. (1984) *Distinction: A Social Critique of the Judgement of Taste*, London: Routledge and Kegan Paul.

Bourdieu, P. (1993) *The Field of Cultural Production: Essays on Art and Literature*, Cambridge: Polity.

Bowlby, R. (1985) *Just Looking: Consumer Culture in Dreiser, Gissing and Zola*, New York: Methuen.

Bowlby, R. (1993) *Shopping with Freud*, London: Routledge.

Bowlby, R. (2000) *Carried Away: The Invention of Modern Shopping*, London: Faber and Faber.

Branson, R. (1999) 'Virgin: the virtues of a diversified brand', in F. Gilmore (ed.) *Brand Warrior: Corporate Leaders Share Their Winning Strategies*, London: HarperCollins Business, pp. 229–240.

Brown, N. and Michael, M. (2002) 'From authority to authenticity: the changing governance of biotechnology', *Health, Risk and Society*, 4(3): 259–272.

Butler, J. (1990) *Gender Trouble: Feminism and the Subversion of Identity*, New York and London: Routledge.

Callon, M. (1986) 'Some elements for a sociology of translation: domestication of the scallops and the fishermen of St. Brieuc Bay' in J. Law (ed.) *Power, Action, Belief: A New Sociology of Knowledge?*, London: Routledge and Kegan Paul, pp. 196–229.

Callon, M. (ed.) (1998a) *The Laws of the Markets*, Oxford: Blackwell.

Callon, M. (1998b) 'Introduction: the embeddedness of economic markets in economics', in M. Callon (ed.) *The Laws of the Markets*, Oxford: Blackwell, pp. 1–57.

Callon, M. (1998c) 'An essay on framing and overflowing: economic externalities revisited by sociology', in M. Callon (ed.) *The Laws of the Markets*, Oxford: Blackwell, pp. 244–269.

Callon, M. (1999) 'Actor-network theory: the market test', in J. Law and J. Hassard (eds) *Actor Network Theory and After*, Oxford: Blackwell, pp. 181–195.

Callon, M. and Law, J. (2003) 'Qualculation, agency and otherness', paper presented at Economics at Large workshop, New York University, 14–15 November.

Callon, M., Meadel, C. and Rabeharisoa, V. (2002) 'The economy of qualities', *Economy and Society*, 31(2), (May): 194–217.

Caminiti, S. (1998) 'Ralph Lauren: the emperor has clothes', *Fortune*, 137(9) (11 November): 80–89.

Carrell, S. (2003) 'Politically correct down to a T: the rise of ethical chic', *The Independent on Sunday* (London), 7 September, p. 3.

Carrera, R. (1991) *Swatchissimo: The Extraordinary Swatch Adventure*, Geneva: Antiquorum Editions.

Carrier, J. G. (1998) 'Abstraction in Western economic practice', in J. G. Carrier and D. Miller (eds) *Virtualism: A New Political Economy*, Oxford: Berg, pp. 25–48.

Castells, M. (1996) *The Rise of the Network Society*, Oxford: Blackwell.

Castells, M. (2000) 'Materials for an exploratory theory of the network society', *British Journal of Sociology*, 51(3): 5–24.

Caves, R. E. and Murphy, W. F. (2003) 'Franchising: firms, markets and intangible assets', in F. Hoy and J. Stanworth (eds) *Franchising: An International Perspective*, London: Routledge, pp. 81–102.

Caygill, H. (1998) *Walter Benjamin: The Colour of Experience*, London: Routledge.

Cochoy, F. (1998) 'Another discipline for the market economy: marketing as a performative knowledge and know-how for capitalism', in M. Callon (ed.) *The Laws of the Markets*, Oxford: Blackwell, pp. 194–221.

Cochoy, F. (2002) *Une Sociologie du Packaging ou l'Ane de Buridan Face as Marché*, Paris: PUF.

Coombe, R. (1998) *The Cultural Life of Intellectual Properties: Authorship, Appropriation and the Law*, Durham, NC: Duke University Press.

Cornish, W. R. (1999) *Cases and Materials on Intellectual Property*, 3rd edn, London: Sweet and Maxwell.

Crook, S. (1998) 'Minotaurs and other monsters: "everyday life" in recent social theory', *Sociology*, 32 (3): 523–540.

Dant, T. (1999) *Material Culture in the Social World*, Buckingham, UK: Open University Press.

Davis, J. (2001) *Intellectual Property Law*, London: Butterworths.

Davis, J. (2003) 'Ethics girl', *The Independent on Sunday. The Sunday Review* (London), 28 September, pp. 15–16.

Day, J. (2001) 'Analysing the allure of orange', www.MediaGuardian.co.uk (accessed 5 March).

de Certeau, M. (1998) *The Practice of Everyday Life*, Berkeley: University of California Press.

De Landa, M. (1996) 'Markets and antimarkets in the world economy', in S. Aronowitz, B. Martinsons and M. Menser (eds) *Technoscience and Cyberculture*, London: Routledge, pp. 181–194.

Debord, G. ([1967] 2002) *The Society of the Spectacle*, trans. D. Nicholson-Smith, New York: Zone Books.

Deleuze, G. (1986) *Cinema 1: The Movement Image*, London: Athlone Press.

Deleuze, G. (1989) *Cinema 2: The Time Image*, London: Athlone Press.

Deleuze, G. and Guattari, F. (1994) *What is Philosophy?*, trans. H. Tomlinson and G. Burchell, New York: Columbia University Press.

Deleuze, G. and Guattari, F. (1999) *A Thousand Plateaus: Capitalism and Schizophrenia*, trans. B. Massumi, London: Athlone Press.

Doane, M. A. (1989) 'The economy of desire: the commodity form in/of the cinema', *Quarterly Review of Film and Video*, 11(1): 23–33.

Donegan, L. and Webster, P. (2002) 'McTrouble', *Observer* (London), 20 October, p. 20.

Dratwa, J. (2000) 'The precautionary principle: stakes and options for policy making', mimeo, Paris: Centre de Sociologie de l'Innovation, Écoles des Mines.

Dreyfuss, R. C. (1990) 'Expressive genericity: trademarks as language in the Pepsi generation', *Notre Dame Law Review*, 65: 397–424.

du Gay, P. (1996) *Consumption and Identity at Work*, London: Sage.

du Gay, P. (ed.) (1997) *Production of Culture/Cultures of Production*, London: Sage.

du Gay, P., Hall, S., Janes, L., Mackay, H. and Negus, K. (1997) *Doing Cultural Studies: The Story of the Sony Walkman*, Milton Keynes, UK: Open University Press.

Eckert, C. (1978) 'The Carole Lombard in Macy's window', *Quarterly Review of Film Studies*, 3(1): 1–21.

Elmer, G. (1998) 'Diagrams, maps and markets: the technological matrix of geographical information systems', *Space and Culture*, 3: 49–65.

Elmer, G. (2000) 'The politics of profiling', in R. Rogers (ed.) *Preferred Placement*, Amsterdam: Jan van Eyck Akademie Editions, pp. 65–73.

Elmer, G. (forthcoming) *Profiling Machines: Mapping the Personal Information Economy*.

Ewen, E. (1980) 'City lights: immigrant women and the rise of movies', *Signs*, 5(3): S45–S65.

Featherstone, M. (1991) *Consumer Culture and Postmodernism*, London: Sage.

Feenberg, A. (1991) *Critical Theory of Technology*, New York: Oxford University Press.

Feenberg, A. (1999) *Questioning Technology*, London: Routledge.

Felstead, A. (1993) *The Corporate Paradox: Power and Control in the Business Franchise*, London: Routledge.

Firat, F. A. and Shultz, C. (1997) 'From segmentation to fragmentation: markets and marketing in the post-modern era', *European Journal of Marketing*, 31(3/4): 183–207.

Firat, F. A. and Venkatesh, A. (1993) 'Postmodernity: the age of marketing', *International Journal of Research in Marketing*, 10: 227–244.

Forty, A. (1986) *Objects of Desire: Design and Society since 1750*, London: Thames and Hudson.

Franklin, S., Lury, C. and Stacey, J. (2000) *Global Nature, Global Culture*, London: Routledge.

Fraser, M. (2002) 'What is the matter of feminist criticism?', *Economy and Society*, 31 (4): 606–625.

Fraser, M. (forthcoming) *The Value of Ethics*.

Frow, J. (2001) 'Invidious distinction: waste, difference and classy stuff', *UTS Review*, 7(2) (November): 21–31.

Frow, J. (2002) 'Signature and brand', in J. Collins (ed.) *High-Pop: Making Culture into Popular Entertainment*, Oxford: Blackwell, pp. 56–74.

Gabriel, I. (1995) 'The unmanaged organization: stories, fantasies, and subjectivity', *Organization Studies*, 16(3): 477–499.

Gaines, J. (1991) *Contested Culture: The Image, the Voice and the Law*, London: bfi Publishing.

Giddens, A. (1990) *The Consequences of Modernity*, Cambridge: Polity Press.

Goffman, E. (1961) *Encounters: Two Studies in the Sociology of Interaction*, Indianapolis: Bobbs-Merrill Educational Publishing.

Goffman, E. (1971) *Frame Analysis: An Essay on the Organization of Experience*, Chicago: Northeastern University Press.

Granovetter, M. (1985) 'Economic action and social structure: the problem of embeddedness', *American Journal of Sociology*, 91(3): 481–510.

Grant, J. (1999) *The New Marketing Manifesto: The 12 Rules for Building Successful Brands in the 21st Century*, London: Orion Business Books.

Haraway, D. (1997) *Modest Witness@Second Millennium*, London and New York: Routledge.

Haraway, D. (1999) *How Like a Leaf: An Interview with Donna Haraway*, London: Routledge.

Hardt, M. and Negri, A. (2000) *Empire*, Cambridge, MA: Harvard University Press.

Hart, S. (1998) 'The future for brands', in S. Hart and J. Murphy (eds) *Brands: The New Wealth Creators*, Basingstoke, UK: Macmillan Business, pp. 206–214.

Harvey, D. (1990) *The Condition of Postmodernity*, Oxford: Blackwell.

Hatfield, S. (2003) 'What makes Nike's advertising tick', *Guardian* (London), 17 June p. 15.

Haug, W. F. (1986) *Critique of Commodity Aesthetics: Appearance, Sexuality and Advertising in Capitalist Society*, Cambridge: Polity.

Hayek, F. (1945) 'The use of knowledge in society', *American Economic Review*, 35(4), (September): 519–530.

Hayles, K. N. (1999) *How We Became Posthuman: Virtual Bodies in Cybernetics, Literature and Informatics*, Chicago: University of Chicago Press.

Hebdige, D. (1988) *Hiding in the Light: On Images and Things*, London: Comedia.

Heidegger, M. (1977) *The Question Concerning Technology*, trans. W. Lovitt, New York: Harper and Row.

Heller, A. ([1970] 1984) *Everyday Life*, London: Routledge and Kegan Paul.

HHCL (1994) *Marketing at a Point of Change*, London: HHCL.

Hill, A. (2000) 'Sport couture', *Guardian* (London), 4 August, pp. 8–9.

Hochschild, A. (1983) *The Managed Heart: Commercialization of Human Feeling*, Berkeley: University of California Press.

Holloway, R. (1999) 'Levi Strauss: focus on the legend . . . and record-breaking global sales', in F. Gilmore (ed.) *Brand Warriors: Corporate Leaders Share Their Winning Strategies*, London: HarperCollins Business, pp. 63–78.

Hosokawa, S. (1984) 'The Walkman Effect', in R. Middleton and D. Horn (eds) *Popular Music*, vol. 4: *Performers and Audiences*, Cambridge: Cambridge University Press, pp. 165–180.

Hoy, F. and Stanworth, J. (eds) (2003) *Franchising: An International Perspective*, London: Routledge.

Ihde, D. (1995) 'Image technologies and traditional culture', in A. Feenberg and A. Hannay (eds) *Technology and the Politics of Knowledge*, Bloomington and Indianapolis: Indiana University Press, pp. 147–158.

Jackson, P., Lowe, M., Miller, D. and Mort, F. (2000) (eds) *Commercial Cultures: Economies, Practices, Spaces*, Oxford: Berg.

Jameson, F. (1991) *Postmodernism, or, The Cultural Logic of Late Capitalism*, London: Verso.

Johnson, R. (1986) 'The story so far: and further transformations', in D. Punter (ed.) *Introduction to Contemporary Cultural Studies*, London: Longman, pp. 277–313.

Julier, G. (2000) *The Culture of Design*, London: Sage.

Keat, R., Whiteley, N. and Abercrombie, N. (1994) *The Authority of the Consumer*, London: Routledge.

Keller, K. L. (1998) *Strategic Brand Management*, Saddle River, NJ: Prentice-Hall.

Kelly, K. (1998) 'I do have a brain', interview with Martha Stewart, *Wired*, August, pp. 114–115.

Kerin, J. (1999) 'The matter at hand: Butler, ontology and the natural sciences', *Australian Feminist Studies*, 14(29): 91–104.

Klein, N. (2000) *No Logo*, London: Flamingo.

Klein, N. M. (1993) *Seven Minutes: The Life and Death of the American Animated Cartoon*, London: Verso.

Klein, N. M. (2000) 'Animation and animorphs: a brief disappearing act', in V. Sobchack (ed.) *MetaMorphing: Visual Transformation and the Culture of Quick-Change*, Minneapolis and London: University of Minnesota Press, pp. 21–40.

Knorr Cetina, K. (1997) Sociality with objects: social relations in postsocial knowledge societies', *Theory, Culture and Society*, 14(4): 1–30.

Knorr Cetina, K. (2000) 'Post-social theory', in G. Ritzer and B. Smart (eds) *Handbook of Social Theory*, London: Sage, pp. 520–537.

Knorr Cetina, K. (2003) 'How are global markets global? The architecture of a flow world', paper presented at Economics at Large workshop, New York University, 14–15 November.

Knorr Cetina, K. and Bruegger, U. (2002) 'Global microstructures: the virtual societies of financial markets', *American Journal of Sociology*, 107(4) (January): 905–950.

Koehn, N. F. (2001) *Brand New: How Entrepreneurs Earned Consumers' Trust from Wedgwood to Dell*, Boston: Harvard Business School Press.

Kopytoff, I. (1986) 'The cultural biography of things: commoditization as process', in A. Appadurai (ed.) *The Social Life of Things: Commodities in Cultural Perspective*, Cambridge: Cambridge University Press, pp. 64–94.

Krauss, R. (1999) *'A Voyage on the North Sea': Art in the Age of the Post-medium Condition*, London: Thames and Hudson.

Krausse, J. (1998) 'Information at a glance: on the history of the diagram', *Oase*, 48: 3–30.

Krippendorff, K. (1994) 'Redesigning design: an invitation to a responsible future', in P. Tahkokallio and S. Vihma (eds) *Design: Pleasure or Responsibility?*, Helsinki: University of Art and Design Helsinki UIAH, pp. 138–162.

Krippendorf, K. and Butter, R. (1984) 'Product semantics: exploring the symbolic qualities of form', *Innovation*, Spring, pp. 4–9.

Kwinter, S. (1998) 'The hammer and the song', *Tijdschrift voor architectuur OASE Architectural Journal*, 48: 31–43.

Kwinter, S. (2001) *Architectures of Time: Toward a Theory of the Event in Modernist Culture*, Cambridge, MA: MIT Press.

Lash, S. (2002) *Critique of Information*, London: Sage.

Lash, S. and Lury, C. (forthcoming) *The Global Culture Industry: The Mediation of Things*, Cambridge: Polity.

Lash, S. and Urry, J. (1994) *Economies of Signs and Spaces*, London: Sage.

Lasn, K. (1999) *Culture Jam: The Uncooling of America*, New York: Morrow.

Latour, B. (1987) *Science in Action*, Milton Keynes, UK: Open University Press.

Latour, B. (1996) 'On interobjectivity', *Mind, Culture and Activity*, 3(4), Available online: www.ensmp.fr/~latour/articles (accessed 11 June 2003).

Latour, B. and Woolgar, S. (1986) *Laboratory Life: The Construction of Scientific Facts*, Princeton, NJ: Princeton University Press.

Law, J. (1984) *Organizing Modernity*, Oxford: Blackwell.

Law, J. (2002) *Aircraft Stories: Decentering the Object in Technoscience*, Durham, NC: Duke University Press.

Lee, B. and LiPuma, E. (2002) 'Cultures of circulation: the imaginations of modernity', *Public Culture*, 14(1): 191–213.

Levy, S. and Garder, B. (1955) 'The product and the brand', *Harvard Business Review*, March–April, pp. 33–39.

Leyshon, A. (2003) 'Scary monsters? Software formats, peer-to-peer networks and the spectre of the gift', *Environment and Planning D: Society and Space*, 21(5): 533–558.

Lunney, G. S., Jr. (1999) 'Trademark monopolies', *Emory Law Journal*, 48(2): 367–487.

Lury, C. (1993) *Cultural Rights: Technology, Legality and Personality*, London: Routledge.

Lury, C. (1999) 'Marking time with Nike: the illusion of the durable', *Public Culture*, 11(3): 499–526.

Lury, C. (2001) 'Whose brand is it anyway?', *Identity Matters 17*, BamberForsyth, pp. 6–7.

Lury, C. (2002) 'Portrait of the artist as a brand', in D. McClean and K. Schubert (eds) *Dear Images: Art, Copyright and Culture*, London: Ridinghouse and ICA, pp. 310–329.

Lury, C. (2003) 'The game of Loyalt(o)y: diversions and divisions in network society', *Sociological Review*, 51(3) (August): 301–320.

Lury, C. (in press): 'The installation of sensation: movement, media and the law in the global culture industry', in L. Moran and E. Sandon (eds) *Law's Moving Image*, Chicago: University of Chicago Press.

Lury, C. and Warde, A. (1996) 'Investments in the imaginary consumer: conjectures regarding power, knowledge and advertising', in M. Nava, A. Blake, I. MacRury and B. Richards (eds) *Buy This Book: Studies in Advertising and Consumption*, London: Routledge, pp. 87–102.

Lury, G. (1998) *Brandwatching*, Dublin: Blackhall Publishing.

Lury, K. (2002) 'A time and a place for everything: children's channels', in D. Buckingham (ed.) *Small Screens: Television for Children*, London: Leicester University Press, pp. 15–38.

Lyon, D. (2001) *Surveillance Society: Monitoring Everyday Life*, Milton Keynes, UK: Open University Press.

McClintock, A. (1995) *Imperial Leather: Race, Gender, and Sexuality in the Colonial Contest*, London: Routledge.

Mackenzie, A. (2002) *Transductions: Bodies and Machines at Speed*, London: Continuum.

McLuhan, M. (1997) *Understanding Media: The Extensions of Man*, London: Routledge.

Macpherson, C. (ed.) (1978) *Property: Mainstream and Critical Positions*, Oxford: Blackwell.

McRobbie, A. (1998) *British Fashion Design: Rag Trade or Image Experience?*, London: Routledge.

McRobbie, A. (1999) *In the Culture Society: Art, Fashion and Popular Music*, London: Routledge.

Manovich, L. (2001) *The Language of New Media*, Cambridge, MA: MIT Press.

Manovich, L. (2003) 'The poetics of augmented space: learning from Prada', Available online: www.manovich.net (accessed 20 May 2003).

Manzini, E. (1989) *The Material of Invention*, London: Design Council.

Marks, L. U. (2000) 'Signs of the time: Deleuze, Peirce and the documentary image', in G. Flaxman (ed.) *The Brain Is the Screen: Deleuze and the Philosophy of the Cinema*, Minneapolis: University of Minnesota Press, pp. 193–214.

Marzano, S. (2000) 'Branding = distinctive authenticity', in J. Pavitt (ed.) *Brand.new*, London: V&A Publications, pp. 58–59.

Massumi, B. (1999) 'Notes on the translation and acknowledgements', in G. Deleuze and F. Guattari (eds), *A Thousand Plateaus: Capitalism and Schizophrenia*, London: Athlone Press.

Massumi, B. (2002) *Parables for the Virtual: Movement, Affect, Sensation*, Durham, NC: Duke University Press.

Mauss, M. (1976) *The Gift*, New York: Norton.

Meech, P. (1996) 'The lion, the thistle and the saltire: national symbols and corporate identity in Scottish broadcasting', *Screen*, 37(1): 68–81.

Meyer, M. W. (1994) 'Measuring performance in economic organizations', in N. J. Smelser and R. Swedburg (eds) *The Handbook of Economic Sociology*, Princeton, NJ: Princeton University Press.

Michael, M. (2000) *Reconnecting Culture, Technology and Nature*, London: Routledge.

Micklethwait, J. and Wooldridge, A. (2003) *The Company: A Short History of a Revolutionary Idea*, London: Weidenfeld and Nicolson.

Miller, D. (1987) *Material Culture and Mass Consumption*, Oxford: Blackwell.

Miller, D. (2000) 'The birth of value', in P. Jackson, M. Lowe, D. Miller and F. Mort (eds) *Commercial Cultures: Economies, Practices, Spaces*, Oxford: Berg.

Miller, P. (1998) 'The margins of accounting', in Callon, M. (ed.) *The Laws of the Markets*, Oxford: Blackwell, pp. 174–193.

Mitchell, A. (2001) *Right Side Up: Building Brands in the Age of the Organized Consumer*, London: HarperCollins Business.

Mol, A. (1999) 'Ontological politics: a word and some questions', in J. Law and J. Hassard (eds) *Actor Network Theory and After*, Oxford: Blackwell and the Sociological Review, pp. 74–89.

Mol, A. (2002) *The Body Multiple: Ontology in Medical Practice*, Durham, NC: Duke University Press.

Mollerup, P. (1997) *Marks of Excellence*, London: Phaidon Books Ltd.

Molotch, H. (2003) *Where Stuff Comes From*, London: Routledge.

Monbiot, G. (2003) *The Age of Consent: A Manifesto for a New World Order*, London: Flamingo.

Moor, L. (2003) 'Branded spaces: the scope of "new marketing"', *Journal of Consumer Culture*, 3(1): 39–60.

Moore, C. (2000) 'Streets of style: fashion designer retailing within London and New York' in P. Jackson, M. Lowe, D. Miller and F. Mort (eds) *Commercial Cultures: Economies, Practices, Spaces*, Oxford: Berg, pp. 261–278.

Morse, M. (1990) 'An ontology of everyday distraction', in P. Mellencamp (ed.) *Logics of Television: Essays in Cultural Criticism*, Bloomington: Indiana University Press, pp. 193–222.

Morse, M. (1998) *Virtualities: Television, Media Art, and Cyberculture*, Bloomington and Indianapolis: Indiana University Press.

Mort, F. (1996) *Cultures of Consumption: Masculinities and Social Space in Late Twentieth Century Britain*, London: Routledge.

Mort, F. (1997) 'Paths to mass consumption: Britain and the USA since 1945', in M. Nava, A. Blake, I. MacRury and B. Richards (eds) *Buy This Book: Studies in Advertising and Consumption*, London: Routledge, pp. 15–33.

Mort, F. (2000) 'The commercial domain: advertising and the cultural management of demand', in P. Jackson, M. Lowe, D. Miller and F. Mort (eds) *Commercial Cultures: Economies, Practices, Spaces*, Oxford: Berg, pp. 35–54.

Mottram, S. (1998) 'Branding the corporation', in S. Hart and J. Murphy (eds) *Brands: The New Wealth Creators*, Basingstoke, UK: Macmillan Business, pp. 63–71.

Mulligan, M. and Authers, J. (2003) 'Coffee culture comes to the coffee-growers', *Financial Times* (London), 4 September, p. 14.

Murphy, J. (1998) 'What is branding?', in S. Hart and J. Murphy (eds) *Brands: The New Wealth Creators*, London: Macmillan Business and Interbrand, pp. 1–12.

Narration (2002) *Need to Know*, London: Foreign Policy Centre.

Nava, M. (1995) 'Modernity's disavowal: women, the city and the department store', in M. Nava and A. O'Shea (eds) *Modern Times: Reflections on a Century of English Modernity*, London: Routledge, pp. 38–76.

Nickson, D., Warhurst, C., Witz, A. and Cullen, A.-M. (2001) 'The importance of being aesthetic: work, employment and service organization', in A. Sturdy, I. Gruglis and H. Wilmott (eds) *Customer Service: Empowerment and Entrapment*, New York: Palgrave, pp. 170–190.

Nixon, S. (1997) 'Exhibiting masculinity', in S. Hall (ed.) *Representation: Cultural Representations and Signifying Practices*, London: Sage, pp. 291–336.

Nixon, S. (2000) 'In pursuit of the professional ideal: advertising and the construction of commercial expertise in Britain 1953–64', in P. Jackson, M. Lowe, D. Miller and F. Mort (eds) *Commercial Cultures: Economies, Practices, Spaces*, Oxford: Berg, pp. 55–76.

Nixon, S. (2003) *The Culture of Advertising*, London: Sage.

Norman, D. (1988) *The Design of Everyday Things*, New York: Doubleday.

Novosedlik, W. (1995) 'Branding as mythology', *Eye*, 19: 36–43.

O'Connell, S. (2003) 'Jean Genius', *Guardian Weekend* (London), 20 January, pp. 8–9.

Olins, W. (1989) *Corporate Identity*, London: Thames and Hudson.

Panesar, S. (2001) *General Principles of Property Law*, Harlow, UK: Pearson Education.

Pavitt, J. (2000a) 'In goods we trust', in J. Pavitt (ed.) *Brand.new*, London: V&A Publications, pp. 18–51.

Pavitt, J. (2000b) (ed.) *Brand.new*, London: V&A Publications.

Peirce, C. S. (1978) *The Philosophy of Peirce: Selected Writings*, ed. J. Buchler, London: Kegan Paul.

Perry, N. (1998) *Hyperreality and Global Culture*, London: Routledge.

Peters, T. (1999) *The Brand You 50: Fifty Ways to Transform Yourself from an 'Employee' into a Brand That Shouts Distinction, Commitment, and Passion!*, New York: Alfred A. Knopf.

Pettinger, L. (forthcoming) 'Brand culture and branded workers: service work and aesthetic labour in fashion retail', *Consumption, Markets and Culture*, 7(2).

Pine, B. J. and Gilmore, J. (1999) *The Experience Economy: Work Is Theatre and Every Business a Stage*, Boston: Harvard Business School Press.

Porter, C. (2003) 'Looking good, being good', *Guardian Weekend* (London), 17 May, p. 57.

Poster, M. (2001) *What's the Matter with the Internet?*, Minneapolis: University of Minnesota Press.

Quinn, M. (1994) *The Swastika: Constructing the Symbol*, London: Routledge.

Ritzer, G. (1993) *The McDonaldization of Society*, Thousand Oaks, CA: Sage.

Rochberg-Halton, E. (1986) *Meaning and Modernity: Social Theory in the Pragmatic Attitude*, Chicago: University of Chicago Press.

Rodowick, D. N. (1994) 'Audiovisual culture and interdisciplinary knowledge', http://www.rochester.edu/College/FS/Publications/AVCulture. Also in *New Literary History*, 26 (1995): 111–121.

Rodowick, D. N. (1997) *Gilles Deleuze's Time Machine*, Durham, NC: Duke University Press.

Rodowick, D. N. (2001) *Reading the Figural, or, Philosophy after the New Media*, Durham, NC: Duke University Press.

Royle, T. (2000) *Working for McDonald's in Europe: The Unequal Struggle?*, London: Routledge.

Rushton, S. (2003) 'Nice and easy does it', *The Independent on Sunday, The Sunday Review* (London), 28 September, pp. 8–12.

Saussure, F. de (1983) *Course in General Linguistics*, London: Duckworth.

Shabi, R. (2003) 'The card up their sleeve', *Guardian Weekend* (London), 19 July, pp. 15–23.

Shields, R. (1997) 'Flow', *Space and Culture*, 1: 1–5.

Shields, R. (2003) *The Virtual*, London: Routledge.

Simmel, G. ([1907] 1990) *The Philosophy of Money*, ed. D. Frisby, London: Routledge.

Simon, H. A. ([1969] 1981) *The Sciences of the Artificial*, Cambridge, MA: MIT Press.

Slater, D. (2002a) 'Capturing markets from the economists', in P. du Gay and

M. Pryke (eds) *Cultural Economies: Cultural Analysis and Commercial Life*, London: Sage.

Slater, D. (2002b) 'From calculation to alienation: disentangling economic abstractions', *Economy and Society*, 31(2) (May): 234–249.

Slater, D. and Tonkiss, F. (2001) *Market Society: Markets and Modern Social Theory*, Cambridge: Polity.

Smith, P. (1997) 'Tommy Hilfiger in the age of mass customization', in A. Ross (ed.) *No Sweat: Fashion, Free Trade, and the Rights of Garment Workers*, New York: Verso, pp. 249–262.

Sobchack, V. (1992) *The Address of the Eye: A Phenomenology of Film Experience*, Princeton, NJ: Princeton University Press.

Spillane, M. (2000) *Branding Yourself*, London: Pan Books/Macmillan.

Stafford, B. M. (2001) *Visual Analogy: Consciousness as the Art of Connecting*, Cambridge, MA: MIT Press.

Stengers, I. (1997) *Power and Invention. Situating Science*, Minneapolis: University of Minnesota Press.

Storper, M. (2001) 'Lived effects of the contemporary economy: globalization, inequality and consumer society', in J. Comaroff and J. L. Comaroff (eds) *Millennial Capitalism and the Culture of Neoliberalism*, Durham, NC: Duke University Press, pp. 88–124.

Strathern, M. (1999) *Property, Substance and Effect: Anthropological Essays on Persons and Things*, London: Athlone Press.

Strathern, M. (2002) 'Externalities in comparative guise', *Economy and Society*, 31(2) (May): 250–267.

Szersynski, B. (1997) 'The varieties of ecological piety', *Worldviews: Environment, Culture, Religion*, 1: 37–55.

Taussig, M. (1999) *Defacement: Public Secrecy and the Labour of the Negative*, Stanford, CA: Stanford University Press.

Taylor, W. (1993) 'Message and muscle: an interview with Swatch titan Nicolas Hayek', *Harvard Business Review*, March–April, pp. 98–110.

Thomas, N. (1991) *Entangled Objects: Exchange, Material Culture and Colonialism in the Pacific*, Cambridge, MA: Harvard University Press.

Thrift, N. (1997) 'The rise of soft capitalism', *Cultural Values*, 1: 29–57.

Thrift, N. (1998) 'Virtual capitalism: the globalisation of reflexive business knowledge', in J. G. Carrier and D. Miller (eds) *Virtualism: A New Political Economy*, Oxford: Berg, pp. 161–186.

Thrift, N. (1999) 'The place of complexity', *Theory, Culture and Society*, 16: 31–70.

Thrift, N. (2000) 'Performing cultures in the new economy', *Annals of the Association of American Geographers*, 90(4): 674–692.

Thrift, N. (2001) '"It's the romance, not the finance that makes the business worth pursuing": disclosing a new market culture', *Economy and Society*, 30(4): 412–432.

Thrift, N. (forthcoming) *Knowing Capitalism*, London: Sage.

Tomlinson, A. (1990) 'Introduction: consumer culture and the aura of the commodity', in A. Tomlinson (ed.) *Consumption, Identity and Style: Marketing, Meanings and the Packaging of Pleasure*, London: Routledge, pp. 1–40.

Torremans, P. (2001) *Intellectual Property Law*, 3rd edn, Bath: Butterworths.

Tung, C. C. (1999) 'Orient Overseas Container Line: growth reflecting the rise of the Asia Pacific economies', in F. Gilmore (ed.) *Brand Warriors: Corporate Leaders Share Their Winning Strategies*, London: HarperCollins Business, pp. 79–92.

Turkle, S. (1996) *Life on the Screen*, New York: Weidenfeld and Nicolson.

Urry, J. (2000) *Sociology beyond Societies: Mobilities for the Twenty-first Century*, London: Routledge.

Urry, J. (2003) *Global Complexity*, Cambridge: Polity.

Vanderbilt, T. (1998) *The Sneaker Book: Anatomy of an Industry and an Icon*, New York: New Press.

Vidal, J. (2003) 'Retail therapy', *Guardian Society* (London), 26 February, pp. 8–9.

Vision of the Future (1996) Eindhoven: Philips Corporate Design.

Vitellone, N. (2003a) 'The rush: needle fixation or technical materialization?', *Cultural Values*, 7(2): 165–177.

Vitellone, N. (2003b) 'The syringe as a prosthetic', *Body and Society*, 8(3): 37–52.

Vlovine, J. (2003) 'Multicoloured frock shop', *Guardian, G2* (London), 30 June, pp. 12–13.

Waldrop, M. (1994) *Complexity*, London: Penguin.

Warner, M. (1987) *Monuments and Maidens: The Allegory of the Female Form*, London: Picador.

Webster, K. K. (2003) 'Branding your employees', www.brand.channel (accessed 18 January 2003).

Wernick, A. (1991) *Promotional Culture: Advertising, Ideology and Symbolic Expression*, London: Sage.

Whitehead, A. N. (1967) *Science and the Modern World*, New York: Free Press.

Whitehead, A. N. (1977) *Nature and Life*, Westport, CT: Greenwood.

Whitehead, A. N. (1978) *Process and Reality*, corrected edition, New York: Free Press.

Williams, G. (2000a) *Branded? Products and Personalities*, London: V&A Publications.

Williams, G. (2000b) 'The point of purchase', in J. Pavitt (ed.) *Brand.new*, London: V&A Publications, pp. 185–211.

Williams, R. (1974) *Television: Technology and Cultural Form*, London: Fontana/Collins.

Willigan, G. (1992) 'High performance marketing: an interview with Nike's Phil Knight', *Harvard Business Review*, July–August, pp. 90–101.

Wilson, E. A. (1998) *Neural Geographies: Feminism and the Microstructure of Cognition*, London: Routledge.

Winship, J. (2000) 'Culture of restraint: the British chain store 1920–39', in P. Jackson, M. Lowe, D. Miller and F. Mort (eds) *Commercial Cultures: Economies, Practices, Spaces*, Oxford: Berg, pp. 15–34.

Zelizer, V. (1998) 'The proliferation of social currencies', in M. Callon (ed.) *The Laws of the Markets*, Oxford: Blackwell, pp. 58–68.

Zizek, S. (1997) *The Plague of Fantasies*, London: Verso.

Web sites

www.brandchannel.com
www.buildingbrands.com
www.interbrand.com
www.latour.net
www.lovemarks.com
www.mcdonalds.com
www.mcspotlight.org
www.manovich.net
www.orange.com
www.transparency.org
www.wnim.com (Issue 14, for research report on colours)

Legal cases

Aristoc Ltd v. *Rysta Ltd* (1945)
Arsenal Football Club plc v. *Reed* (2002)
British Sugar plc v. *James Robertson & Sons Ltd* (1996)
Canon Kabushiki Kaisha v. *Metro-Goldwyn Meyer* (1995)
Claeryn/Klarein, Benelux Court of Justice (1975)
Jellinek's Application (1946)
Lancer Trade Mark (1987)
Libertel Groep BV v. *Benelux-Merkenbureau* (2003)
Lloyd Schuhfabrik Meyeer and Co. GmbH v. *Klijsen Handel BC* (1999)
Philips Electronics BV v. *Remington Consumer Products* (1998)
Sabel BV v. *Puma AG, Rudolf Dassler Sport* (1998)
Swizzels Matlow Ltd's Trade Mark Application (1999)
Wagamama v. *City Centre Restaurants* (1995)

Index